Schooling in the Middle Years

By Mervyn Taylor and Yvonne Garson

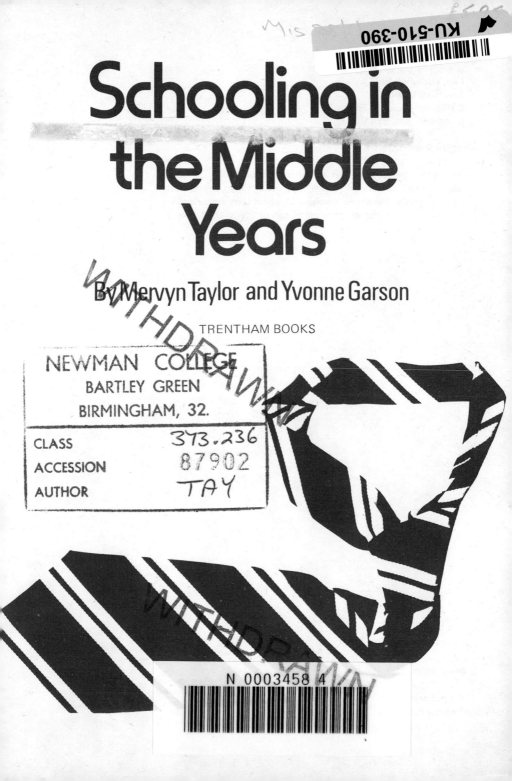

TRENTHAM BOOKS

© Trentham Books 1982

First published 1982 by
Trentham Books
30 Wenger Crescent, Trentham,
Stoke-on-Trent, ST4 8LE.

ISBN: 0 9507735 1 4

cover design by Cal Swann FSIAD Kite Graphic Design

Set and printed in Great Britain by:
Bemrose Press Ltd./Cheshire Typesetters, Chester.

Contents

ACKNOWLEDGEMENTS

Any book is the result of a team effort with many people working hard behind the scenes. We would like to acknowledge our debt to all those teachers who completed our lengthy questionnaires and to our colleagues at the University of Keele and the National Union of Teachers for their help and advice. Our particular thanks go to Phil Robinson and Professor Alan Blyth for their helpful and constructive comments on the manuscript and to Professor John Eggleston for his continued support and encouragement during the period of the research. We are grateful to the University of Keele for financing the project.

Handling the large quantity of data would have been impossible without the help of staff at the University of Keele's Computer Centre especially the punch card operators who worked their way through 25,000 cards. Our final thanks go to our typists Pauline Harrison and Barbara Wiggins who patiently deciphered our handwriting. As always, the errors which remain in the book are the fault of the authors and no-one else.

Preface

This book is the result of the first ever large scale survey undertaken into the English middle school — a comparatively new feature to emerge onto our educational landscape. The research began as a basic fact finding operation into current practices in middle schools — how they are staffed and how the curriculum is organised — together with an analysis of their perceived advantages and disadvantages over the more traditional pattern of schooling, but as the work proceeded such large differences began to emerge between the various kinds of middle schools that the enterprise gradually evolved into a comparative study. In fact there is no such creature as *the* English middle school; rather it is a concept which varies in its application not only according to the age range of pupils taught, but in the philosophical beliefs of its teachers.

The book begins with two introductory chapters, the first briefly tracing the development of middle schools, the second outlining the educational arguments which accompanied their gestation and birth. The results of the survey comprise Chapters 3 to 7 and follow in broad plan the pattern of questions presented in the questionnaire. Wherever possible the data is presented in tables which, for the sake of easier reference are kept together at the back of the book, and the text attempts to pick out the major points revealed by the figures; sometimes however, in order to reduce the number of tables, information is given in the text only. Also data which is considered of lesser importance or which is less informative has been placed in the Appendices so that the main body of the text remains as uncluttered as possible.

Chapter 8 also presents unique data in that this was obtained from upper schools to which middle school pupils transfer and it attempts to look at the middle schools, their advantages and their shortcomings, from the viewpoint of the upper school head teachers; this is the first time also that a large scale exercise of this kind has been carried out.

The head teachers and their colleagues who responded to the questionnaire were left a section at the end to write their own unstructured comments about a number of important questions covering middle schools and these notes form the basis of Chapter 9.

The final chapter in the book takes a broader perspective assessing the nature and extent of the problems which middle schools are likely to face in the future; the outlook for such schools is considered to be rather bleak and it seems unlikely that many will survive to see the twenty-first century.

CHAPTER 1

The Beginning of Middle Schools

'In the best of all socialist worlds every child of secondary school age would be attending a purpose built, all-through comprehensive. Since, however, the nation has neither the money, nor indeed the unanimity to apply this ideal immediately, there must be compromise'.

This extract from the leading article in the Times Educational Supplement of May 6th, 1966 was written after Anthony Crosland, then Secretary of State for Education and Science, had announced that he had reconsidered the cautious approval he'd given to middle schools in Circular 10/65, and would view LEA proposals for such schools more favourably in the future. The quotation, however, has a wider significance when viewed in historical context for it provides the key to the question as to why we have middle schools in Britain today; the answer lies in the fact that middle schools are compromise schools borne out of the classically English way of inching forward through the gradual ad hoc adjustment to conflicting opinions and pressures.

It is difficult in the early eighties, especially during a period of retrenchment in education, to comprehend just what conditions were like in the 1960s, particularly in the early part of the decade, when unparalled expansion and opportunity within the system were the norm. Yet only if we can capture some feeling of the cut and thrust of the debates of that period and examine the diverse opinions and pressures on decision makers of the time, will it be possible to understand how the gestation and birth of the English middle school came about.

The basic political force in education during the 1960s was for reforms leading to a more equitable and egalitarian system of schooling, for there was widespread discontent with the practice of separating pupils at aged 11 into those few who went to grammar schools and the many who went to some other kind of school, either a technical school or more usually a secondary modern school — what Lady Wooton, a leading Labour peer, called 'the dump of the secondary modern school. It takes the rump, it takes the leavings. It is, of course, socially the dump as well as, theoretically at any rate, intellectually'.[1]

This view was typical of that held by many people both inside and outside the Labour Party and such a change in the perception of the tripartite system within the space of a couple of decades was remarkable since it was this form of organisation, based on the Norwood Report, which was urged upon local authorities by the Labour Government after the Second World War. Circulars such as Number 73 (December, 1945) and Number 90 (March, 1946) sent out by the Minister of Education all underlined the necessity for building and development to proceed according to the tripartite system. At that point in time the Labour Government was particularly keen to encourage the development of grammar schools, for these provided free places for pupils based on merit alone and not merely the ability to pay, as had been the case before the 1944 Act; thus the grammar schools provided greater educational opportunity for bright working class children.

During the following twenty years, however, there was a persistent and gradual rise of disillusionment in a system which divided the nation's children at the tender age of 11 into 'the haves' and 'the have-nots' and the demand for an end to selection for secondary education became irresistable because there were so many injustices in the operation of such a system. Not only were the actual instruments of selection, the intelligence tests, attracting increasing criticism by psychologists and sociologists such as Simon (1953) and Floud et al. (1956), but there was also concern at the different procedures of selection adopted by local education authorities and the wide variation in the proportion of places offered at grammar schools. It became all too clear that obtaining a place at a grammar school was not based solely on a particular agreed level of ability required in a pupil, but also on such pragmatic considerations as the available buildings on the one hand and the numbers of children in a particular age cohort on the other.

All this conspired to make the 11+ selection procedure in practice something of a national lottery, though it was also considered by many as offensive in principle to determine a child's future at the age of eleven. There were, of course, a large number of people who were opposed to a change in the system, who thought, as did Lord Newton,[2] that one could not for ever opt out of competition. '. . . sooner or later one had to learn one was more stupid than one thought or than one's parents thought'.[3] Even this somewhat pessimistic view, however, was being challenged by the increasing number of children at secondary modern school who, rejected as failures by the 11+ examination, were staying on beyond the statutory leaving age and were successfully taking examinations at 'O' level. For example in July 1963 Sir Edward Boyle, then Minister of Education, claimed in the House of Commons that voluntary staying on had risen during the life of that Parliament from about one-third to nearly two-thirds of the pupils in secondary modern schools.[4] Thus the traditional demarcation lines which were believed to separate pupils into two or three neatly defined groups were breaking down in practice and it made it even more difficult to accept the contradictions in the system.

In addition to this groundswell of opinion for a fairer educational system there were other pressures at work in the 1960s and it was these, combined with the movement towards comprehensive education, which were responsible for the evolution and development of the middle school. These pressures can be put together under three main groupings. Firstly, there were demographic pressures caused by the expanding school population and manifested in such practical problems as the availability of buildings and teachers, the need to expand the provision for higher education and the recommendation to raise the school leaving from 15 to 16 years. Secondly, there were growing pressures and strains in the relationship between central and local government especially after 1964. Thirdly, there were pressures arising from educational theories concerning the most appropriate age for the transfer of pupils from primary to secondary school, and the best form of re-organisation along comprehensive lines. We shall take each of these strands and consider them separately, though in real life of course, all the differing strands were bound together to form a dynamic interlocking political, social and economic fabric.

The major pre-occupation for the Ministry of Education in the 1960s was the same as had been since the end of the war, namely that of providing roofs over heads for a continually expanding school population — a logistical problem of unprecedented size and difficulty. By 1961 the number of pupils in maintained primary and secondary schools had risen by close on one million since 1945 to a fraction under seven million; by 1976 the number of pupils had risen to just under nine million giving the largest ever school population in British history. To have continued to carry out the necessary improvements in the education service after 1961 with a school population which was stable or only slightly expanding would have been a major enterprise but to achieve this with an extra two million pupils being absorbed into the system transformed it into a gargantuan one. Not only did successive governments and the local authorities have to find the necessary finance but they also had to undertake the sophisticated planning and organisation so that the basic physical and human resources could be brought on stream at the right time and in the right places.

To begin with, many of the nation's schools in the early 1960s were in a deplorable state, this despite tremendous efforts in the previous 15 years which had produced over three million new school places. The 1962 School Building Survey (DES, 1965) revealed that over three-quarters of a million primary school children were housed in schools built before 1875; over six thousand primary schools lacked a warm water supply for pupils to wash in and for two hundred primary schools there was no piped water at all. Well over half Britain's primary school children had to use outside lavatories, often at great inconvenience, as this example from two schools in Islington shows: 'The children had to walk over 100 yards right round one of these schools and across the playground to get to the outside lavatories'.[5] One can imagine that this would be quite an experience for a seven year old on a cold January morning. One-quarter of the primary schools had no central heating system and over one-third didn't even have a staff room. Secondary schools fared considerably better than the primaries, but even so a third of these had outside sanitation and one-quarter were on sub-standard sites. All in all, of the thirteen categories of defect listed in the survey, three-quarters of the nation's children were in schools which exhibited one or more of these defects. The estimated cost in 1962 of bringing all maintained primary and secondary schools up to standard amounted to a staggering

£1,368 million and this did not include the finance required to build new schools to cater for the expanding school population caused by the rising birth rate and the larger proportion of children staying on at school beyond the minimum leaving age of 15.

Another indication of the magnitude of the buildings problem in this period was the number of children still attending all-age schools which provided continuous education under one roof for children aged five to fifteen. The 1944 Act proposed their abolition stating that a local authority should provide primary and secondary education in separate schools, yet in 1963 there were still 130,000 children being educated in 474 all-age schools; in fact the last of these schools did not disappear until 1971 — 27 years after the 1944 Act.

The necessity to provide additional accommodation and to renew many of the existing school buildings meant that a continuing investment in the education service was required. In 1963 5% of the Gross National Product was being spent on education — an increase over the 1951 figure of 2% which involved a much smaller resource base — and new schools were being produced at the rate of ten per week, but still this did not satisfy the demand. In 1964 a massive investment programme was announced to provide an additional 800,000 new school places within the space of four years, a £200 million injection which would increase the nation's stock of schools by a staggering 10%, and this time the primary schools, the cinderellas of the system, were to get a fair share of the money too.

An additional problem which exacerbated the buildings shortage was the commitment to raise the school leaving age from fifteen to sixteen years. The leaving age was raised from fourteen to fifteen years in 1947 and was the first of the major reforms of the 1944 Act to be implemented. However, the Act also laid down that as soon as it was practicable the school leaving age should be raised to sixteen years, although in view of the pressure on resources caused by the steadily rising birth rate the reluctance of successive Ministers to announce a specific date for implementation was understandable, in spite of pledges made to the cause in principle. For example, in the middle of 1963 Edward Boyle quite clearly laid the blame for the lack of a specific target date for raising the leaving age on the increasing numbers of pupils: 'We are facing a population explosion in the schools. The figure of the prospective school population is now markedly different from any previously imagined'.[6] An additional turn of the screw to increase still further the pressure on the Government came in October 1963 with the publication of the Newsom Committee's Report. Set up two years previously to advise on the education of pupils aged thirteen to sixteen of average and less than average ability, its principal recommendation was that there should be an immediate announcement from the Government raising the school leaving age to sixteen years for all pupils starting secondary school from 1965 onwards. Again the importance of demographic trends and their effects on building resources was illustrated in a rider to the main recommendation which declared that if the leaving age was raised in 1969-70 then the number of fifteen year olds involved would be relatively small. In the Queen's Speech to the new Parliament in November 1963 there was still no announcement, but in the following January Edward Boyle did keep the historic promise and fixed the date, not for 1969-70 as Newsom had recommended, but rather for 1970-71 when it was estimated that sufficient buildings would be available. In the event, of course, the date was deferred in January 1968 until 1972-73 as part of a set of measures designed to reduce expenditure on education due to a series of ever more serious financial crises.

Two further logistic problems were in evidence in the 1960s. The first of these was the general shortage of teachers; this did not have as direct an effect on the formation of middle schools as did the shortage of buildings, but the indirect effect was considerable because funding new colleges of education to increase the supply of teachers diverted finance away from the schools building programme.

Other sectors of higher education were also competing for funds in response to the Robbins Report, published in 1963, which advocated that there should be a place available in higher education for all young people who could satisfy the entrance requirements. In terms of numbers of students this would involve a doubling of the places available from 216,000 in 1963 to 560,000 by 1980-81 with intermediate targets of 328,000 in 1967-68 and 392,000 in 1973-74. The estimated cost of this expansion, unprecedented as in the primary and secondary sectors, was a capital programme of £1420 million in 17 years. These figures, considered alongside those already examined for the other sectors in the system, give some idea of the scale of the financial commitment to education in the 1960s. Huge sums of money were being sucked into all sectors of education because of the need to provide accommodation for large numbers of pupils and students.

This, then, was the logistic scenario of education in the early 1960s — an expanding birth rate necessitating a massive building programme to provide new schools, a commitment to replace or renovate many old and decrepit schools; the promise of a change in the school leaving age further exacerbated the problems; finally, higher education was also expanding as a natural consequence of expansion lower down the system, and it too swallowed up astronomical sums to provide buildings and equipment in universities and colleges. These were the physical constraints and demographic facts which formed the background against which the re-organisation of secondary education on comprehensive lines took place, out of which the middle school directly sprang.

Turning now to the pressures for reform which were in evidence in the 1960s, the most powerful arguments and the greatest emotion centred mainly on the question of selection. Those who were dissatisfied with the 11+ examination were divided into two groups. On the one hand were those opposed to selection in any form within the compulsory education period and they favoured a move towards fully comprehensive secondary education. On the other hand, there were those who believed that the selection process at 11 years was unfair and unsound, not because of any wish for greater egalitarianism, but rather because it was too early an age to be able to ascertain with any degree of certainty what a child's aptitudes might be. This group did not wish to abolish selection in

5

secondary education, but rather they favoured postponing the age of selection to twelve or thirteen, and thus the question of the best age of transfer to secondary education and, by implication, the most appropriate age spans for schools to contain, became an important part of the education debate of the period.

The Leicestershire Plan was a prime example of an early experimental scheme which sought not to abolish selection, but rather to postpone it to an age when children might be selected more successfully for a type of schooling best suited to their needs. The scheme began as an experiment in 1957 in two urban areas of the county, one near to Leicester at Oadby and Wigston, the other in south-west Leicestershire at Hinckley. It became a plan for the whole county in 1959 and the re-organisation was completed in 1969. All children transferred from their primary schools at the age of eleven to high schools, which were the former secondary modern schools, where they remained until they were fourteen years old; then a choice had to be made either to continue in the high school until the statutory leaving age of fifteen years or transfer to an upper school if the pupil was prepared to stay on at school to age sixteen or beyond; these upper schools were the old grammar schools. One can see that this was not a fully comprehensive system but it did postpone, at least in theory, the selection process for three years, though of course internal selection process would have been in operation throughout the pupil's stay in the high school. So the scheme abolished the 11+ and replaced it with a 14+ though to be fair the selection procedure was based on criteria quite different from those used at age eleven. The plan seemed to be particularly successful for it appeared to satisfy a wide range of demands such as those of parents for an end to the 11+; it was able to utilise existing buildings, concentrating expensive equipment where it was most needed; it gave secondary modern teachers some contact with able children and although reducing the age range of children in contact with the former grammar school teachers it nevertheless gave them a larger number of older pupils; finally a great advantage was that the scheme avoided the creation of very large schools thought necessary for the new 11-18 comprehensive schools in order to provide viable sixth forms.

The Leicestershire scheme was not without its critics many of whom felt that the bright children would not be sufficiently stretched in the former high schools largely because they would not come into contact with the really good academic teachers. The latter would tend not to be drawn to such schools because they were smaller, and thus would not be able to pay scales high enough to attract them. Furthermore, the interruption of external examination courses two years before their completion would tend to make the upper school something of a cram factory compensating for time 'lost' in the high school. It was for reasons such as these that in 1963 Edward Boyle pronounced that he was '... doubtful whether ... this is the right method for other parts of the country'.[7] Research published a couple of years later by Eggleston (1965) confirmed the still limited opportunities which the Leicestershire scheme conferred upon working class children. However, the importance of this scheme to the development of middle schools is that it broke down the traditional age ranges of the secondary school and demonstrated that transfer between schools could take place successfully at ages other than eleven even though it maintained the traditional divide between primary and secondary education.

There soon followed other proposals by LEAs which altered the traditional pattern of the 11-18 grammar/technical schools and the 11-15 secondary moderns. For example, the Croydon Plan envisaged the creation of a junior college to replace the traditional grammar school sixth form and Stoke-on-Trent also suggested a college for its sixth formers underpinned by junior high schools organised in two stages from 11-13 and 13-16 years. Yet another proposal was the Doncaster Plan, a modification of the Leicestershire scheme, envisaging the creation of high schools to which all pupils transferred at 11 years followed by a system of parental choice at 13; those children whose parents were willing for them to remain at school for a five year course leading to 'A' levels taken at 18 years, and whose teachers recommended it, would transfer to a grammar technical school while the remaining pupils, leaving at 15 or 16 years, would stay on in the former high schools. However, in these latter schools a full range of academic courses would be available leading to 'O'-level and CSE examinations, thus allowing pupils to transfer to an appropriate sixth form course if desired. In this scheme there was still postponement of selection rather than its abolition, although the distinctions between the groups of children are made less sharp. However, like all the other plans, although it allowed transfer between schools at ages other than eleven the traditional break between primary and secondary schooling was maintained. It was left to the West Riding to break through this particular barrier.

The proposals of the West Riding (Clegg, 1963) were drawn up to meet the demands for comprehensive education made by the separate divisions within the authority and suggested that there should be three blocks of education for 5-9, 9-13 and 13-18 year olds. All children would enter school at the start of the term after their fifth birthday, and a reception period of voluntary and often part-time attendance would introduce reception children to school before they began in real earnest. At 8+ or 9+ pupils would transfer from a primary to a middle school for four years and at the end of this period they would all move on to a secondary school. As can be seen this plan was more radical than the other three-tier schemes not only because it planned for fully comprehensive education without any selection at all, but also because it proposed a school which sat astride the traditional primary/secondary divide.

The report itself was drawn up after the West Riding Education Committee had called for an investigation into the feasibility of a distinct type of schooling for the 9-13 age range and the teachers, lecturers, inspectors and advisers who were consulted believed that the standard of primary education had risen so remarkably in recent years that it was a mistake to cut it short at 11. Furthermore there was concern that examination pressures were forcing specialisation on children too young to be able to cope with it effectively.

As these proposals stood, they were in direct contravention of the 1944 Act because they failed to hold the distinction between primary and secondary education exactly in the same way as did all-age schools. Local authorities, therefore, were not allowed to build or adapt schools for children in the 9-13 age range. However the report stated that '. . . the law is so peculiar that the scheme is put forward in defiance of it in order that the Minister may be pressed to consider the issues involved'. There is no doubt that at the time in question the idea of transfer at 13+ was gaining in popularity and more and more people were coming round to the view that both intellectually and psychologically 13 was the best age for the 11+. However, even though the West Riding's plans were tentative and localised there were many who thought that such radical changes affected school buildings, and hence public money and that the law should act as a brake on too much chopping and changing. On educational grounds too there was some disquiet at the implication that primary schools had all the answers so that its influence should be extended while secondary schooling, being the menace, should have its influence curtailed. In spite of these disquiets, however, the Minister for Education, Edward Boyle, took up the challenge and an Act of Parliament came into being on July 31st 1964 which amended the 1944 Act with respect to the traditional divide at 11+ between primary and secondary education. This date can be regarded as the birthday of the English middle school.

The 1964 Act deftly steered a middle course between experiment and conservation for although it allowed a change in the age ranges of schools, and thus in the age of transfer between schools, it still maintained the traditional division of compulsory schooling into primary and secondary elements. This was achieved by stipulating that any proposed new school which broke with the traditional transfer age should be deemed as either a primary school or a secondary school, a situation which exists to this day. As the middle school had thus to be placed within either the secondary or primary stages the spirit of the 1944 Act was maintained even though the letter was changed. Also the 1964 Act referred to new schools only and so it was not possible for local authorities to alter the age ranges of existing schools, although of course there was nothing to prevent any LEA from proposing to close an existing school and re-open it as a new school with different age ranges. There was little doubt, therefore, that as it stood the 1964 Act would not allow 'our school organisation to be exposed to every crackpot scheme'.[8]

Three months after the passing of the 1964 Act the Conservative Government was replaced by the Labour Government which was to retain power until 1970. The new government heralded a marked change in educational policy, for the Labour Party were committed to introducing a fully comprehensive system of education and the abolition of selection. During their term of office the Conservative Government had allowed a policy of a hundred flowers — an opportunity for local authorities to experiment with many different schemes of education — for even the Conservatives recognised the problem of the 11+ selection and the great anxiety it aroused in a large number of parents and their children. Even though the 11+ was electorally unpopular the Conservatives were caught on the horns of a dilemma because the solution to the

11+ problem involved its abolition and with that would come the end of the grammar schools — an event which the Tories could not accept. Hence central government appeared to lay back and not initiate any reforms of secondary education, but rather left this to local authorities who could initiate their own proposals to which central government was not unsympathetic; it was in this way that many comprehensive schools were established under a Conservative Government.

The change in style and policies was signalled by the issue in July 1965 of Circular 10/65 which the new Secretary of State for Education, Anthony Crosland sent to all LEAs requesting them, if they had not already done so, to prepare and submit plans for re-organising secondary education in their areas on comprehensive lines; and the document provided some clear guidelines on the methods by which this could be achieved. The Circular is often portrayed as an example of central government wielding the big stick to the local authorities, and of course there is no doubt that Circular 10/65 was meant to exert pressure on the local authorities, and also many people found it difficult to adjust to central government taking the initiative after it had adopted such a laissez-faire attitude for such a long time under a Conservative administration. However, it is also wothwhile noting that it can be viewed as a necessary instrument of rationalisation on what was rapidly becoming a rather chaotic and disorganised education system with a multiplicity of different schemes appearing up and down the country. As Crosland himself remarked, one of the reasons for listing acceptable proposals was to escape a patchwork pattern which would place an intolerable strain on parents and teachers who frequently had to be geographically mobile.[9] Some coherent national strategy was essential, and in any case the Labour Government claimed, perhaps rather over optimistically, that 74% of the nation's children were in areas that had adopted, were adopting or were contemplating comprehensive schemes — 'There is no power or indeed intention to impose, but the tide is irresistible'.

Circular 10/65 proposed six types of acceptable plan though two of them were to be considered as interim — that where all children transferred at 11 years to a junior comprehensive and then at age 13 or 14 years some pupils moved away to another school while the remainder stayed put (the Leicestershire scheme, in fact); the other interim scheme was a variant of the Leicestershire plan in that at age 13 or 14 years all the pupils moved on to another school, but which one depended on whether or not the child wished to remain beyond the compulsory school leaving age. The remaining four schemes were regarded as fully comprehensive — the all-through 11-18 school; a two tier arrangement whereby all pupils transferred at 11 years to a junior comprehensive and then all pupils transferred at 13 or 14 years to a senior comprehensive; an 11-16 school combined with a form college for pupils over 16 years old and finally,

'(vi) A system of middle schools which straddle the primary/secondary age ranges. Under this system pupils transfer from a primary school at the age of 8 or 9 to a comprehensive school with an age range of 8 to 12 or 9 to 13. From this middle school they move on to a comprehensive school with an age range of 12 or 13 to 18'. (DES, 1965. p.2)

As was mentioned at the beginning of this chapter the most favoured scheme was the all-through comprehensive school:

If it were possible to design a new pattern of secondary education without regard to existing building, the all-through comprehensive school would, in many respects, provide the simplest and best solution'. (Ibid.)

Of the remaining three fully comprehensive schemes the one proposing middle schools was regarded as a very limited option for in paragraph 21 of the Circular it is stated that whereas middle schools would give considerable benefits in that they would lead to an end of selection and would allow the possibility of smaller all-through comprehensive schools, the Minister intended to give his approval to no more than a 'very small number'. The reasons given for this were stated in a later paragraph (number 30) namely that local authorities should regard the age of transfer from primary to secondary education as the traditional one of 11+ and that plans should be prepared on this basis except where a limited departure from this had been agreed with the Secretary of State. This caution was undoubtedly due to three main causes. The first was the fact that it was in the spirit of the 1964 Act that the introduction of middle schools should not drive a coach and horses through the traditional distinction between primary and secondary education enshrined in the 1944 Act. Secondly, the scheme was totally untried; as there were no middle schools in existence at that time no-one could pronounce with any degree of certainty whether such schools would work. Thirdly, there was the influence of the Plowden Committee which was set up in August 1963 to consider the whole subject of primary education and, in addition, the transition to secondary education. Anthony Crosland at that stage realised that Lady Plowden's Report was a good distance away from completion and so for all intents and purposes it was best not to disturb the status quo pending any recommendations on the age of transfer which the Committee might make.

From all of this, therefore, it can be seen that the arrival of the middle school on the educational scene was a very hesitant one; the 1964 Act gave it a limited and circumscribed birth, and its first birthday, celebrated by Circular 10/65, was a typically cautious and restrained affair. There was no green light for the mushrooming of middle schools which was to take place later. What, then, caused this to happen?

To find the answer to this it is necessary to look at a debate on education and technology which took place in the House of Commons on 25th April 1966. Mr. Eric Lubbock, the Liberal Member for Orpington, raised a question in the context of comprehensive schooling concerning the West Riding system,

'. . . which, it appears, has some advantages in communities like mine. The education officer, in his report to the committee in the London Borough of Bromley says:

"It is understood that the Department (meaning the DES) is most unlikely to accept a proposal of this sort"

that is, of the West Riding type —

"unless, while wanting to change, a local authority finds no other system administratively practicable".

This must be the education officer's interpretation of one passage in Circular 10/65, that is paragraph 22, where the Secretary of State says that he does not intend to give his approval to more than a very small number of such proposals in the near future, the reason being that he wants to wait until the Plowden Report is made and he can see what the Plowden Committee recommends about the age of transition. But from an Answer given to a Question just before the Summer Recess last year it appeared that the attitude of the Department was beginning to change and that a larger number of West Riding type schemes might be acceptable to the Minister. I should like to ask him what his present policy is on the subject, because it strikes me that the West Riding system has certain advantages particularly to boroughs like mine . . . The only reason for my intervention this evening was to ask the Secretary of State, in his winding up speech, to say something further about his thoughts, on the West Riding system and whether he would accept more than the very small number of such schemes which he stated in Circular 10/65 he was willing to accept' (Hansard, 25.4.66. p.472).

Towards the end of the debate, the Secretary of State gave his reply:

'The hon. Member for Orpington asked what the attitude would be now, as opposed to last July when the circular went out, to schemes for 9-13 middle schools on the lines of the West Riding. He is right in supposing that our attitude has shifted in the light of experience since the day when we used the language in the circular. We would now be more willing than we were then to consider, possibly, 9-13 schemes. We would still ask to be shown that these schemes could produce a clear advantage in terms of teachers and buildings, but supposing that they could, we should be more inclined than it appeared from the circular to approve such schemes'. (Ibid., p.494)

One month later, in May, Circular 13/66 was issued outlining the Secretary of State's plans for school building for raising the school leaving age to sixteen. It is in this context, that paragraphs 4 and 5 of the circular should be read. These made two points, namely that since the issue of Circular 10/65 it had become apparent that some authorities would find it easier to introduce comprehensive education if the age of transfer was changed from 11+; secondly, that for some authorities it might be easier to provide facilities for raising the school leaving age if the age of transfer was changed as this would lead to 'a consequent reduction in the age range of secondary schools which would have to accommodate extra pupils'. (DES, 1966. p.3)

So although a national decision on transfer ages had to await the Plowden Committee (not to report for another six months) Anthony Crosland thought that there were a number of 'urgent practical reasons' why LEAs should be given flexibility in this matter:-

'He (the Minister) will therefore regard a change in the age of transfer for the time being as a matter for local option, and he is prepared to consider proposals from authorities on this basis. He will however expect authorities' proposals for making changes in the interim to be justified by reference to some clear practical advantages in the context of reorganisation on comprehensive lines, or the raising of the school leaving age, or both'. (ibid.)

So we have a dramatic U-turn on middle schools provision within the space of about 9 months and the question we must ask is why was this. There are two main reasons for this change of policy. The first, as is usually the case, was financial, for there is no doubt that the huge amount of finance required to service an ever expanding education service committed to comprehensive re-organisation to an enlargement of higher education and to raising the school leaving age was placing an almost intolerable burden on the public purse. Even in July 1965, a week or two after Circular 10/65 was issued, the government was forced to cut back on expenditure in education; this was limited in the first instance to capital expenditure postponements for six months in colleges of education, technical colleges and universitites and of cut backs in sports and recreation facilities and in the youth service. Only the school building programme escaped unscathed, but undoubtedly the pressure was on to save money and reduce expenditure wherever possible. Some idea of the continuing pressure on financial resources can be gauged from the fact that in 1967 the government had to take the politically very unpopular decision to postpone the raising of the school leaving age from 1970-71 until 1972-73 simply because the resources were not available to meet the earlier deadline. There was pressure too from LEAs who wanted a more flexible approach to the execution of government policy, or more cash to be able to do the job properly; after all Circular 10/65 in effect only gave LEAs three ways of achieving comprehensive re-organisation and many found that they could not cope with the limitations of buildings in their areas given the restricted amount of government finance. For a number of areas, therefore, middle schools looked to be a quite attractive proposition for with a year or two lopped off their entry existing secondary schools would be able to accommodate the extra children produced by raising the leaving age with a minimum of additional building; any further accommodation which was needed could be confined mainly to the primary sector where it was considerably cheaper. In any case according to the 1962 Building Survey investment in primary school buildings was long overdue.

The second reason for this policy change was related to the findings of the Plowden Committee. It was becoming public knowledge during 1966 that the Committee was going to recommend some changes in the age of transfer from primary to secondary education. For example in February the TES was able to state in a leading article, 'If, as is widely rumoured, the (Plowden) Committee intends to recommend the age of transfer be moved to 12 . . .'; the Report was expected by June but was not presented to the Secretary of State until the end of October and was not published until the beginning of 1967. So even though the Secretary could not make any public pronouncements on the age of transfer and indeed had to be seen to be waiting for the Committee's recommendations, privately he must have been aware for a considerable time of the contents of the report concerning the age of transfer. This in itself gives a particularly apt illustration of Bacon's phrase 'For knowledge itself is power' because with the fore knowledge that Plowden was going to recommend changes based on well argued, sound educational criteria, the Secretary of State was able to propose changes on the transfer age based on financial and administrative expediency knowing that his educational flank was well covered. It was a classical piece of political manoeuvring allowing greater flexibility for those LEAs who wanted and could make use of it while at the same time appearing cautious and not imposing a uniform system on the country as a whole ahead of Plowden. The episode reveals just how much the English education system progresses and changes through compromise and 'ad hocery'.

Attention can finally be turned on the effects of the Plowden Report which, when published early in 1967, confirmed earlier speculation by proposing a change in the age of transfer from primary to secondary education. The reasons for the Committee's decisions will be explored in Chapter 2 and here we shall consider the recommendation itself and the implications of that decision. The Committee decided that the age of transfer should be raised from 11+ upwards, but to what age involved another debate as to whether it should be 12+ or 13+; in the end the finely balanced arguments were thought to tip the scales just in favour of 12+, hence this age was to replace the traditional one of 11+.

In paragraph 393 the Report outlined the need for a single nationwide age of transfer because of the requirements of a mobile labour force – it did not want to see children who left a secondary school in one area having to go back to a primary school if they moved to another area. So even though the Report recommended a transfer age of 12+, it suggested that the national transfer age should be decided upon the basis of available buildings and this might be 13+ instead. That recommendation of Plowden was never implemented and a national policy was never announced. Why was this so? The answer can be found in constraints and difficulties which the education system was experiencing at that point in time. Firstly, the Plowden Report was third in line behind two other influential reports of the decade – the Robbins and Newsom Reports both of which, as we have seen, produced recommendations which involved a huge financial burden on the country in expanding higher education and in raising the school leaving age. Secondly, the plans for reorganising comprehensive education were, by 1967, well under way and although some LEAs complained to the Minister that they could only reorganise if a change in transfer ages was allowed, there were many also who complied with Circular 10/65 and this, coupled with the fact that a large building programme had already been planned and executed in the first half of the decade, meant that a wholesale change affecting the nation's primary schools was simply impracticable. The nation had run out of steam and out of money; the Plowden Report was too late to have any major influence on the national structure of the educational system, though within the primary sector, of course, its influence was enormous; had the Report come three or four years earlier then the face of English education may well have been very different with 8 to 12 or 9 to 13 schools being the rule rather than the exception. However, by recommending a change in transfer ages it paved the way for local authorities to adopt a middle school organisation if it suited their particular needs even though a national change in the transfer age was impossible because of administrative and financial constraints. Thus the combination of circumstances at national and local level assured that middle schools would have a marginal status.

In this introduction we have tried to show that the arrival of middle schools on the English educational scene was due to a combination of many different factors the chief of these being the need to expand rapidly the national educational provision in a period when resources were limited. The move to comprehensive education, the raising of the school leaving age, the demands of further and higher education all placed great burdens on the Exchequer and the middle school seemed to provide an economical alternative to more expensive schemes. Although a national move towards middle schools could not be supported as too great an investment had already been made in plant based on the traditional primary/secondary divide, the Plowden Report provided legitimation on educational grounds for individual local authorities who wished to introduce middle schools on financial and administrative grounds.

Notes

1. *Times Educational Supplement*, 2.8.63.
2. Lord Newton, formerly Peter Legh M.P. for Petersfield, was Minister of State for Education in the Hume Government from April 1st, 1964 until the Government fell in October of that year.
3. *Times Educational Supplement*, 2.8.63.
4. 'Questions in Parliament', *Times Educational Supplement*, 12.7.63.
5. *Times Educational Supplement*, 1.2.63.
6. 'Questions in Parliament', *Times Educational Supplement*, 12.7.63.
7. *Times Educational Supplement*, 1.3.63.
8. *Times Educational Supplement*, 8.5.64.
9. *Times Educational Supplement*, 12.3.64.

CHAPTER 2

The Educational Arguments

Although the case has been proposed in the previous chapter that middle schools developed primarily as a consequence of political and economic pressures, nevertheless it is important that the educational arguments be considered too, for it must be remembered that even though new types of school may be brought into existence on the grounds of administrative convenience, their success or failure as institutions is judged on how well they fulfil certain educational aims. The strongest arguments for the establishment of middle schools came from the West Riding of Yorkshire in the early 1960s, and in particular from Alec Clegg, the County's Chief Education Officer, yet it was the Plowden Report which justified, on educational grounds, the setting up of middle schools. As Edwards (1972) notes, many LEAs had to make decisions about the type of comprehensive education they wanted to introduce into their areas before Plowden was published and so for this and other reasons outlined in Chapter 1 the Plowden Report's effect was mainly on the development and organisation of middle schools rather than their initial establishment. It is thus useful to examine the arguments which Plowden considered because they crystallise so much of the educational debate which helped to shape the pattern of middle school evolvement.

The ages and stages of primary education are considered by Plowden in paragraphs 344 to 407 and the question of raising the age of transfer to secondary education is considered in paragraphs 365 onwards. This section begins by noting that, ' "11+" seems now as firmly fixed in Englishmen's minds as 1066'; a brief historical account is then given as to why the traditional age of transfer became 11 that it gave 'scholarship winners' from elementary schools the chance to spend five years in the grammar schools and also that it allowed a 'secondary' education, within an elementary system, of at least two years before most pupils left school at 14.

As there were in the early 1960s a large number of different schemes for secondary re-organisation being canvassed by LEAs and pressure groups the Plowden Committee decided to examine the question of transfer age 'from first principles' taking into account the evidence on children's development, evidence from the inspectorate, other associations and individual witnesses; other factors considered were the arguments for the Leicestershire Plan and for 9-13 schools; discussions were also held with class teachers and head teachers from different types of primary and secondary schools and visits were made by members of the Committee to a variety of schools, including those with an age range of 11-13. From this welter of evidence the Report then considered the arguments for and against changing the age of transfer to secondary school.

First of all, however, were presented four 'good arguments against a change'; two of these were academic, one social and one which advocated the status quo because from the primary schools' view there was little to be gained from interfering with an already proven system, especially as many of the nation's primary schools were in the van of educational thought and practice. Why disturb such a successful sector when to do so might check the very advances which distinguished it? The academic arguments related mainly to secondary education, for transfer at age 11 enabled teachers to get to know their pupils very well before subject choices had to be made and thus the most suitable and best informed decisions could be taken; furthermore, the existing system allowed 11 and 12 year old pupils to be taught by specialist teachers, particularly in maths and science. There was also a sound argument for retaining an 11+ transfer age on social grounds, for by moving into a new school before the onset of puberty the pupils were given time to settle down and meet the storm and stress of adolescence within a familiar environment.

On the other side of the coin there were solid reasons for advocating an upward change in the transfer age, though it must be said that many of these were because of apparent defects in the education then being provided by secondary schools; however great play was also made of the idea that there was a distinctive period of middle childhood and that the 11+ transfer 'cut across this phase of learning and the attitudes to it'. The Report continues:—

> 'An unselfconscious period in art, dramatic movement and writing, for example may last till 12 or 13. Many children, too, at the top of the primary school develop confidence in devising experiments and using books in specific situations (often unrelated to "subjects"). Their progress may be slowed down by premature emphasis on class instruction, adult systematisation and precision in secondary schools' (para. 371).

Whereas the secondary school was seen to be antithetical to this phase, the primary school was viewed as sympathetic, especially as the curriculum in the 1960s had been widened in a number of directions and now frequently included a foreign language for example; even subjects themselves had been extended from simple nature study to more complex science, and from arithmetic to mathematics; it was argued, therefore, that the new and enlightened curriculum of the upper primary school provided sufficient basis for a distinctive middle school curriculum. Some psychological justification was also afforded by the followers of Piaget, who claimed that because the powers of abstract thought developed somewhat later on in adolescence, this gave credence to postponing transfer until nearer that phase of formal operational thought.

Continuing the case for change, it was argued that from the secondary school side the age of 11 was too early for important educational decisions to be taken, especially as many of the (then) new comprehensives operated a selective system within the school which was just as divisive as when the 11+ examination separated children between schools: 'This rigidity inside comprehensive schools may be unnecessary and may be temporary; but it has to be taken into account' (para 372). This is hardly the basis on which to advocate a national change in the transfer age, though it does illustrate the difficulties which faced the Plowden Committee with regard to the way in which the curriculum was organised for junior pupils in the secondary schools; this was a period of great upheaval with no settled pattern of secondary education and there was little indication of how the internal organisation of comprehensive schools would eventually develop, especially as many of them at this period had to co-exist and compete with grammar schools. It was additionally argued too that because an increasing number of pupils were remaining at school to 16 and 18 years, the most highly qualified staff were being drained away from the junior pupils who were thus not receiving the benefits of specialist teaching; this problem was exacerbated, however, because even though the pupils were not getting contact with the specialist staff, the curriculum was still being organised as if they were, and thus the pupils in the early years of the secondary school were getting the worst of all worlds – no specialist teachers yet an unnecessarily over specialised curriculum.

Apart from these academic arguments there were also social reasons for changing the age range of secondary schools, for it was felt by many educationalists that having 11 and 18 year olds within the same institution made it difficult to cater adequately for the needs of either. Older adolescents were keen to distance themselves from the younger pupils in school while the younger children were frequently overwhelmed by the older pupils and felt left out of things; this could be seen particularly in some extra-curricula activities such as sport and drama, and frequently the younger pupils were not adequately catered for by support facilities such as libraries.

Other arguments advanced by Plowden for change included that of avoiding the over large secondary school caused by the move towards comprehensivisation and the raising of the school leaving age; a much more sensible approach would be to reduce the size of the secondary school by removing the pupils at the lower end – an argument, it will be remembered, which was a principal one advocated in Circular 13/66.

All in all the Plowden Committee felt that the 11 and 12 year olds fitted 'less well than they did' into a secondary school pattern and therefore it considered that the case was made out for pupils of this age to be spent in a primary school. The Committee then examined whether the age of transfer should be fixed at 12 or 13 years. Consideration was first given to the advantages of both ages – that either would protect pupils from the downward extension of external examination pressures and yet would give adequate time in the secondary school to prepare for CSE or GCE; however a disadvantage of transfer at 13 would be that the non-examination pupils, who became labelled the Newsom children, would only spend 2 years and 2 terms in the secondary school – a period considered too short by many teachers; for these pupils transfer at 12 would be more advantageous.

17

As regards the curriculum either age of transfer would be suitable for subjects such as english, home economics and art; transfer at 12 would be a slightly better age as far as modern languages was concerned. However, the real problém areas for transfer at 13 would be the practical subjects such as handicraft, science and PE for these would require a major investment in specialist accom-modation and specialist teachers; staffing would be a much greater problem in a 9-13 than an 8-12 school because a higher level of specialist expertise would be required. Such arguments, of course, were concerned more with administrative and economic constraints than educational aims, though on the positive side the Committee did also consider whether transfer at 12 or 13 would provide the kind of middle school which they wished to see: in paragraph 381 the Plowden Report describes the ideal middle school — an influential section as it provided a model for middle school development in the 1970s:.

'A school with semi-specialist accommodation shared between cognate subjects, and teachers skilled in certain areas of the curriculum rather than in single subjects, could provide a bridge from class teaching to specialisation and from investigation of general problems to subject disciplines. The influence of semi-specialist teachers primarily concerned with the older pupils might be reflected in more demanding work being given to nine and ten year-olds, while the primary tradition of individual and group work might advan-tageously be retained for a longer period than at present . . .'

To provide for this transition either 12 or 13 would be suitable, the Report claimed, with no intrinsic advantage to either age group, yet each was not with-out problems also for the danger of making 12 the age of transfer would be that it would not provide a sufficient stimulus and challenge to teachers to make the school distinct from a primary; a 13 year transfer age, on the other hand, might have the opposite effect and such a middle school, becoming secondary orien-tated, 'would forget that it was still a primary school' (p.384).

The arguments for a transfer age of either 12 or 13 were thus evenly balanced, yet on nearly every count, according to Plowden, there was a slight advantage in favour of the 12 year transfer age, and so the Report recommended that transfer at age 12 would give the ideal middle school.

The question which we can now ask is how convincing were the arguments put forward by Plowden for a change — a national change — in the age of transfer to secondary education?

The first point which needs to be stressed is that any proposal which advocates changes in the age of transfer from one educational institution to another, be it from infant to junior, secondary to tertiary or primary to secondary is handi-capped by the simple fact that there is never any one age of transfer which is correct either for all individual children or all systems of education; many countries have different age ranges within their schools and yet educate their pupils as successfully as any other. Thus to advocate a change in the age of transfer from primary to secondary school by a year or two can rarely be sup-ported by strong arguments and politicians are unlikely to be moved from the status quo by educational arguments unless these present a clear and overwhelming case for change; this the protagonists for middle schools in general and the Plowden Committee in particular were never able to do, for the development of pupils − physically, mentally, socially and emotionally − is a continuous and evolving process and any interruption caused by institutional changes is bound to break that continuity.

'The answer to the question "What is the appropriate age of transfer?" (from primary to secondary education) must be that there is no one "correct" age'.

This was the conclusion of Nisbet and Entwistle (1966, p.89) in their carefully considered book on the age of transfer to secondary education and underlines the point that any age chosen to transfer pupils from one institution to another is arbitrary and will not of itself ensure success or failure of the constituent organisations. These problems of the arbitrariness of any transfer age and the relative weakness of educational justifications were exacerbated by the very nature of the Plowden Report itself which approached the question rather like a judge in a courtroom summing-up with the case for and against a change presented alongside each other with supporting evidence; the conclusions reached by the Committee were that the arguments did just about tip the scales in favour of raising the age of transfer, though whether to 12 or 13 presented yet again some finely balanced arguments. This hardly provides the basis for a strong and overwhelming case on which to advocate a nationwide change in the age of transfer, causing yet more upheavals in the system already in a state of some turmoil due to the change-over to comprehensive education. Plowden's influence in this context, therefore, was limited to providing sufficient educational justification for those local authorities whose administrative and financial situation favoured a middle school system.

Another consideration is that the problem of transfer was explored within the broader context of the whole of primary education and in particular the age of entry into the infant school. The Report advocates the raising of the age of entry to infant school from the term following a child's fifth birthday to the September following a child's fifth birthday and it could be argued that once this recommendation had been made the Committee were forced to raise the age of entry to secondary school to provide an adequate and acceptable length of schooling in the infant and primary sectors; thus, as in most organisations, decisions taken in one part of the education system are found to have consequences, both intended and unintended, for other parts.

Another area to examine in this evaluation is the opinions of teachers surveyed by the Plowden Committee to ascertain the profession's views on the major questions considered. 3000 questionnaires were sent to a random sample of teachers of which 2239 were returned, giving a 75% response rate. The breakdown of the sample replying is given as follows:−

	number	%[1]	
Infant	358	16.0	82.1% Primary Sector
Infant and Junior	808	36.1	
Junior	672	30.0	
Secondary Modern	185	8.3	16.4% Secondary Sector
Secondary 'Other'	181	8.1	
Others	35	1.5	
	2239	100.0	

It can be seen that the secondary sector is very much under-represented in this sample and no distinction is made between grammar and comprehensive schools; for many of the questions exclusively concerned with the organisation and development of primary education this does not matter too much, but for those questions concerning the age of transition and which involved pupils traditionally educated in the secondary sector the view points of secondary teachers are seriously attenuated and a much larger sample and a more sophisticated breakdown of the number of teachers in secondary schools should have been made available — after all the terms of reference to the Central Advisory Council specifically included consideration of the transition to secondary education and this should have meant close consultation with secondary, as well as primary, school teachers.

Considering first of all the age of transfer from infant to junior school 58%[2] of primary teachers favoured a continuation of this at age 7, though a substantial minority of 37% thought that transfer at 8 years would be more suitable. Examination of the figures by type of school, however, reveals that junior school teachers, both heads and assistants, were overwhelmingly in favour of the status quo with 70% wishing to retain transfer at 7; it was, in fact, the teachers in infant schools, particularly the head teachers, who favoured raising the age of transfer to junior school. Of interest in passing is that only 3% of all primary teachers were in favour of a transfer age of 9.

With regard to secondary school transfer the primary school teachers were more evenly divided with 36% favouring retention at 11 while a slight majority — 40% — wanted to see this raised to 12 and again it was the head teachers who formed the largest group in favour. As one would expect the majority of secondary teachers (53%) thought that transfer should be retained at 11, though of the remainder there was a fairly even split between those wanting 12 as the age of transfer (23%) and those who wanted to see it raised to 13 (18%).

A similar phenomenon can thus be observed with regard to the transfer between infant and junior and junior and secondary schools — that is teachers, and especially head teachers, in the institution from which the children transfer

1. Added by present authors.
2. All figures have been rounded off.

wanted to keep their children for an extra year, while those teachers to which the children were moving were against losing their bottom age range of children. Whether the desire to keep the children for another year in both types of school was due to the perceived need to give them more time to master the basic skills and to provide more appropriate help for slow learners, or because many teachers thought his change would enhance the status of infant and junior school teachers, it is difficult to say; perhaps, as is often the case, it was a bit of both.

Whereas the Plowden Report does not give the secondary teacher responses to the question concerning the age of transfer from infant to junior school, no such inhibition is present in giving the primary teacher's views on what should be the minimum length of time necessary for a secondary school course; a division of interests is naturally revealed for 51% of primary school teachers felt that four years was sufficient while only 38% of secondary teachers did. About 28% of primary teachers felt that five years was the minimum length necessary, but 44% of secondary teachers – the majority – stuck to the five year secondary course.

Finally, and perhaps most revealingly, are the results given to the question 'Should children in the first two years of the secondary school have a) a general class teacher b) a gradual introduction to specialisation or c) full specialist teaching from the first?' An overwhelming majority of primary school teachers (72%) felt that there should be a gradual introduction to specialist teaching with the remainder divided equally between the other two categories a) and c); surprisingly, however, even 49% of the teachers in secondary schools favoured a gradualist approach and among the head teachers this proportion jumped to 62%. It is to this question that a more detailed analysis of the secondary teachers responses would have been especially valuable to see how grammar, comprehensive and secondary modern schools varied.

However, these figures do indicate a commitment to practice in the lower forms of secondary schools which is rather different from that presented in the first volume of Plowden which saw secondary schools in general as dedicated to subject specialisation as soon as the pupils entered the school gate. This is perhaps typical of the Plowden Report in its approach to the transfer problem, for it compares the best and most progressive practices available in the primary sector with the most traditional forms of organisation found in the secondary sector; at best only scant attention was given to the widespread changes in thinking and practice which were taking place along with comprehensive education, and at worst, secondary schools were stereotyped in the mould of the old fashioned grammar school which was fast disappearing.

The final point to consider, almost by way of footnote, is the so-called 'Plowden Paradox'; the growth and development of children is examined by the Report basing its statements largely on the work of Tanner, and it shows the strong trend towards earlier maturity of pupils and an increase in their physical size at all ages.

This trend, however, gives rise to a paradox with respect to the recommendations given concerning the age of transfer to secondary education, for if pupils are maturing earlier why should it be necessary for them to be kept in primary school for a year longer? On the basis of the physiological evidence it would appear more logical to recommend a reduction in the age of transfer to 10 years rather than increase it to 12.

By the end of the year in which Plowden was published the Secretary of State had approved 22 schemes for secondary re-organisation on comprehensive lines with middle schools as an integral part of the system; one year later, in 1968, 40 such schemes had been approved and it was in this year also that the first middle schools opened in the West Riding of Yorkshire and the London Borough of Merton. The growth in the number and distribution of middle schools during the 1970s has been particularly well documented by Blyth and Derricott (1977) and it is intended here merely to give an indication of the extremely rapid rise in their number from 15 schools in 1969 to 140 in 1970, 348 in 1971 and over 400 in 1972. From 1973 to 1974 the number doubled from 686 to 1212 and although the second half of the decade has seen a tailing off in the rate of growth, nevertheless the total for 1978 is 1690 schools.

Such a rapid transformation from a limited number of experimental schools to a national network inevitably gave rise to a number of problems not the least of which was the sheer necessity of providing appropriate curricula for a new type of school with which teachers were totally unfamiliar. Thus a large number of curriculum projects were undertaken which were relevant to the middle years of schooling including such major programmes as 'Combined Science' (1970), 'Science 5-13' (1972) and 'History, Geography and Social Science 5-13' (1975); the general problems of curriculum planning and organisation were covered by such Schools Council projects as 'The Curriculum in the Middle Years' (Working Paper No. 55, 1975) and 'Education in the Middle Years' (Working Paper No. 42, 1972). Blyth and Derricott estimate that in whole or part 37 projects covered the middle years of schooling which represented an investment in curriculum development of about £2m. Running parallel with these major projects, however, were an enormous number of regional and local schemes which were drawn up by teachers and advisers working together and it would be true to say that at both national and local level most of the energy and resources expended within middle schools has been in the sphere of curriculum development.

In order to give further help and support to teachers in the emerging middle school sector a number of conferences were organised by the DES, the most important of which were held in Warwick in 1967 and Exeter in 1968. At the Warwick Conference, whose proceedings were later produced as Schools Council Working Paper No. 22, the emphasis of the speakers was very much on the positive attributes of middle schools and delegates were urged to take advantage of the new opportunities for experiment and innovation which these new schools would allow. Many curriculum theorists saw the emergent middle school as a suitable vehicle for their particular interests; for example, Dennis Lawton wanted middle schools to turn out good social scientists, and Tim McMullen pressed hard for them to be centres for resource based learning; it was Arthur Razzell, however, who waxed most lyrical at the opportunities provided by the new middle school: —

'Bernard Shaw wrote, "You see things as they are and ask, 'Why?'", I dream things that never were and ask, "Why not?".' It will be something of this capacity to capture a wide and clear vision, and then attempt to turn that vision into a reality that will help to create the exciting middle school' (Razzell, 1969; p.15).

The optimism and visionary zeal of this speaker was counter-balanced by more jaundiced views from the floor of the conference and in the discussion groups between practising teachers it was clear that they perceived a world entirely different from that portrayed by the platform rhetoric. In these groups one finds doubts, hesitancy, problems and questions – Would the 9-13 schools be a better proposition than the 8-12's? What would be the particular problems of middle schools in rural areas? Would especially bright children receive sufficient specialist teaching for their needs? Would the size of schools limit the number of scale posts and so be unable to attract good teachers? Would teachers in middle schools receive the ancillary help and support which colleagues in secondary schools have? The Warwick Conference seemed to parallel at the micro-level the conflicts which were encountered at the macro-level in the establishment of middle schools; at the macro-level were the educational justifications versus the economic and political determinants, while at the micro-level were the theoretical rationales for the middle school curricula set against the economic constraints which could inhibit the development of such programmes.

In the early days then, the official attitudes to middle schools were really quite favourable and in addition to the organisation of conferences and the stimulus to curriculum development the DES published two pamphlets in 1970, one called 'Launching Middle Schools' detailing the experiences of the West Riding and the other 'Towards the Middle School' – a more general document covering the curriculum, organisation of the school, buildings and equipment and even sample timetables to help teachers preparing for middle schools. 'It seemed that middle schools had come to stay and that they enjoyed a wide measure of benevolent interest' (Blyth and Derricott, ibid., p.25). However in more recent years, as theory has given way to practice, a rather less favourable attitude can be discerned in official DES publications which seem at best only lukewarm towards middle schools and at worst distinctly hostile. A case in point would be the report on 'Gifted Children in Middle and Comprehensive Secondary Schools' (1977) in which middle schools were accused of not even thinking about the problem of gifted children; furthermore middle schools appeared to be ill-equipped with resource material, such as libraries, to provide the necessary stimulus for such children and the lack of specialist staff was a further handicap. In general the report claimed that a three tier system made it inherently more difficult to provide for the needs of gifted children and there was hardly a word which gave encouragement to middle school teachers. Even in art, where middle schools might have been expected to show some signs of excellence and innovation, combining the best of primary and secondary approaches, the report states,

'Many, especially those in middle or intermediate schools, are without specialist help and important opportunities for the growth of skills and insight are lost' (DES 1977, p.52).

A similar unenthusiastic attitude can also be detected in 'Curriculum 11-16' (DES, 1977) where in Supplementary Paper Number 2 on Mobility and the School Curriculum the difficulties caused by local and regional variations in the curriculum are examined; the problem is shown to be difficult enough with a conventional primary/secondary transfer age, but with the introduction of middle schools with a whole variety of different age ranges, the problem becomes very much worse.

In the Green Paper – 'Education in Schools – A Consultative Document' (1977) two further problems are raised – the first concerning the range of the curriculum offered in middle schools and the second on the difficulties of transition between schools. On the curriculum the report acknowledges that to a greater extent than in other types of school the size of middle schools is a critical feature in determining the range and depth of the work which can be provided, especially in science, modern languages and handicrafts, because of the problem of providing specialist teachers: 'Many middle schools, including the smaller 9-13 schools, are unable to allocate more than one post to each of these specialisms, and some none' (p.9). In a recent National Union of Teachers' commentary on this section of the Green Paper (NUT, 1979) there can be detected from the middle school teachers a sharp feeling of betrayal by the DES, who having sired this particular offspring now seem unwilling to provide the necessary environment to ensure its survival. The following quotation illustrates the point.

'The Department (i.e. the DES), it would seem, having approved and even encouraged the establishment of middle schools, is now aware of the problems of understaffing but is not prepared to give the lead to LEAs in order to counteract them. The problem is particularly acute in those authorities which have created combined first and middle schools (5-12) by a stroke of the administrator's pen, but have done nothing to provide a still small school with the necessary resources to develop its new image' (NUT, 1979, p.5).

On the difficulties involved in transition between schools the Green Paper picks out middle schools as having certain problems in this area:

'A middle school system with careful co-ordination between the phases of schooling can work well . . . It can, however, cause some difficulty for pupils who transfer in and out of the area. Since middle schools are in a minority, transition is a matter to which local education authorities and teachers in such areas need to give special consideration' (ibid., p.9).

Here middle schools, far from easing the continuity between primary and secondary education, between non-specialist and specialist teaching, are viewed as creating additional and particularly difficult problems.

Such changes in the attitude towards middle schools are the more remarkable for the speed with which they have occurred though some of this may be attributed to the very difficult financial climate in which middle schools have had to establish their identity. In 1977 Blyth and Derricott felt sufficiently confident to write:

'However, being over 1500 in number, they (i.e. middle schools) are numerous enough to be firmly embedded in the educational system . . . they cannot simply, like Day Continuation Schools, vanish' (Blyth and Derricott, 1977, p.190).

Today, such a feeling of security and confidence is absent, for not only have middle schools failed to gain a separate status necessary for their particular needs and their continued growth and development, for they are still deemed as either primary or secondary under the 1964 Education Act, but also some recent publications have emphasised their minority position and marginal status with such titles as 'Middle Schools — High Road or Dead End?' (Burrows, 1978) and 'Middle Schools — Deemed or Doomed?' (NUT, 1979). The optimism at the beginning of the decade has given way to considerable despondency.

'Without a good proportion of specialist staff the 9-13 school in particular, and the 8-12 less so, begins to lose part of its fundamental character. Once there is a possibility that specialist teaching is at a minimum the accusations that the middle school is simply a prolongation of the primary stages cannot be contradicted' (NUT, 1979, p.5).

If that becomes the norm then the case for the continuation of middle schools as a distinctive form of education for pupils in the middle years of childhood ceases to exist.

CHAPTER 3

The Design of the Research

The amount of research that has been carried out in middle schools is relatively small due to the fact that they have been in existence for only a short period of time and also because most of the involvement and interest in middle schools has been centred on the development of appropriate curriculum materials. The research which has been undertaken is generally small in scale, often consisting of case study work examining, for instance, the organisation of a particular school or models of curriculum organisation and local transfer schemes (e.g. Meyenn and Tickle, 1980; Razzell, 1979; Gorwood, 1979; Campbell, 1973; Nicholson, 1970). Much of this work is descriptive but no less important for that since this kind of research has been a most important vehicle for the dissemination of information about middle schools and thus has played a major part in shaping their growth and development.

There are, however, some major gaps in the research on middle schools especially in terms of the scale of work which has been undertaken and frequently there are assumptions and statements made in the literature and the educational press based only on the evidence of case study work and these need to be quantified with a larger number of schools. There is very little survey material available about middle schools and those surveys which have been carried out are again rather small in scope often covering one particular problem in one particular area. For example, Working Paper 42 (1972) reports on investigations into teachers' views about problems in the middle years of schooling, yet the number of middle school teachers involved in this survey was only 48 out of a total of 1,390 — less than 3½% of the sample. Similarly, the Assistant Masters' Association's survey of 1974, though focusing on important aspects of the structure of middle schools such as staffing, grouping of pupils and the organisation of the curriculum, nevertheless was conducted only in those schools which had an AMA membership and since this was not one of the larger teacher organisations, replies were received from only 40 9-13, and 11 8-12 schools — a mere 5% of the 1974 total. Little has changed, in fact, since 1972 when Edwards wrote:

'The alleged advantages of the middle school system are, as yet, only in the minds of their advocates since they have not been supported by any experimental data' (Edwards, 1972, p.85).

It was felt by the present authors that such a deficiency ought to be remedied and that middle schools had been a part of the educational scene long enough for some kind of stock-taking exercise to be carried out comparing the organisational patterns and problems of different kinds of middle schools. It was decided, therefore, to undertake some form of large scale survey, although initially the form which this might take was undecided. A number of options were considered, such as the detailed surveying of all the middle schools in one particular region, a random sampling of all middle schools in the country and some sort of stage sampling, with a large number of schools being questioned at a general level with a further, detailed, in depth analysis being undertaken on a smaller selected group of schools.

In the end the decision on the form which the survey was to take was greatly influenced by the fact that the total number of middle schools in the country was not too large and that all could be contacted by post; furthermore such a project would just about be within range of the modest financial resources available. Such a survey would have the great advantage that any sample of middle schools which was obtained would be a sample, not of a wider sample, but rather of a total population — a most unusual situation in educational research. The advantages of a survey which attempted to contact all of the nation's middle schools were counter-balanced by corresponding disadvantages, the most significant of which was that information could not be obtained from a variety of teachers, but that the data collection would have to be restricted to the head teachers; it was simply beyond the team's financial resources to do otherwise. The decision was made, therefore, to send a questionnaire to all of the middle schools in the country excluding those schools which did not straddle the traditional primary/secondary division at age 11; thus the junior high schools in the 11-14 age range were excluded such as those in Croydon, Gateshead and Leicestershire; in the latter county also one or two 10-14 schools were not contacted because these were essentially part of the Leicestershire Scheme and were not middle schools in the traditionally accepted sense of the term.

The two basic aims of the survey were firstly, to obtain information about current practices in middle schools and secondly, to provide comparative data from the various types of middle school which had developed over the decade. The questionnaire, a copy of which can be found in Appendix 1, was divided into eight broad sections, each one dealing with a particular aspect of middle school organisation. A list of these sections is given below, together with an abbreviated description of the major topics covered in each part.

1. Background Information

Questions asked here concerned the size of school, its date of opening, denomination, the number of feeder first schools and number of high schools to which middle school pupils were sent. Such information was basic data designed to establish the nature of the sample of schools obtained and to establish the place of middle schools within the broader perspective of infant and secondary education.

2. Staffing

From our informal conversation with colleagues in schools it emerged that staffing was one of the most vital areas in establishing the distinctive character of middle schools and so questions asked in this section concerned the number of staff and the number of scale posts, the provision made for specialist and remedial teaching and pastoral care, the time spent by subject specialists teaching their own subject and the way in which additional staff resources might be used by the head teacher.

3. Grouping of Pupils

The questions here were concerned with the basis on which pupils were grouped for social/administrative and teaching purposes and to establish whether any different patterns of organisation were adopted as pupils progressed through the school.

4. Organisation of the Curriculum

The basic concern of this section was to assess the extent to which children in the middle school were exposed to subject specialists, what their role was and to assess the extent to which nationally and locally produced curriculum project materials were being used in middle schools.

5. Assessment Procedures

An attempt was made in this section to ascertain on what basis pupils were grouped on entry to the school and to establish the extent to which standardised tests and formal examinations were used on the various age groups of pupils.

6. Links with Other Schools

Information on links with other schools is included in other parts of the questionnaire (e.g. Section 1) but a separate section was included to examine the nature of the liaison between first and upper schools and to find out which members of staff were involved in this crucial aspect of middle school organisation.

7. Ethnic Minority Groups

A small section was included in the questionnaire on ethnic minority groups because some authors (e.g. Blyth and Derricott, 1977) had suggested that middle schools had particular advantages with regard to the social development of children in early adolescence. It was thought that it would be useful to ascertain the views of head teachers on this topic, especially from those schools who had a sizeable proportion of ethnic minority pupils.

8. General Organisation

The last section of the questionnaire comprised a miscellany of questions covering a variety of topics such as the type and organisation of the parent-teachers association, provision of pastoral care for pupils over 11 years old, the nature and frequency of 'problem pupils' and the out of school activities provided by the school. The last four questions covered the aims of middle schools, the perceived problems and advantages of middle schools and the way they were likely to develop in the future; they were open-ended to allow head teachers to respond to the questions, if they so wished, in their own way.

Once the broad areas for inclusion in the questionnaire had been decided, consideration had to be given as to whether or not it would be possible to compile a different questionnaire to send to each type of middle school; there was no doubt that separate questionnaires would have had many advantages especially as questions could be tailored more closely to the organisational patterns existing in the different schools and thus the quality of data collected would have been superior than with a single questionnaire; however, such a procedure would have involved the production of at least four different questionnaires and possibly five — one each for the 8-12, 9-13, 10-13 and 5-12 schools and also one for the combinations of other ages such as 8-13 and 9-12. Such an undertaking, necessitating such high printing costs, was again beyond the resources available and so it was decided to compose one questionnaire to cover all the different types of middle schools.

The work on drafting the questionnaire was begun in Easter 1978 after numerous and lengthy consultations with colleagues in middle schools, upper and first schools, advisers, administrators and other research workers and a preliminary questionniare was piloted on a number of middle schools in Staffordshire and the West Midlands during May and June. A final version, taking into account the numerous helpful comments and advice obtained during the piloting, was printed and assembled during the summer so that it would be ready to send out to schools during the early part of the new school year.

One of the most difficult parts of the whole exercise was obtaining an up-to-date list of middle schools, especially as new middle schools were opening each year as schemes for re-organising secondary education progressed through their development. The majority of our addresses were obtained from the Education Authorities Directory (1978) although many middle schools, especially those covering the age ranges 5-12 and 8-12, were not listed there and so information had to be obtained from individual local authorities who very kindly sent us lists of schools in their areas.

The questionnaires, together with an accompanying letter explaining the purposes of the survey, were distributed to all middle schools for which we had addresses in October 1978 and it was hoped that head teachers would respond by the end of November or Christmas at the latest; a follow up letter was sent out (in January 1979) to all schools not returning the questionnaire and the date for completion of any late returns was extended to the end of March.

Much of the previous research on middle schools has tended to look at these schools in isolation from the other schools with which they are in contact, a rather surprising feature when it is considered that these schools are very much 'in-between schools' linking feeder first with upper schools. It would have been desirable to extend the survey to the first schools which send on pupils to middle schools so that a more complete view of the system could be obtained; however the number of first schools was too great to allow this, but it was possible to survey the upper schools especially as these numbered around 500; hence a smaller questionnaire was circulated in October 1978, after an initial pilot study, to all head teachers of upper schools receiving pupils from middle schools.

The Upper School Questionnaire asked for basic information concerning the size and origin of the school and the numbers of middle schools feeding it. A section on staffing was included to give some idea of the range of subject specialists available and the ancillary help which was provided. The most important aspect of the questionnaire was that dealing with transfer from the middle schools, especially as this might affect the organisation of the curriculum and so a number of questions were asked to ascertain how pupils were grouped on entry to school and what changes took place in this initial grouping during the first year; data was also sought on the nature of the information about pupils which was sent on from the middle schools, as well as details concerning the quality of liaison between schools. A final open-ended section, allowing head teachers to respond to questions covering the advantages and disadvantages of a three tier system, was included to give the heads an opportunity of recording their own personal views about the middle school system especially as it affected their own school organisation.

The replies from both middle and upper school questionnaires were coded onto data sheets and from them to punch cards for use on the University of Manchester's Regional Computers, the CDC 7600 and the 1900, to which the University of Keele's Computer Centre is linked. All the data analysis was carried out using Versions 6 and 7 of SPSS (Nie et al, 1975).

Characteristics of the Sample

The basic details of the middle school sample only will be presented in this section and information concerning the upper schools responding to the questionnaires will be found in Chapter 8.

The number of schools returning the questionnaires is given in Table 3.1 with the figures divided into the four main age ranges of middle schools. The fifth category 'Other' in that table consists of one 10-14, three 8-13 and five 9-12 schools and also includes four schools undergoing re-organisation which, in addition to having pupils of middle school age, also have older pupils; one such school, for example, has a year group of pupils aged 15 who are working their way out of the system as well as pupils of 9-13 years. Altogether returns were obtained from schools in 29 counties and 19 metropolitan areas (see Appendix 5).

The percentage of the total number of middle schools which these returns represent is shown in Table 3.2, which is arranged according to the criteria used in Statistics in Education, Volume 1, Schools (HMSO, 1981), so that the proportion of the total number of middle schools which the sample consists of can be accurately calculated; this table shows that in the two major categories — schools deemed primary and schools deemed secondary — the numbers responding to the questionnaire represented over 50% of all the nation's middle schools which were in existence in 1978; within that overall figure a particularly high response rate of 60% was obtained from the 10-13 schools.

On the other hand the lowest and most disappointing response was from the first and middle schools with under 30% returning their completed questionnaires. The decision to include the combined schools in the survey was a difficult one to take because the questionnaire was least well suited to this form of middle school organisation; however, on balance it was thought that it would be valuable to attempt to collect data from these schools especially in view of Burrows' (1978) opinion that their ultimate fate looked uncertain. Many first and middle schools are very small schools, often in rural areas with the head teacher spending a good deal of time in ordinary classroom teaching, and the thought of coping with a large and detailed questionnaire clearly proved too daunting a task for many of them. Even though the number of 5-12 schools responding to the questionnaire fell short of 30%, the actual number of schools comprising the sample was over 100 and so it is possible to gain some insight into the methods of organisation and the problems experienced by these schools, though the inferences drawn must be treated with some degree of caution.

The crucial question which has to be asked about any piece of survey research is the extent to which the cases in the sample are representative of the population from which they are drawn. Absolute numbers do not matter; the critical factor is rather how typical of the population the sample is. For the Keele survey of middle schools the same question must be asked concerning the schools which returned the questionnaire — how representative are they of all the middle schools in England and Wales? The theoretical answer to this question, even though over 50% responded, is that it is not possible to say, for unless a sample is drawn at random from a population it is not possible to guarantee its representativeness; certainly the data may not be representative of all those head teachers who forget to return questionnaires or throw theirs in the waste-paper basket.

However, as with most research in the social sciences, one has to be satisfied with less than perfect results and it is possible to make some assessment of the validity of the survey data by triangulation which involves comparing data produced in the survey with similar data obtained from other sources and seeing how far the pieces of evidence match. The first such comparison can be made with respect to the sizes of middle schools and the data for this are given in Table 3.3; the figures are presented in such a form to enable them to be placed alongside the DES figures (HMSO, 1981) for 1978, and from this table it can be seen that the percentage of all middle schools in each of the categories used by the DES is very similar to the percentages for each category in the Keele sample — in fact the percentage usually differs by no more than 5%, and frequently a good deal less. The only exception to this is for schools in the 401-600 category and for those deemed primary there is a deviation downwards in the survey of 5.8% and for the schools deemed secondary the shortfall is 8.9%; this band of schools is slightly under-represented in the Keele survey, though the differences are really quite small. In all other respects the information given in Table 3.3 shows that the sample data is very similar to the population data with the modal band for the 8-12 schools being 201-300 pupils and that for the 9-13s and 10-13s being considerably larger at between 401-600 pupils. The extent to which schools under 200 pupils can maintain their character as a middle school, separate and distinct from that of a primary school, would seem rather dubious since to provide the necessary resources, both physical and human, would be very expensive in such a small establishment. However, in 1978 there were 90 such schools representing about 13% of all the middle schools in the country.

The data for first and middle schools cannot be presented alongside the DES figures as the numbers given in the Keele survey are for the middle school element only and so exclude the number of children who are aged 5-8 in the school — numbers which the DES figures include. However, a separate table is given for the combined schools so that the percentage of schools in each band responding to the questionnaire can be seen (Table 3.4).

CHAPTER 4

The Background of Middle Schools

The period of greatest expansion for middle schools was between the years 1971/72 and 1974/75 with the number of new schools deemed secondary (mainly 9-13 and 10-13 schools) reaching its peak in 1972/73 with over 100 new schools being opened; the peak year for the opening of the other middle schools was one year later in 1973/74 when well over 400 new schools came into being. Examination of the survey data presented in Table 4.1 reflects quite closely this period of expansion with well over 50% of the schools in the sample opening between 1971 and 1975; further inspection shows that the sample also follows the national trend for the peak year of new school openings with the largest percentage of 9-13 schools (22.1%) opening in 1972 and the largest number of 8-12 (31.7%) and combined (32.7%) schools coming into existence in 1973.

Most of the 8-12, 9-13 and 10-13 schools in the sample are non-denominational though in the case of 5-12 schools a much larger proportion are Church schools, the majority being Church of England with 28.2% being so designated (see Table 4.2). Taken in conjunction with Table 4.3, showing the population area from which middle schools draw their pupils, it can be seen that a much larger proportion of the 5-12 schools in the sample are situated in villages, thus supporting Burrows' (1978) claim that many of these schools are voluntary, usually Church schools in rural areas, or small primary schools in towns. He goes on to relate further that many of these 5-12 schools were founded before the days of state participation in their localities which in recent years could not afford to pay the price for new separate first and middle schools. The majority of 10-13 schools are town schools with 8-12s and 9-13s coming largely from both town and suburban areas.

A further distinctive feature of the 5-12 schools is that a larger percentage of these draw on areas of private housing, again reflecting their village and suburban character; however looking at the overall pattern shown in Table 4.4 one can see that, as expected, about half of all the schools (43.7% to 57.7%) draw their pupils from a mixture of both council and privately owned housing. Worthy of note is the fact that the percentage of 9-13 schools which take pupils from predominantly private housing areas is lower than for any other type of school which ties in with evidence shown in Table 4.3 showing that there are more 9-13 schools than other middle schools located in the inner areas of large cities.

As well as showing quite different patterns of distribution with respect to geography and demography middle schools also exhibit quite marked variations in their origins, as the data given in Table 4.5 demonstrates. The overwhelming majority of 5-12 and 8-12 schools were originally primaries, with just under a quarter being purpose built new schools; a very small proportion only of combined schools (5.5%) had their origins in secondary schools, while 13.2% of 8-12s are adapted from secondary schools. The ancestry of the 10-13 schools is almost a mirror image of that for the 5-12s as nearly 70% of the sample are former secondary schools and only one school in the survey is adapted from a primary school. The 9-13 schools reveal a much more evenly balanced picture, for although a majority of these are former secondary schools there are still a significant number (nearly 30%) which started life as primary schools, and a quarter of the 9-13 schools, the largest percentage in any group, are in purpose built premises. Looking at the middle school sector as a whole, however, three-quarters of the schools are adapted from buildings designed for and used by other age ranges, which gives an appropriate illustration of the constraints outlined in Chapter I and shows the economic advantages of re-organising secondary education based on a three-tier system; considerable savings were made by being able to adapt existing buildings.

Of particular interest also is the percentage of schools which have some part of their premises open plan, for there exists an intimate relationship between the styles of learning and the type of environment created by school architecture. In the Building Bulletin 35 (DES, 1966) plans and designs for new and adapted middle schools reveal an emerging philosophy that, by blending the best of primary and secondary education, they should develop a distinctive style and character; in practice this meant that the curriculum was conceptualised in broad areas rather than narrow subject divisions which the example of Delf Hill, given in the Building Bulletin, illustrates: —

> 'It is expected that a curriculum will develop in which pupils . . . will come to spend about 30 per cent of their time in the broad field of scientific, mathematical and environmental studies; 30 per cent in the field of language, literature and religion; 20 per cent of their time making and doing things with many kinds of materials; and 20 per cent in a variety of activities concerned with music, movement, drama, gymnastics and games' (DES, 1966, p.137).

To complement this flexi-curriculum were ideas about how the pupils' learning would be organised and here again the stress was on providing space and therefore opportunity for pupils to move freely from one activity to another unhindered by the confines of the four walls of the traditional classroom; this was to be replaced by a new concept — the base — again illustrated by Delf Hill:

> 'It is anticipated that four small groups of teachers will be responsible for four main groups of 105 pupils. Each of these groups will therefore have a "base" where they can meet together, keep their clothes and belongings, and display their work. Throughout the day, however, it is expected that the pupils will be working partly in their own centres, partly elsewhere . . . there

will not be standardised working groups, but a changing pattern of groupings, some as small as three or four; some of eighteen or twenty; others of thirty, forty or even sixty or more depending on the aptitudes of the pupils and the work they are doing' (ibid., p.138).

Such a philosophy, reflecting Bernstein's (1971) weak classification of subject areas and the encouragement of pupils to choose freely between different topic areas, finds its physical manifestation in the open plan school and many of the middle schools, adapted as well as purpose built, were designed on these lines. Table 4.6 reveals that just under half of the survey's 9-13 and 10-13 school buildings have some part of their accommodation open plan, while about one-third of the 5-12 and 8-12 schools are so arranged. Of those schools which do possess some form of open plan arrangement it is the craft and science areas which are designed in this way, though in the case of the open plan 5-12 schools, it is more likely to be the whole building which is open plan rather than a particular area.

Although open plan schools are based on a particular educational philosophy, they also have the added advantage of being cheaper to build, or rather allow more facilities to be provided for the same amount of money, a not inconsiderable bonus when providing new buildings, or adapting old ones, at a time of severe financial restraint.

The specialist facilities which are available to middle school children appears to be a crucial ingredient in forming the particular style and character of this type of education, for if these are not provided then the school remains little more than an extended primary; this requirement for some provision of specialist facilities is acknowledged in Building Bulletin 35:

'A school with an upper age limit of 12 must have much in common with the primary school — but should enjoy some extended facilities for older pupils to use and develop their capacity for learning.

The facilities which immediately come to mind are those for science, crafts, language teaching and music' (DES, 1966).

The Bulletin then goes on to add a sensible note of caution, however, when it adds:

'It would be wrong as well as extravagant to look for specialist accommodation of the type normally to be found in secondary schools which is not, in any case, particularly adapted to meet the needs of their younger pupils' (ibid., p.2).

For pupils transferring at age 13+ the case for specialist teaching facilities is stronger — 'There should be a stronger infusion of the disciplines characteristic of the secondary school' (ibid., p.3); the Bulletin gives little grounds for optimism that these could be provided for in its comments about converting junior schools it states:

'The ordinary junior school lacks spaces furnished and equipped for some of the special work described. It is not practicable to meet all the claims which might be posed in a single school and deliberate choices and compromises have therefore been made' (ibid.).

No list of specialist facilities necessary for a 9-13 school is given in the same way that one is provided for those schools with 12+ as the age of transfer.

The questions which can here be asked are what specialist facilities are available in the different kinds of middle schools and what do head teachers feel to be particularly lacking, if anything, by way of building resources. Some answers to these questions may be found by referring to Tables 4.8 and 4.9, and immediately one can see the contrast between different kinds of middle school described in Building Bulletin 35; however it can also be seen that there are considerable deficiencies in the 5-12 and 8-12 schools even in those four areas of science, craft, language and music listed in the Bulletin. Looking at Table 4.8 in detail nearly all the 9-13 and 10-13 schools in the survey possess craft facilities and most of the 8-12s do also, but the 5-12 schools show a considerable drop with nearly half possessing no craft facilities at all; this trend can be observed throughout the table, though the differences between types of school for some of the specialist facilities are greater than others. In the case of music, for example, nearly twice as many schools transferring pupils at 13+ have specialist facilities than those transferring at 12+, and even within those latter schools it is the 5-12s who are the least well endowed with less than one-third having specialist music facilities. With regard to science facilities the contrast is even greater, though in this case the 8-12s do a little better than for music. The problems of science, or lack of it, in the junior school are emphasised in the Primary School Survey (DES, 1978) and the data presented here would seem to indicate that for the 5-12 and 8-12 schools similar difficulties prevail, though one is also forced to ask why more of these schools possess specialist facilities for doing home economics than for doing science. True, it is probably easy to place a cooker next to a sink and define this as a specialist teaching facility, but only a modest expenditure is required to create a specialist science facility suitable for children up to 12 years old yet two-thirds of the 5-12s and nearly half of the 8-12 schools possess no such resource. Is it any wonder that the organisation of science teaching in many middle schools is made so much more difficult for both pupils and teachers because of the lack of basic science facilities?

For physical activities Table 4.8 illustrates the same trend as shown for other facilities, though in respect of outdoor facilities the contrasts between schools are not so marked — a situation which is the same for outdoor teaching resources. Another interesting feature revealed in Table 4.8 is the small percentage of any middle school type possessing language laboratories, especially as this area of the curriculum was considered so important in the early Building Bulletin, No. 35; the reason for this low frequency may, however, be in the results of research published by the NFER (Burstall, 1974) which showed that beginning a language at 8 years in the primary school had no effect on achievement later on in the secondary school; while there may be many interpretations as to why this lack of achievement occurred, there is no doubt that the publication of 'Primary

French in the Balance' has halted the development of foreign language teaching in the primary and middle years of schooling.

If one takes the evidence from Table 4.8 as a whole it shows quite clearly that those schools who transfer at 13+ are quite well endowed with specialist teaching facilities but that many 8-12 middle schools have few extra resources and that the majority of the 5-12s possess little more than the facilities one would expect in a normal primary school.

The final question in the first part of the survey asked head teachers to specify what additional buildings they would want for their school, given that they had funds for the purpose. This was an open ended question and the response rate for these types of question tends to be lower than for those where there is just a box to tick for the answer. Table 4.9 shows that about 20% or more of the schools desired more general classroom space, a rather surprising request in view of the shortage of specialist facilities available in many schools. However many of the specialist facilities in middle schools are not large enough to take a full class of children and so more general space is required to give flexible groupings of pupils so that specialist facilities can be used.

A large number of schools appear to want better gymnastic facilities — many schools are without any gym at all, and those which have some specialist accommodation usually find it is doubling up as a school hall and dining room, and hence has a restricted access. The same holds for changing and showering facilities for even though schools may have had a school hall adapted for PE, frequently there are totally inadequate changing facilities and sometimes pupils have even to change in their own classrooms. Again, this is something which might be acceptable, if not ideal, for the primary school child, but for older pupils already into early adolescence this seems a particularly pressing problem.

One particularly interesting feature revealed by Table 4.9 is the number of schools requesting additional science laboratories — a not unexpected finding considering the small number of 8-12 and 5-12 schools possessing these; however if one compares the numbers here with those percentages given in Table 4.8 one finds that a large number of schools without laboratory facilities are not requesting them. Why should this be so? Perhaps an explanation can be found in the origin of these schools, especially the 5-12s, whose teachers are mainly ex-primary teachers and who do not perceive the middle school as a place for specialist science teaching; that is, they regard these middle schools, at least with respect to science, as more like the primary school, though as the primary school survey showed the teaching of science there was inadequate too. The important point about middle schools which this reply reveals is that within the 5-12 and 8-12 schools there are quite different perceptions of what the curriculum for the middle school pupil should be. Some 9-13 and 10-13 schools are requesting provision for extra laboratory space rather than the setting up of new laboratories, especially in those schools where the present facilities cater for only half a class.

Overall, Table 4.9 shows that, with the exception of PE facilities where 9-13 and 10-13 schools seem particularly deficient, there is a far greater need for specialist facilities in the 5-12 and 8-12 schools as can be seen in their demand for additional facilities for music, craft and laboratory subjects; these were seen to be the problem areas in Building Bulletin No. 35 and also in the Plowden Report though it does seem somewhat ironic that although the Plowden Report recommended that 8-12 schools should be established because they would require less additional specialist facilities than 9-13 schools, it is the latter which now seem better equipped for their functions as middle schools rather than 8-12s many of which have still not got the modest additional buildings to make them distinctive from a traditional 7-11 primary school.

CHAPTER 5

The Staffing of Middle Schools

The majority of heads and deputy heads in middle schools are men, the data from the Keele survey confirming the figures presented by Blyth and Derricott (1977, p.189), though there are variations in the percentages between schools. For example, the combined school has a greater proportion of women heads than do other types of school — 20% as compared to less than 10% — which would suggest the view that where children are younger and where there are most women teachers, then women do have a greater chance of becoming head. However, it is interesting to note that generally in middle schools, where women teachers outnumber the men, it is still the latter who have less difficulty in reaching the highest position. Both the 5-12 and 8-12 schools have larger numbers of women deputy heads (40.0% and 34.6% respectively) than do the 9-13 and 10-13 schools (21.0% and 27.3%); of course, the latter two types of school are, on average, larger than the 8-12 and combined schools and so can appoint more than one deputy and when this occurs the most common pattern is for one man and one woman to fill these positions (Table 5.2).

In the early years of middle schools, according to Edwards (1972), considerable importance was attached to the idea of the head teacher actually being involved in teaching so that, 'he or she could fully appreciate some of the school's problems'. This was thought necessary because there were no precedents to go by as head teachers only had experience in other types of schools but not middle schools, and so the view was expressed that being involved in teaching would assist the heads in establishing themselves in their new role as well as helping their new schools to become efficient institutions. Now, some years later, differences between the four types of school have emerged with the 5-12 heads teaching the most — on average for 8 hours per week — and the heads of 10-13 schools the least — for about 6 hours per week (see Table 5.3). Some effects of size may be evident here because the larger 9-13 and 10-13 schools require more administration and therefore make greater demands on the head, thus restricting his availability for teaching. A number of heads indicated that they cannot time-table a regular teaching commitment for themselves as they often have to cover for staff absences due to illness or in-service work because cuts in local authority expenditure have limited the number of relief or supply staff available; in addition, some head teachers are reluctant, on ideological grounds, to include regular teaching as part of their role.

41

The average numbers of teachers in the different types of school are given in tables 5.4 to 5.7; in the case of the 5-12 schools this figure includes all the staff for the 5-8 year olds as well as those of the middle school aged children as head teachers claimed that their schools are not organised in such a way as to clearly delineate first and middle school teachers. The 9-13 schools have an average of 18.9 teachers which is comparable to the 20.6 teachers in the 10-13 schools; the 8-12 schools are smaller with only 12.0 teachers while the combined schools have nearly the same number (10.7) to cover the larger age range. Some important differences can thus be observed in the staffing provision between those schools transferring at 12+ and those at 13+. The mere presence of a larger number of adults in the 9-13 and 10-13 schools provides a broader base of expertise from which to plan and implement the curriculum. Both Edwards (1972) and Blyth and Derricott (1977) draw attention to the complexity of the roles of staff in small middle schools; the NUT pamphlet (1979) also considers the problems of small middle schools where, 'despite the enthusiasm and the dedication of the staff (the size) inhibits the development of middle school objectives' — a situation bound to get worse as pupil numbers further decline. The role expectations for staff in middle schools are much wider than those in the traditional primary school because of the presence of older children, and in a small school especially, it is difficult for staff to meet these needs; even the larger schools may experience problems because many local authorities have based their calculations for the staffing ratio on a traditional conception of provision for children of this age range. The NUT has put forward a powerful argument against these rather strict staff/pupil ratios:—

'They usually mask the actual teaching situation by reducing to generalities the deployment of teachers in school. Comparability between small and large schools with identical ratios will often disguise variations in curricular width. Class size statistics provide a useful check on the level of staffing. But if a school's work is to be properly planned it is the organisation and curricular patterns which must determine staffing levels, not the reverse'. (NUT, 1979, p.15).

The need for a more flexible staffing formula to meet the needs of individual middle schools is essential because of their widely differing ideologies, but is very difficult to implement under the rather rigid present day administrative procedures which still classify middle schools as either 'deemed primary' or 'deemed secondary'.

Turning now to the characteristics of teachers in middle schools one can see that there are twice as many women as men teachers in the 8-12 schools and an even larger ratio in the 5-12 schools with an average of 2.8 men and 7.9 women, although the younger children are certainly all taught by women. The difference in the proportion of men and women decreases in the 9-13 and 10-13 schools where on average there are only approximately two more women teachers than men. The Plowden Report (p.145) expressed the hope that 'Middle schools might well attract more men than junior schools have done, which would probably give them a more stable staff'. This certainly appears to have happened as the ratio of male to female teachers in all middle schools exceeds the ratio of one man in five found in the sample of schools surveyed in the Plowden Report. Furthermore, the Report hoped that middle schools might also attract more graduates. According to Plowden (Vol. 2, p.229) primary schools are largely staffed by non-graduates — a case which also exists in middle schools though there are significant numbers of graduates as well. However, the suggestion made by Burrows (1978, p.185) that one-half to two-thirds of the staff in the 9-13 middle school have degrees is not supported by the data in the Keele survey, and the ratio of graduates to non-graduates is much more modest; in the 9-13 and 10-13 schools the ratio is about one graduate to every three non-graduates and in those schools transferring at 12, the proportion is approximately one to four.

These differences in the proportion of graduates in middle schools can be partly explained by the way in which such schools have developed, many 9-13 and 10-13 schools evolving from secondary schools and the 8-12 and combined schools originating in primary schools. Table 5.8 indicates the previous experience of middle school staff and shows that a much larger proportion of teachers in the 9-13 and 10-13 schools have secondary experience. Also the 9-13 and 10-13 schools have a teaching force with a more varied background than those schools transferring at 12+ which tend to be dominated by teachers with only primary school experience. A relatively small proportion of teachers in middle schools have specific middle school training, but it is worth noting that again it is the 13+ transfer schools which have the largest percentage.

Although the numbers of graduates in middle schools may be accounted for by historical development and administrative factors, such as the retention of the same staff when schools changed their age-range, there is also the point that this distribution may reflect positive choices made by the teachers involved. There is no doubt that middle schools do provide an attractive alternative to the secondary school where children are often perceived to be less motivated and also the curriculum is dominated by the demands of public examinations; the middle schools do have an age-group of children who are often enthusiastic and well motivated, and this, combined with the possibility of some subject specialisation, is appealing for many teachers.

To examine the career prospects of teachers in middle schools necessitates a detailed look at the availability and distribution of scale 2 and above posts in the schools (Table 5.9). Head teachers are allowed sufficient autonomy to decide how to allocate scale posts within the limits of points awarded by each local authority; generally, the size of school determines the number of scale posts available and therefore the larger 9-13 and 10-13 schools are able to allocate more scale 3 and 4 posts than either of the 5-12 and 8-12 schools can. Although there are more scale posts available in the schools with older pupils, and this may provide a sufficient incentive to attract some graduates into the schools, discussion with heads and teachers in middle schools have revealed certain problems that these figures alone do not disclose. Expectations of promotion are higher in the 9-13 and 10-13 schools and because of their larger size a greater number of teachers actually obtain such posts, but the proportion of individuals obtaining a scale 3 or 4 post are no greater than in the smaller 8-12 schools. So any appearance of a better position in the larger school is illusory and because of higher expectations may lead to career frustration. Blyth and Derricott (1977, p.189) also perceived this to be a problem in middle schools where the middle range opportunities – the scale 3 posts – are more difficult to obtain than they are in secondary schools.

To describe accurately the functions of teachers holding scale posts in middle schools is extremely difficult for a number of reasons. Firstly, even though a particular job may carry the same title, the job specification may vary enormously from school to school. Secondly, the qualifications and experience of individual teachers affects the nature of the actual task performed to a far greater degree in middle schools than in other schools; for example, the experience which a teacher has in teaching a particular subject will influence quite considerably the range and depth of material taught, as well as the amount of advice which can be given to colleagues. Thirdly, the facilities which a school has available also exerts an influence on the teacher's role, especially in the practical subjects. Fourthly, the pastoral, administrative and teaching duties have different emphasis in different middle schools and are apportioned in different combinations to indivivual members of staff. All these factors make it very problematical to compare staffing functions in different middle schools. Burrows (1978) and Blyth and Derricott (1977, p.50) conceptualise the organisation of staffing duties in terms of a model which separates out pastoral and subject responsibilities, the administrative tasks such as year teacher or year co-ordinator cutting across those of subject specialist responsibility; the resulting grid provides a large number of posts of responsibility for which in most middle schools no scale posts are actually available, and thus individual teachers are frequently involved in more than one role, the actual number and extent of overlays depending on the size of school. In many smaller middle schools, therefore, the grid model is quite inappropriate as there are so few teachers. All this presents especially difficult problems for the head teacher in allocating scale posts in such a way as to maximise the efficient running of his own particular school while at the same time satisfying the legitimate career aspirations of the teachers.

Such problems also present difficulties for the survey researcher, and so caution must be exercised in the interpretation of the data given in Table 5.10. The term 'specialist teacher', for example, presents enormous difficulties of definition within the middle school context. In secondary schools, by way of contrast, the roles of the specialist teacher are more clearly delineated and well understood because most of the teachers are specialists and with a few exceptions, such as when absent colleagues are covered, they do not teach subjects other than their own; a secondary school teacher is assumed to have been trained to teach his own subject and not others. In junior schools also the role of the teacher is quite clearly defined and where specialist teachers do exist it is to cover subjects such as music, physical education, art, craft and french which need some particular expertise in addition to that gained during general training.

However, these additional subjects slot relatively easily into the normal programme of basic general teaching run by the class teacher. In recent years both primary and secondary sectors have made concessions towards each other's domain with some secondary schools initiating programmes of integrated studies, especially for the younger pupils, and some primary schools use the skills of an individual teacher to increase the depth of knowledge of the pupils in a particular subject area. Nevertheless, these are viewed as interesting variations to the traditionally established pattern of teaching.

The middle school 'specialist teacher' has a much more complex set of roles which do not fit in easily with the models of the primary or secondary school. As Blyth and Derricott (1977, p.64) points out:

'Middle school teachers cannot follow either the traditional class teacher pattern of the junior school or the traditional subject teacher pattern of the secondary school'.

The Plowden Report (p.146) also offered some suggestions as to the needs of middle schools and claimed that they would require:

'teachers with a good grasp of subject matter, but we do not want the middle schools to be dominated by secondary school influences'.

However, it is impossible to dispense with the two types of curricular model — primary and secondary — as the points of reference for the middle school subject specialist. Drawing on the analyses made by Edwards, Blyth and Derricott, Burrows and Plowden for example, it would appear that two important dimensions of the middle school teacher's role are flexibility and adaptability and so it may be best to conceptualise the roles of middle school teachers as covering a continuum, with the generalist at one extreme and the single subject specialist at the other; in between are the semi-specialist teachers who may, for example, claim some expertise in a particular subject, or who may have specialist skills across a number of subjects. Certainly all of these combinations exist in middle schools both from sheer necessity, when the number of teachers is small, and actual preference, to create a new type of teacher. In this survey, therefore, the term 'subject specialist' covers a wide spectrum of different roles.

A very high percentage of each school type employs some subject specialists and in some cases this is a shared responsibility with administrative and pastoral duties (see Table 5.10). In those schools which do give a scale 2 or above post solely for specialist subject teaching, it is the 5-12s who have the lowest number though in many 8-12 schools there are combination posts awarded because of the smaller size. In the 8-12 and combined schools many subject specialists carry out their functions along with other duties, thus supporting Burrows' (1978, p.180) claim that the size of those schools makes 'the full subject specialist less common' than in the 9-13 schools. The contrast between the types of school is also brought out in Table 5.11 which provides a more detailed breakdown of the distribution of the scale posts for specialist subjects. Again the size of the school is an important influence and it is interesting to note that nearly one-quarter of

9-13 schools give 10 or more scale posts for specialist subjects in marked contrast to the small percentage in the combined and 8-12 schools, where the majority have between 3 and 5 posts. In addition to size, however, there is a clear influence of philosophy too, and it is quite apparent that in most of those middle schools transferring at 13+ the contribution of specialist staff is considered vital for the implementation of the middle school curriculum.

Differences between schools can also be found in the distribution of scale posts for reasons other than subject specialisation. For example, more of the 9-13 schools than any other type offer scale posts for year co-ordinators, and the relatively low percentage of 10-13 schools offering scale posts for this function alone suggests that in these schools this duty is combined with other responsibilities. Also noteworthy is the very small number of 10-13 schools giving scale posts for 'resources' possibly because being more secondary orientated each subject area looks after its own resources which are not shared to the same extent as in other middle schools.

Looking now at specific subjects for which scale posts are given in middle schools, Table 5.12 reveals some quite interesting distributions. The NUT (1979) claim that english, mathematics and science are regarded as the highest status subjects and therefore attract the largest number of scale posts, and the data in Table 5.12 shows that more schools give scale 3 posts for these subjects than many others, though it reveals also the very high percentage of schools awarding scale 3 posts for art and craft – over 10% of the 8-12 schools and more than 25% of the 9-13 and 10-13 schools.

The 10-13 and 9-13 schools naturally have more scale posts to offer than do the combined and 8-12 schools and so differences between those schools transferring at 12+ and those transferring at 13+ are usual. However, two areas of the curriculum where differences are not as great as one would expect are music and PE which have scale 3 posts in over 10% of 8-12 middle schools. This may be due to the necessity of having to pay more to attract staff in shortage subjects, especially as most generalist teachers lack the expertise to cope with these two areas. The distribution of scale posts in foreign languages presents an interesting pattern for there is roughly the same percentage of 12+ schools giving scale 2 posts for languages, maths and english, but the percentage of schools giving scale 3 posts for languages is a good deal less than for english and maths; also fewer schools transferring pupils at 13+ give scale 3 posts for languages than for maths and english, but the position is reversed for scale 2 posts. It would appear, therefore, that foreign language teachers, especially in 13+ transfer schools, have about the best chance of anyone in middle schools of obtaining a scale 2 post, but that their chances of getting a scale 3 are limited.

The distribution of scale posts for foreign languages in middle schools has to be understood in the context of an overall shortage of modern language teachers – a situation which also exists for science. The science curriculum presents considerable difficulties for middle schools because of the separate subjects involved and these schools are rarely in the position of being able to choose what they would like. In the majority of secondary schools receiving pupils at 11+ the first year children would be introduced if not to the separate disciplines of physics, chemistry and biology than to an integrated science programme designed by the various specialist teachers and would spend a proportion of their timetabled science lessons in a laboratory, but in the majority of middle schools science is handled in a rather different way. First of all the majority of science teachers have a firm grounding in only one branch of science and although there is common ground between the sciences, in reality it is much more difficult for them to teach, organise and co-ordinate an introductory general science programme which includes all the sciences than it is to treat them separately. Also, the middle school science teacher does not have the advantage of being in a science department where problems of the curriculum can be discussed with colleagues. Secondly, the laboratory facilities necessary for teaching 'secondary' science are often not available in many middle schools and so create further constraints for the middle school science teacher. So, although it is possible to run a 'secondary' type science curriculum for older pupils in middle schools it is often extremely difficult to do so. The alternatives also present problems chiefly because there is so little published innovatory material in science suitable for children of this age group; there is plenty for younger secondary school pupils because the schools have fully equipped laboratories and also some for primary schools which do not need to develop so great a depth as do middle schools. Of course, the assumption is also frequently made that there is a suitably qualified specialist to select and manage the curriculum, yet the Keele survey shows that many combined and 8-12 schools do not give a scale post for science – over 50% in each case – and so the science curriculum could well be the responsibility of a scale 1 teacher or be taught by a generalist. For pupils in these schools it could be argued that a 'primary' type, class based, science curriculum is sufficient, although it must be remembered that primary science has many deficiencies, as revealed by the Primary School Survey (HMSO, 1978); however, for older pupils in the schools transferring at 13+ it is hard to justify the lack of specialist and experienced teaching. In the 9-13 schools there are more than 20% which do not give a scale 2 or above for science teaching, and in the 10-13 schools the figure is over 10%.

Other areas of the curriculum also suffer from similar staffing problems and it is clear that many combined and 8-12 schools do not give extra remuneration for certain important subject areas. For example, although more schools give scale 3 posts for maths and english than for many other subjects there are still large numbers which give no special allowance at all for these basic subjects. This may be indicative of a primary ethos in the schools transferring at 12+ for in primary schools all teachers are deemed to be experts at teaching maths and english; however, even some 9-13 (22.5%) and 10-13 (12.2%) schools do not have a mathematics specialist with a scale 2 or above post. Obviously it would be foolish to assume from this data that those schools without a maths specialist do not teach maths or do not teach it well, but the figures give some indication of the priorities of middle school organisation and illustrate how few scale posts there are available in the smaller schools. Of course, it must be remembered that the absence of a scale 2 post in a subject area does not necessarily preclude a school from having a teacher who has responsibility for that subject, but it shows that in some middle schools a member of staff is carrying the responsibility for subject organisation, yet is not receiving the remuneration and status which would normally accompany such a role.

The subject specialist in all types of middle school has a variety of tasks to do in addition to teaching his subject and some indication of these is given in Tables 5.13 to 5.15 revealing yet again differences between the 12+ and 13+ transfer schools. Table 5.14 gives the time spent by subject specialists teaching their own subject or, if they are also class teachers, it indicates the time spent with classes other than their own, and this shows that subject specialists in the 9-13 and 10-13 schools spend two or even three times as much time teaching their specialism as do the specialists in the 8-12 and combined schools; furthermore in these latter schools it is much more likely for the subject specialists to teach only their own classes and so their expertise is not available for other classes in the school (see Table 5.13). Thus the very conception of a subject specialist in these schools must be rather different from that normally understood by the term and must chiefly involve duties other than that of teaching.

An indication of these other duties is given in Table 5.15 and this shows that subject specialists have a heavy involvement with curriculum planning, advising their colleagues and liaising with the upper school. All four categories of middle school are involved with these activities, yet it is again the 9-13 and 10-13 schools which have the largest percentages. Considering the data from Tables 5.10 to 5.15 some idea may be gained of the enormity of the task facing these middle school subject specialists. Their position is frequently not as clearly defined nor do they have the authority of a head of subject department in a secondary school. Advising and directing colleagues who may well be unacquainted with, and unskilled in, their particular subject is really only possible if the advice is sought in the first place. Liaison with upper schools, particularly when there are a number of them, is a time consuming task and often has to take place after school hours, as does all planning and servicing of equipment for practical subjects. In quite a number of middle schools there is only one subject specialist in a particular field to cover all these different aspects of the job and in some instances this specialist may well be a probationary teacher or a relatively inexperienced teacher with a scale 1 post. There seems little doubt that in many middle schools, but for dedicated teachers, some subjects would have vanished completely from the curriculum under a burden of overwork, lack of facilities and shortage of ancillary, non-teaching staff.

Part-time teachers have become scarce in all schools as stringent cuts by many LEAs have caused part-time jobs to be a luxury, a situation which will have become even worse since the survey was completed. Most of the part-time teachers are non-graduate women and the 10-13 schools have the fewest part-time staff with the combined and 8-12s having, on average, the most. In some instances, notably foreign languages and music, there is reason to suppose that this part-time support is not in addition to full-time specialist staff, but is a substitute for it. It is interesting to note the relatively large percentage of middle schools using part-time teachers for class teaching duties, as this may release another teacher for specialist teaching. This would indicate that part-time teachers are of especial importance in middle schools because they give much needed flexibility to the system and there is no doubt that whatever particular use the school makes of these teachers — either for broadening the base of expertise or strengthening already existing programmes — their loss through financial expediency will be greatly felt. Peripatetic teachers are very seldom used by any schools except for instrumental music tuition and, in some LEAs, for foreign language teaching.

Non-teaching staff in middle schools vary both in their number and the job they are required to do. Many schools have only part-time secretarial assistance which may amount to only a few hours per week in smaller schools. This must affect the way in which head teachers can carry out their duties and define their own roles within the school for adequate administrative help in the office obviously alleviates the head of many routine chores which can be dealt with by an efficient secretary. General assistants are used in some schools to help with administrative tasks as well as act as librarians, workshop technicians and laboratory assistants. Indeed, some schools because of their small size cannot employ different individuals to fill all the particular jobs and so the general assistant has to spread his time thinly over a number of different areas.

Laboratory assistants are the expected norm in every secondary school, whereas even in the 9-13 and 10-13 schools where there are laboratories only 39% have these personnel and so the teachers have little or no assistance in the time consuming job of setting up and clearing away apparatus. Also, few middle schools have workshop technicians and where they do exist it is likely to be in the 9-13 and 10-13 schools for heavy craft is taught in few combined and 8-12 schools. This lack of assistance which is so time-saving and which makes teaching so much more efficient is worth considering in terms of the total appeal of the job to teachers — it certainly adds a considerable amount to the workload in practical subjects.

It can be seen therefore that there are major differences in staffing policy between middle schools deemed primary and those deemed secondary. The combined and 8-12 schools have in essence retained a traditional primary organisation with some additional specialist teaching for the older pupils and although there may be teachers in many of these schools who wish to develop more specialisation they are prevented from doing so because of the practical constraints of small schools, lack of equipment and staffing ratios unfavourable to flexibility and thus the basic class teacher arrangement is the simplest to maintain. In reality, therefore, choices of organisational patterns and deployment of teachers to maximise their skills and job satisfaction are rarely afforded to many head teachers in 5-12 and 8-12 middle schools. By contrast the 9-13 and 10-13 schools have felt the necessity for a more specialised approach to the curriculum and in the main have managed to implement this, though with many difficulties; for example, many teachers have had to undertake onerous tasks to make this possible. No matter what personal rewards individuals may feel about teaching this age group in middle schools — and many teachers are very positive about these — the arrangement and maintenance of the curriculum into subject areas as well as at the same time maintaining some generalist teaching is extremely problematical and is likely to remain so until some concessions are made by local education authorities towards better staff/pupil ratios.

CHAPTER 6

The Organisation of the Middle School Curriculum

Middle schools do not vary greatly in the ways in which they group pupils for pastoral and teaching purposes. Blyth and Derricott (1977) claim that pupils in middle schools 'are likely to be less rigidly separated than in secondary or even junior schools' and that 'middle-schools have been born with a propensity towards non-streaming' (p.55).

Indeed, the majority of schools group their pupils for registration purposes in mixed ability classes; none of the 5-12 schools stream for this purpose and only 4.5% of the 8-12s stream the last two years. Streaming, however, is used more widely in the 9-13 and 10-13 schools, as Table 6.1 shows.

The organisation of teaching groups is very similar to that of registration or pastoral groupings with only about 1% more of the 9-13, and 3% more of the 10-13, schools streaming their pupils for all subjects thus supporting Blyth and Derricott's supposition that the most frequently found pattern of grouping is non-streamed. A more common arrangement found in all types of middle school is some kind of setting to cater for individual subject requirements within an overall framework of mixed ability grouping. This pattern is a result not only of ideological preference but is also due to other factors such as the size of school. Larger schools with more members of staff obviously have greater potential flexibility in their grouping practices whereas the smaller schools, such as many of the combined and 8-12 schools, cannot sustain such variety and thus pupils remain in mixed ability groups taught by one class teacher.

The older pupils in all types of middle school are more frequently placed in ability sets for teaching purposes, though the proportion does vary with different subjects. For example, pupils are set for their mathematics lessons more frequently than for any other subject, while science, even in the final years of the 9-13 and 10-13 schools, is taught predominantly in mixed ability classes. Generally speaking, the 9-13 and 10-13 schools are able to regroup their pupils in a variety of different ways and reflect more closely the needs and interests of the pupils – a situation only possible where the numbers of pupils and staff involved make this practicable (Table 6.2).

Table 6.3 reflects the differences in size of the four main types of middle school. The 5-12 schools have the smallest numbers of pupils for any one particular age group as they are mainly 1 or 2 form entry schools. The 8-12s are bigger on average and the 9-13s even larger with the majority at 3 or 4 form entry. However, the largest year groups are in the 10-13 schools where over 70%

of the schools have a five form entry or more. This large year group which in the 9-13 and 10-13 schools is used as an organisational unit allows the possibility of greater flexibility in grouping pupils for various teaching subjects and explains the largest numbers of schools of this type which set their pupils. Large numbers of children of the same age, more resource facilities and staff provide a broader base from which to organise a curriculum.

Average class sizes for the top two years in each school do not vary significantly from one type of school to another — none fall below 22 pupils nor do any rise above 28. Where there is a difference of class size within a year-group, none of the maximum numbers — except in two instances — rise above 31. Obviously setting has not allowed schools to alter class sizes to suit the needs of different subjects and groups of children — something which would be extremely difficult in many schools as staffing ratios would not provide enough teachers for the smaller groups.

Middle schools have a wide variety of subjects in their curricula and frequently include minority subjects such as home economics, social studies, drama, and environmental studies as well as the traditional core subjects of mathematics, english, science, art and craft, music, a foreign language and physical education. This breadth of curriculum was advocated in the Plowden Report. Humanities teaching is timetabled under a variety of guises, sometimes clearly carried out in some schools as an integrated area of study including aspects of english and environmental science, whereas in others history and geography are clearly delineated as separate subjects. In the chapter on Aspects of the Curriculum, the Plowden Report points out that for the older pupils 'the conventional subjects become more relevant' and that 'some children can then profit from a direct approach to the structure of a subject'. Both Gittins and Plowden gave support to the development of broad areas of study in primary schools with the accompanying discussions about the problems of block-timetabling and flexibility.

If some subjects are selected for a more detailed examination, then clear differences may be observed in the curriculum for pupils of the same age but in different types of middle school (Table 6.4). Home economics and drama are only taught in a minority of schools to younger pupils but in the case of the former, the incidence increases with age and it is taught to older pupils in about half of the middle schools, whereas drama teaching — surprisingly low — seems to depend on an overall school policy with no great differences for age.

Foreign language teaching occurs in comparable frequencies in both types of school that transfer at 12+ and there is a steady increase with age of pupils in the percentages of schools that teach a foreign language; however, it is worth noting that over 20% of 11 year olds in these schools do not learn a foreign language. The difficulty of obtaining and keeping foreign language teachers is severe for many middle school heads for not only is there a scarcity of french teachers, but cutbacks in staff have often meant that the foreign language teacher, if part-time, cannot be retained. Science teaching also occurs more frequently on the timetable as pupils get older. 10% more of the 11 year olds are taught science in the 8-12 than the combined schools and reflecting on the lack of facilities and staffing problems in the generally smaller combined schools, this is not altogether surprising. So, taking foreign languages and science together, it is possible to compare the situation in those schools transferring pupils at 12+ with those transferring at 13+. More 9 year olds in the 9-13 schools do both subjects than in the other two types of school and although the differences between the schools is still marked with older pupils, the gap does close and this is due to the 5-12 and 8-12 deploying their specialist staff and resources to the older pupils, thereby safeguarding their curriculum; a consequence of limited staff resources in this case, however, frequently means that the expectations of the Plowden Report with regard to the enrichment of the middle school curriculum for younger pupils cannot be realised.

Looking now in more detail at the way in which the curriculum is organised with respect to the generalist-specialist teacher continuum, head teachers were asked to estimate the percentage of time which their pupils of different ages spent with specialist teachers, the definition of such personnel being left to the responding head teacher. Again the four types of middle school fall into two groups with those having pupils until 13 organising their teaching differently from the combined and 8-12 schools; pupils in the latter have about half as much contact with specialists as in the 9-13 and 10-13 schools. The largest differences occur for pupils aged 11 and perhaps Table 6.5 illustrates more clearly than many others the very different educational experiences which pupils are exposed to in the various schools; an eleven year old pupil in a 9-13 school is likely to experience a very different style of teaching from one in an 8-12 school – the differences being due partly to differences in ideology and partly to economic and organisational constraints.

There are some interesting variations in the degree to which individual subject specialisation is distributed in middle schools. For example, specialist teaching in english and mathematics shows a familiar pattern of occurring more in the 9-13 and 10-13 schools than in the 5-12 and 8-12 schools and also the younger pupils are more likely to be taught by specialists; but the number of combined and 8-12 schools where pupils are taught by mathematics or english specialists is unusually low – even in the top year. The similarity to a primary school type of organisation, where teachers are all considered to be 'experts' in english and mathematics, is very close. In the 9-13 and 10-13 schools where there is substantially more specialist teaching in these subjects there also appears to be a different philosophy adopted towards the organisation of the top two years in school; there is a particularly strong concentration of specialist teaching in the top two years – those years which would have been 'secondary' years in the traditional system. However, even though there is a sudden increase in the amount of specialist teaching in english and mathematics at 11 years, the overall percentage frequencies are still lower than for some other subjects, notably foreign languages and science, the figures for which are supplied in Table 6.7. The predictable split between those schools deemed primary and those deemed secondary emerges yet again with significantly more 9-13 and 10-13 schools using specialists throughout the school. However, there is no sudden dramatic intervention of specialist teachers in these subjects at age 11 as there is in english and mathematics and the spread of these specialists appears to have a rather wider distribution in the schools. If one examines the data in Table 6.7 overall, then there must surely be some concern at the very low percentage of older children in combined and 8-12 schools not being taught foreign languages and science by a specialist, and even in 25% of the 9-13 schools the older pupils are not being taught by specialist language staff.

The pattern revealed in the distribution of specialist english, mathematics, foreign language and science teaching, with older pupils being exposed to more specialist teaching than younger, and with 9-13 and 10-13 schools specialising to a greater degree than 5-12 and 8-12 schools, is typical of all other subjects in the middle school curriculum, though in varying degrees. There is one exception to this and that is music, for in all of the middle schools the percentage of specialist music teaching does not vary with the age of the pupils; if a school has a music department then that teacher's expertise is used throughout the school.

The 1970s saw a dramatic increase in the amount of curriculum material available for teaching 8-13 year old pupils; for example, in 1975 the Schools Council listed in their Project Profiles no less than 37 such projects. To what extent have middle schools taken advantage of this curriculum material? Details of the more popular project material is given in Table 6.8 which confirm the observation made by Blyth and Derricott (1977) that there is a relatively low take-up of projects in middle schools, especially in the humanities. For example, 'Time, Place and Society' and the Longman's 'Humanities Project' are found in less than 2% of schools; the low take-up may be due to financial constraints, but many projects were available before the cuts became especially severe and so this is not a wholly convincing argument. Perhaps the answer lies in the very great variety of subject areas indicated within the humanities umbrella and therefore it is difficult to find a curriculum to suit everyone. The NUT hint at this explanation for in their pamphlet they write:

> '. . . as subject areas encompassed within the humanities incorporated such a wealth of potential study areas which could all be considered important, schools should "do their own thing" ' (NUT, 1979, p.35).

By way of contrast science, mathematics and french projects are more frequently used in schools with Nuffield Combined Science being the most popular science project; this is most frequently used in 9-13 and 10-13 schools where the necessary facilities for laboratory work are available. The scheme was actually developed for use in well equipped secondary school laboratories and would be very difficult for the majority of combined and 8-12 schools to use. These latter, however, do not appear to find the Schools Council's Science Five to Thirteen any more attractive even though the material is much more suitable for schools with limited science facilities.

The Schools Mathematics Project is used by over half of all the 9-13 schools with the number decreasing to a mere 10% take-up in the combined schools. Of course, other mathematics courses are available for use by schools, and over one-third of all the middle schools use the Fletcher Mathematics scheme developed in Staffordshire and the Alpha-Beta series is used by nearly 33% of 8-12 schools.

'En Avant' is the most popular project in middle schools for not only do three quarters of the 9-13 schools use this french course but a large number of 12+ transfer schools also use this scheme. The 10-13 schools do not use 'En Avant' as frequently as do the other middle schools and they seem more to favour Longman's Audio Visual Course (39.4%) which is also used by 11.1% of 9-13 schools.

The amount of curriculum development at the local level is similarly low, all the more surprising in view of the large amount of planning which characterised the beginnings of middle schools. However, the data from the survey reveals that less than 5% of all types of middle school use material produced either by local teachers or advisers; and this applies across all subject areas. The conclusions which can be inferred from all of this, therefore, are that middle schools are not particularly innovative and have not adopted radical new methods which many early protagonists envisaged.

Sections 2 (Staffing) and 3 (Grouping of Pupils) of the Questionnaire contained questions concerning the provision for remedial pupils. The term remedial pupils covers pupils with learning difficulties who are likely to need special provision for an extended period of time as well as those whose problems may be more acute, as in the case of recently arrived immigrants and pupils who have difficulties in adjusting to transfer from another school. So even though the term has not been strictly defined and no attempt made to examine the various categories of pupils involved, the evidence gathered does help to ascertain the nature of, and the extent to which, provision for these pupils is made in middle schools.

Of the 10-13 schools, 78.8% have a teacher on scale 2 or above who is responsible for remedial work; this is the highest percentage frequency of any type of middle school, for only 56.9% of the 9-13 schools have such a teacher. As one would expect the figures for scale 2 posts in schools transferring pupils at 12+ are drastically lower with 27.3% of 8-12 and only 19.1% of combined schools having such personnel. In the majority of cases, remedial teaching consists of basic language and number work — traditionally the domain of the primary school teacher — and since the 5-12 and 8-12 schools have more ex-primary teachers, and as they are also likely to stay with their class for more of the day than do teachers in 9-13 and 10-13 schools, it seems reasonable to assume that the onus for helping remedial pupils in these schools falls on the class teacher.

In all the schools, except the 10-13s, remedial help diminishes as the pupils get older and so the remedial specialist concentrates more on the younger pupils with the anticipation of integrating pupils more fully into the mainstream before they transfer to upper schools. The 10-13 schools reverse this pattern and concentrate their main efforts on the 11-13 year old pupils — a pattern which is difficult to explain. Pupils are withdrawn from normal classes for tuition in small groups from the majority of all types of school.

Doing homework is considered the norm for secondary school pupils whereas in the primary school homework may be set occasionally, or perhaps to a few individuals, but rarely is it part and parcel of the primary school ethos. Middle schools, lying at the interface between the two have to decide whether setting regular homework should be a feature of their curriculum and their decision often reflects a particular ideology or genuine preference because such choices are unaffected by financial constraints.

There is a natural trend shown in Table 6.9 in that the frequency of schools giving regular homework increases with age, but a most unexpected finding is that a slightly larger proportion of 5-12s than 8-12s set homework regularly. Yet again, however, the major differences which occur are between schools transferring at 12+ and those at 13+. If one examines Table 6.9 for differences at particular ages then it does show how much middle schools do differ in their approach to the curriculum, especially for those pupils aged 10 and 11; the data clearly provides yet more confirmation of the more secondary orientattions of the 10-13 school with 8-12s, not the 5-12s in this case, being more primary orientated. This information, seen in the context of comments from some upper school head teachers, explains why they are concerned about the variations in style and approach of their feeder middle schools, especially in regard to the inculcation of regular homework habits.

As has been noted at the beginning of this chapter pupils tend to be less rigidly separated in middle schools than in other types of school, although some form of procedure has to be used by all schools to ensure the grouping of pupils in the way that they want, whether it be based on mixed ability, streaming or broad banding. The information used to assign the first year pupils on entering the school to their appropriate groups is given in Table 6.10. Schools may use a combination of different types of information but the largest single source is the feeder school record, although some differences between types of schools occurs; for example more 10-13 schools make use of this than any other type and only just over one-half of the 8-12 schools use the feeder school record to group their pupils.

Standardised tests, whether IQ or attainment, are used by about one-third of middle schools to group their first year pupils and their use differs little between the various types of middle school. An internal test, usually maths or english, is favoured by approximately 20% of 9-13 and 10-13 schools and 16% of 8-12 schools. The age of the pupil seems to play a more significant part in the grouping of first year pupils in the 8-12 school than in any of the others.

Many other methods of grouping were mentioned by middle school head teachers but each of these applied to only a few schools; some heads attempted to keep friendship groups together, others base their first year teaching groups entirely on a random sorting such as alphabetical order; a couple of schools referred to the importance of creating a suitable balance between pupils of the indigenous population and those from ethnic minorities.

Table 6.11 shows that the use of intelligence tests continues to flourish in Britain's middle schools, especially in those transferring at 12+; the incidence of testing in those schools increases considerably with the age of the pupil and for those in their final year 65.5% of combined, and 53.6% of 8-12 schools administer some form of IQ test, usually one of the NFER's verbal series. The number of 9-13 and 10-13 schools giving IQ tests to their pupils is considerably lower with the proportion staying the same at about one-third irrespective of the pupil's age. The difference between the 12+ and 13+ schools in this respect probably reflects the latter's more differentiated curriculum, and with specific subject areas being developed a test of general intelligence is seen to have less relevance.

There were few details recorded by heads on their informal assessment procedures, and only a minority of schools responded. The information given was mainly in connection with basic skills tests such as the Bristol Achievement and the Richmond tests, although these appear to be used in only a small number of schools. Much more information was given concerning formal assessment procedures and the data for this is given in Tables 6.12 to 6.15. These tables show the term and the year in which middle schools make some formal assessment in maths, english, and reading, and certain common features can be found in all four tables. In maths, for example, the incidence of testing increases within the school year from term 1 to term 3 in all types of middle school, and this holds good for standardised and internal tests; the only exceptions to this general rule are the first year in 9-13 and the second year in 10-13 schools where the frequency of schools giving standardised maths tests decreases during the school year. Almost the same pattern exists in the assessment of english, with percentage frequencies being recorded which are similar to those in mathematics. A general feature typical of all types of middle school is that more schools prefer to use their own internal tests for maths and english than a standardised test — a situation that is reversed in the assessment of reading. In the 5-12 and 8-12 schools reading attainment is measured more frequently than maths and english at the beginning of the year for all ages of pupil while in the 9-13 and 10-13 schools this holds good for only the younger pupils, but not for the older pupils in the last two years. A difference also occurs between the combined schools and the other types of schools in that the former has a level of testing in the third term which is similar in maths, english and reading; the remaining schools generally have a lower incidence of assessment in reading than in maths and english in the final term, especially in the upper part of the school. Although there are no major differences in the proportion of schools making formal assessments in maths and english the combined schools generally have a lower proportion involved than those in the other schools, yet have a greater proportion evaluating reading skills — perhaps another indication of a more primary orientation.

Little additional information was given concerning other relevant assessment procedures so that it is impossible to regard these in any significant way; a number of schools mentioned the existence of LEA screening tests especially in reading, and about 4% of schools referred to tests in their final year given in consultation with the upper schools. A significant feature among the 5-12 schools is that 10% are involved in selection procedures to upper schools at either eleven or twelve — a practice which goes directly against circular 10/65.

In conclusion to this chapter on the organisation of the curriculum it can be seen that the size of school, numbers of teachers and resources available are the major influences which shape the curriculum in middle schools. The smaller schools with fewer teachers have little choice in their methods of grouping pupils and thus have not the flexibility to vary the composition and size of teaching groups to meet the needs of pupils in particular subject areas. The number of teachers also determines to a large extent the range of subjects which the middle school can offer, as does the type of teaching available — specialist or generalist. All this shows that the staffing of the school and the curriculum which is taught are so much more intertwined and interdependent in middle schools than in either primary or secondary schools.

The now familiar differences between schools transferring at twelve and those transferring at thirteen are also reinforced by the evidence presented in this chapter. Many 9-13 and 10-13 schools are able to provide a curriculum which genuinely extends primary education into more specialist areas while the 8-12 and combined schools in the main have kept a primary type curriculum taught and managed by a class teacher; for the older pupils some efforts are made by many such schools to provide some limited amount of specialist teaching.

One point which emerges strongly from this chapter is that very few schools enjoy the flexibility of approach mentioned by Blyth and Derricott, Burrows and Gannon and Whalley and that rather the picture is one of attempting to maintain curricular expectations under difficult conditions. It seems hardly surprising in view of this, therefore, that middle schools are not innovatory institutions.

CHAPTER 7

Liaison and Transfer

Of all the areas of middle school organisation, it is perhaps that of liaison with other schools which is the most sensitive for, as the Plowden Report states, 'schools are shy of each other'. Although effective liaison between primary and secondary schools is obviously advantageous to the children moving from one school to another it was in the past not considered essential, for with the clean break model pupils often felt that they could make a fresh start in the secondary school and leave the failings and foibles of the primary years behind them. Grammar schools almost always had to operate a clean break philosophy because it was quite impossible to maintain close liaison with a large number of feeder primary schools many of whom would send on only two or three pupils after passing the 11+ exam. Although some marginal improvement has taken place in the communication between primary and secondary schools it is generally agreed even today that contacts between schools are woefully inadequate and this problem is regularly highlighted in DES publications as, for example, in the Green Paper (HMSO, 1977) which begins paragraph 4.2 with the comment:

'Difficulties of transition within an area often arise because there is insufficient contact between the teachers of a secondary school and those in their contributory primary or middle schools'.

If a lack of contact between schools transferring and receiving pupils at the traditional age of 11 seems fairly typical of the educational system (see also the Plowden Report, paragraph 4.31) then why should this problem appear to be more significant in a three tier system of schooling? The answer to this question lies not in any particular deficiencies of the schools themselves nor of the teachers in them, but rather because middle schools cannot operate the clean break philosophy, characteristic of the traditional divide between primary and secondary education, without seriously interfering with the educational needs of their pupils. There are a number of reasons for this.

Firstly, for many three tier systems there is an additional transition point to that in the traditional primary/secondary school, namely that between the first school and the middle school. There has, of course, long been a division between infant and junior schools but this has been a relatively low barrier for children to cross because one infant school usually feeds one junior school; often the buildings are on the same site so that the move from the infant school means that all the children from one class move across the yard to another classroom and so they are likely to be familiar with the new school and with the staff who will teach them. A middle school, on the other hand, frequently has more than one first school from which it receives its pupils and hence the transfer of pupils takes on a quite different dimension from the easy familiarity which most often characterised the move up from infants to juniors. Pupils in a three tier system, therefore, may have to cope with two major transition points rather than with one in the traditional system.

Secondly, the traditional primary/secondary age divide has meant that over the years school curricula and text books have been tailored to this division and stepping outside this pattern causes problems; for example, expensive text books may have to be purchased for 11-12 year old children who will only use a small part of their contents because the target age range is for 11 to 13 or 14 year olds. More important, as Edwards notes, are the difficulties in maintaining continuity in the curriculum between the middle and upper schools:

'A second tier middle school of either nine to thirteen or ten to thirteen will introduce a distinct break at thirteen in the teaching of major subjects in the curriculum which could be quite serious for pupils who will later be sitting the GCE and CSE examinations' (Edwards, 1972, p.90).

Burrows (1978) highlights this with a nice illustration using foreign languages:

'The first foreign language in this country is traditionally French, and all first and second year upper school pupils are likely to learn it. But what is their starting point to be? If there are six contributory middle schools and there has been no co-ordination there may well be two which have already given their pupils a four year course, one a two year course, one through exigencies of staff on erratic now-we-have-it-now-we-don't provision, one no French at all, and one originally minded school which instead has provided German. What is the languages department of the upper school to do?' (p.197).

The third difficulty arises because middle schools cause the postponement of the age of entry to upper schools and this means that the pupils are nearer to the time when they will take their external examinations. Staff in the upper school often feel that this creates a problem with respect to subject choices and it is frequently claimed that pupils transferring at 13+ have insufficient time to adjust to their new schools before making very important decisions on their choice of subjects; the staff also feel under pressure because they do not know the pupils sufficiently well to be able to give them the best advice. Perhaps this aspect is the most critical of all the transition problems and clearly is the most pressing on those schools which transfer and receive pupils at age 13+·

There has been no shortage of exhortations to the staffs in three tier systems to co-operate more closely together and virtually no limitation on the number of suggestions as to what this might involve. For example, the Plowden Report, in addition to advocating a variety of contacts between teachers in successive stages of education, suggested that LEAs should close their schools for one day to arrange teacher conferences to encourage contact between schools; that pupils should make at least one visit to their new school in the term before transfer takes place and that discussions should take place between primary and secondary teachers to avoid overlap in such matters as text books. Pamphlet 57 (HMSO, 1970) also encourages regular meetings between the staffs of different schools and suggests that with appropriate organisation children from the various schools could be jointly involved in music, drama, school visits and displays of work; furthermore any teacher who spends time with pupils at either side of the divide ought to have an opportunity for visiting the contributory or receiving schools. Culling (1973), in discussing the head teacher's role in the middle school, suggests that he and his staff should visit other schools regularly to share ideas and discuss common problems; above all he ought to maintain close contact with the first schools from which pupils are recruited and the high schools to which they transfer 'so that some continuity of educational progress is developed and there is some feedback from the secondary schools about former pupils'. Burrows supports this, for in the final year in the middle school there has to be a change in the pattern and style of the pupil's work so that he is adequately prepared for life in the upper school; this can only be achieved if the middle school 'is familiar with the objectives and the practices of the upper school, and if teachers from both have talked the problems over together' (p.196).

It is left to the NUT's Middle Schools pamphlet to strike a cautionary note not, one hastens to add, on the desirability of close contact between schools, for the NUT regards the fullest possible liaison between schools as essential at all stages in the system; the problem is perceived rather in terms of the extent to which liaison and staff exchanges are possible for this is entirely dependent on the adequacy of staffing levels in both the primary and secondary sectors as well as on adequate resources such as clerical and secretarial support.

The actual mechanics of organising close liaison between schools and easing the passage of pupils from one school to another is thus a good deal more complex than one might originally think, for it not only involves setting up links between schools at different stages, but also between different schools within the same stage. At the beginning of the middle school movement when new schools were being planned and new curricula were being devised the co-operation among teachers and between them and the LEA was undoubtedly very good, no doubt encouraged by the thought of being closely involved with the birth of a new system. However, as schools began to be established and become concerned with the day to day problems of internal organisation, the development of closer links with other schools frequently took a lower level of priority as this middle school head suggests,

'When we established ourselves as a middle school we were given almost complete freedom to work out our own solutions. We have had long enough to put our own house in order and we now ought to be asking fundamental questions about what we have achieved and where we are going (Blyth and Derricott, 1977; p.112).

One of the major influences on the complexity of the transfer problem is the numbers of schools and pupils directly involved, for if a large number of different schools are concerned then the quality of liaison between them is likely to suffer. It is this topic which we shall turn to first, beginning with the transfer between first and middle schools. Results from the survey are given in Table 7.1 and show the percentages of middle schools which had pupils transferring from the various numbers of feeder first schools. As one would expect there is no transfer problem at all in most of the combined schools since for 90% of these the pupils are in the same school; an unexpected finding, however, was the fact that about 10% of combined schools receive pupils at aged 8 from other first schools to join those which already exist in the school; although this is not a large scale pattern it may nevertheless present some difficulties of integration especially when four or five schools are involved.

The main feature which Table 7.1 reveals is the contrast between schools transferring pupils at 12+ and those who transfer later at 13+; in the case of the 8-12s by far the largest majority receive pupils from just one first school, a situation not unlike the traditional pattern of transfer from infant to junior school. If one includes two feeder first schools this shows that over 80% of the 8-12 schools are covered, compared with only 20% for the 9-13 schools; in the case of the 10-13 schools there were none in the sample which took in pupils from fewer than three first schools. It would seem, therefore, that for the vast majority of 8-12, and a small minority of 9-13, schools there are few problems created by the number of feeders involved. However, for the majority of 9-13 and 10-13 schools one finds that a relatively large number for first schools are involved in sending them pupils — over 60% of the 9-13 and over 80% of the 10-13 schools are taking pupils from four or more schools. Clearly the number of schools feeding a middle school is dictated mainly by the relative size of the transferring and receiving institutions and as has been shown in Chapter 4 schools transferring pupils at 13+ are larger than those transferring at 12+; however, though this may be the explanation of the cause it does little to ameliorate a difficult problem, for quite obviously it becomes increasingly difficult to manage effective communications about pupils with a large number of first schools. For those schools who receive pupils from 8 or more schools the chances of arranging any really close and effective links with regard to the curriculum and the special needs of individual pupils must be rather remote; even arranging meetings so that all of the interested parties can attend can be extremely difficult.

Another factor which influences the complexity of transfer is the extent to which choice is allowed by a local authority for parents to send their pupils to different schools. Some indication of this is given in Table 7.2 and it reveals that it is mainly the 9-13 schools in which this features as a major element. For most of the 8-12 schools the pupils come from particular designated first schools and from areas based upon residence and it is only a minority where parental choice is a prominent feature. For the majority of 10-13 schools it is pupil residence which is the determining factor though in practice some parental choice is allowed. The most usual procedure in authorities which do not specifically give parents a choice of middle schools is for there to be a normal pattern of transfer which is acceptable to the majority of parents, but generous allowance is given to those parents who wish their children to go to a different school. Of course, all this can be achieved with far greater ease in urban rather than rural areas, but it is ironic that where an authority does encourage parents to choose their children's middle schools this does have the consequence of increasing the number of schools involved in the transfer and thus creates considerable difficulties for the teachers to liaise with each other effectively. The effects of the 1980 Education Act on transfer and liaison are discussed in Chapter Ten.

The problems of transfer for middle schools do not end with pupils coming into the school, for being in the middle means that, ideally, close links need to be established with upper schools too and Table 7.3 shows the number of upper schools to which pupils transfer from the middle schools. As with the first school transfer, quite marked differences are revealed between the various types of middle schools, and in this case it is the combined and 8-12 schools for which numbers create the most difficulties. Whereas around 50% of the 9-13s and 10-13s transfer their pupils to one school, the proportion for the other schools is nearer to a fifth and a quarter. About 45% of 5-12s and 8-12s transfer pupils to more than three upper schools whereas only about 25% of 9-13 and 10-13 schools do — and remember that the schools transferring pupils at 12+ are smaller schools than those transferring at 13. The greatest variation seems to occur with the 9-13 schools for although the majority of these transfer their pupils to one or two schools, a significant minority are involved with many more, a few sending pupils to 11 or 12 different upper schools. To speak of maintaining links with this number of schools, to attempt to harmonise curricula in maths, foreign languages and science is well nigh impossible.

A limitation of Table 7.3 is that it does not reveal the number of pupils involved in the transfer between schools and so Tables 7.4 and 7.5 have been drawn up to give some indication of this. Looking first at those schools which transfer pupils at 12 one can see that Table 7.4 reveals a difference between the combined and 8-12 schools, for whereas 55% of the 8-12s send more than 50 pupils to just one school, the combined schools' percentage drops right down to 13. This pattern is again largely a function of size because combined schools seem to send smaller groups of 11-30 pupils more frequently to one upper school.

Another significant feature is that approximately 60% of 8-12 and 5-12 schools distribute groups of less than 10 pupils to a large number of upper schools. About 20% of combined, and just under that percentage for 8-12 schools, send small groups of pupils to 4 or more upper schools — a feature which makes liaison particularly difficult. However, with the 8-12 schools it would appear that the typical pattern of transfer is for a larger group of pupils to be transferred to one upper school, with significant minorities scattered around a handful of upper schools; with the combined school, however, no such large blocks are evident and the pattern seems to be small numbers of pupils sent to a variety of upper schools.

For the 10-13 schools Table 7.5 reveals a much tighter and close knit organisation; for them the norm is for the majority of pupils to move on to one or perhaps two schools and it is quite unusual for more than 3 upper schools to be involved. The 9-13 pattern follows quite closely on that of the 10-13 schools but in this case there is quite a significant number of schools distributing small numbers of pupils to upper schools with about 6% of them sending pupils in groups of less than 10 to more than 6 schools.

A distinction can thus be seen in the patterns of transfer between different kinds of middle schools and their associated first and upper schools. For transfer into the middle school it is the combined and 8-12 schools which have fewer first schools to liaise with and thus the potential problems are likely to be fewer; the 9-13 and 10-13 schools, being larger, have to liaise with a greater number of first schools and thus difficulties in maintaining effective curricular links are more likely to occur. For transfer out of the middle school the situation is completely reversed for here the most fragmented dispersal takes place from the combined schools and the most homogeneous from the 10-13 schools. The 9-13 and 8-12 schools occupy an intermediate position with the 9-13 pattern being closer to the 10-13 schools and the 8-12 transfer closer to that of the combined schools. Many of the 9-13 and 10-13 schools are, of course, larger than those middle schools transferring at 12+ and this alone makes for a more systematic transfer out of the school; also many of them are organised into a restricted pyramid structure where two or three middle schools serve one upper school to form a coherent unit, though often this is at the expense of parental choice.

Table 7.6 reflects this differential pattern of transfer out of the middle schools showing some quite marked contrasts in the reasons for pupil allocation to more than one upper school. For over 40% of the 9-13 schools and nearly 50% of the 10-13 schools transfer is mainly to one school whereas the figures for the 5-12 and 8-12 schools are only half of that. Parental choice features far more widely in all the middle schools other than the 10-13 schools with the largest percentage being that for the 9-13 schools. One feature of Table 7.6 is particularly prominent and that is the number of combined and 8-12 schools which are involved in some form of selection of pupils for upper schools. Although this figure may have decreased since the time when the survey was undertaken it is nevertheless quite remarkable that schools established under the aegis of Circular 10/65 and part of a three tier system of comprehensive education should be involved at the same time in a selective system. The majority of schools involved are the combined schools, chiefly in rural areas, but this feature merely adds strength to the feeling that little attention is given by administrators to the supposed ideals of middle school organisation and, being infinitely malleable, can be tailored to suit whatever administrative pattern is convenient.

The final point to be made concerning transfer is that numbers of schools participating is not the whole story, for even though only a few schools may be involved in any one scheme, liaison may be poor between them; similarly, even though a large number of schools may be involved in the transfer of pupils, contact between the various institutions might be particularly good. The point which the survey data emphasises, however, is that middle schools, because they break continuity at unconventional ages, have problems in liaising with other schools at both the intake and out-take points and that the numbers of schools involved is likely to be a significant factor in exacerbating the difficulties. Furthermore, if more freedom of choice is to be allowed for parents to send their children to different schools then this is likely to make life more difficult for the middle schools rather than easier and also make effective liaison with other schools that much more difficult to maintain.

Of course it is not only the number of schools involved in liaison with middle schools which makes communication a problem, and the way in which the schools and the staff are organised to cope with this can do much to ameliorate potential difficulties. One complete section of the Questionnaire was devoted to this topic, the first question of which asked whether or not schools had a member of staff specifically responsible for continuity between the first and middle school. In all of the 10-13 schools in the sample there is a specific member of staff so designated and in the 9-13 schools virtually all adopt this practice (96.7%). In the case of the 8-12 schools, although the overall figure is high at 82.8%, there are still quite a significant proportion of schools which do not have a teacher specifically concerned with first school liaison. Of those schools which do have a member of staff specifically designated for first school liaison, Table 7.7 gives some indication of who this duty falls upon. For many 8-12 schools it is part of the head teacher's role to liaise with the first school while in the 9-13 and 10-13 schools only a small percentage of heads are so involved; in these latter schools it is primarily the task of the first year co-ordinator to keep in touch with the first school, no doubt partly a reflection of their larger size which enables them to use scale posts for this specific task; in the 10-13 schools it is not infrequently part of the deputy head's job. Perhaps most interesting, however, is the fact that about one-third of middle schools do not use the senior management or first year co-ordinator for this task, but assign this duty to another member of staff — a particular feature of middle schools where teachers have responsibility for more than one aspect of organisation.

How frequently do formal liaison meetings occur between middle schools and their feeder first school? Details of this are given in Table 7.8 which shows that for many of the schools a formal meeting takes place once every year, usually in the summer term before the new pupils are to enter the middle schools in the following September. However, about 40% of the schools have formal meetings more frequently than this which does indicate that many middle schools are working hard to keep open the lines of communication between themselves and the first schools. A possibly worrying figure from Table 7.8 is the percentage of those schools which meet rarely or not at all on a formal basis and one can see that this comprises about one-third of all the 8-12 schools and approximately 17% of the 9-13s. However, caution must be exercised in making inferences from this data for a number of head teachers indicated that there was little call for formal meetings with the first schools as there were so many informal meetings taking place. On the other hand others did say that the infrequency of meetings was due to lack of co-operation among the first school heads.

Turning now to liaison with the upper schools Table 7.9 gives the percentage of middle schools which have a member of staff specifically responsible for this and as with many other areas covered by this survey, the frequency increases as one moves from the 5-12 schools through to the 10-13s, though over 70% of the combined schools do designate a member of staff for this. Differences exist, too, in who the designated member of staff is, for in the smaller 5-12 schools it is the senior management, especially the head teacher to whom this responsibility falls, while in the other types of middle schools senior management plays a relatively small part in this; for them it is the fourth year co-ordinator who frequently takes on the responsibility of liaising with upper schools. Another feature of Table 7.10 is that, as with first school liaison, co-ordinating links with the upper school frequently falls to a member of staff outside senior management and year co-ordinator roles.

One of the many areas covered by the Plowden Report was that concerned with the contacts between teachers in successive stages of education and the point was made that this was a particularly difficult problem for all schools. The suggestion was proposed, however, that given the will to do it co-operative programmes of schools working together were possible, such as teachers spending a proportion of their time teaching pupils in different schools — a much more valuable and fruitful exercise than formal contacts, many of which gave little opportunity for teachers to discuss individual pupils. To what extent have middle and upper schools been able to take up these suggestions made in the Plowden Report?

Table 7.11 shows the number of staff from middle schools doing some teaching in the upper schools and the details given by the schools involved reveal that this consists of staff mainly concerned with music, games and craft; a few of the 8-12 schools have their teachers teaching maths in the upper school and one or two middle school staff are involved in the upper school morning assembly. One can see, however, that this form of contact between middle and upper schools is miniscule and with further pressure on staffing ratios is unlikely to develop. Quite a number of head teachers expressed a desire for such exchanges to take place but wrote that shortages of staff inhibit such arrangements; also there was the added problem for some middle schools of a large number of upper schools, which made such a scheme impracticable.

On the other side of the coin is the pattern of visits by upper school teachers to middle schools and here a slightly more encouraging picture is revealed by the survey, details of which are given in Table 7.12. Overall about 10% of middle schools have upper school staffs teaching in them, though this does vary from 6.1% (10-13) to 14% (9-13). Many parts of the curriculum are represented in this exchange but the main ones are foreign languages, maths and science — areas where middle schools have often experienced considerable difficulties in covering adequately. Additional contacts reported were of upper school staff taking assembly in the middle school and also help given with educational technology.

It would thus appear from the survey data that a significant minority of schools have upper school staff teaching in them and this would appear to be a basis for future developments which would benefit all concerned — pupils and teachers.

There is some evidence from the head teachers' comments that a large number of informal contacts take place between middle and upper school staffs, many concerning the curriculum and sporting events; also many teachers keep in touch through local teacher associations or teachers' centres. One or two schools report that Friday lunchtime in a local hostelry is a popular time for staffs from the various schools to get together but the underlying barrier to informal contacts between teachers is the large number of schools involved. For example, one head teacher reported that he had to deal with seven different upper schools and that, in addition, there was a 12+ selection system; it is difficult to maintain any sort of effective contact with that number of upper schools, let alone informal exchanges. Even if informal contacts can be maintained, frequently this is with just a sample of the upper schools to which any one middle school sends its pupils, a situation revealed by one respondent who had no less than 17 upper schools to which his pupils transferred.

More important perhaps than informal contacts between colleagues in middle and upper schools are the formal liaison meetings which take place to discuss specific subject areas. This is an area of particular significance for middle and upper schools because they break into the continuity of the curriculum at unconventional ages. Table 7.13 gives the figures for schools in the survey holding such formal meetings and Table 7.14 shows the percentage of those schools which have meetings to discuss particular subject areas. Some interesting similarities and differences are revealed. The contrast between middle schools transferring at 12+ and those transferring at 13+ is again quite marked with only about 50% of the combined, and 60% of the 8-12, schools holding such meetings. Table 7.14 reveals that most of the liaison meetings are concerned with maths, english, foreign languages and science; little difference is shown between the types of middle schools for maths and english, but the other areas show quite marked contrast especially in foreign languages and science. The 9-13 and 10-13 schools clearly invest more time here because of the necessity to co-ordinate curricula across different middle schools. The combined and 8-12 schools do not have this problem to the same extent as these subjects are less well developed, and in any case, many upper schools feel that they can 'lose' one year and still make it up, whereas for transfer at 13+ this is clearly impossible. The percentage of schools having liaison meetings for humanities and remedial teaching drops quite sharply with the exception of the 9-13 schools who do seem to maintain quite a vigorous programme of formal contact in these areas. What also emerges from Tables 7.13 and 7.14 is the relative isolation of the combined school. Only 50% of these schools arrange formal subject liaison meetings with upper schools and it is with respect to this number that Table 7.14 should be interpreted. For example, the 60.3% of combined schools which meet with upper schools to discuss science consists of 36 schools — a mere 33% of the total in the sample. This relatively low figure illustrates the problems which face the 5-12 school for many are still centred on class teaching which makes it difficult, both in respect of expertise and time, for staff to meet with science colleagues in the upper school, especially when more than one upper school is involved.

Something more of this predicament is highlighted in the series of Tables 7.15 to 7.18 which attempt to show which personnel in the middle and upper schools are involved in these subject liaison meetings and how frequently these meetings occur. In the combined school (Table 7.15) one can see that it is in foreign languages where the subject specialist alone is most frequently involved and to a lesser extent in science also. For other subjects the responsibility for upper school liaison seems to be a much more devolved responsibility especially in maths and the humanities. For english and maths the fourth year teachers appear to play a quite important role as does the senior staff for remedial teaching.

The person most frequently contacted in the upper school is the subject head of department, especially in the case of foreign languages and science where fewer other staff are involved than the remaining subject areas; there is in nearly all middle and upper schools greater exclusivity in the liaison meetings for foreign languages and science than for any other subject. The general pattern of meetings seems to be about one per year on average, though a sizeable proportion of schools meet less often than this. The most frequent meetings take place among the linguists and scientists.

Table 7.16, concerned with the 8-12 schools, reveals a similar contrast between foreign languages, science and the other subject specialists as was revealed in Table 7.15 for the combined schools. English likewise is seen as a more devolved area of responsibility than other subject areas and senior staff appear to be well represented in subject liaison meetings especially in the remedial area, again a similar pattern to that of the 5-12 schools, however, a difference from that of the 5-12s is the increased importance of the remedial specialist.

In the upper schools the heads of department are more frequently represented than for those meetings with 5-12 schools, though the difference in frequency between modern languages, science and the other subject areas is again maintained. There are fewer combinations of staff involved in the 8-12 meetings also.

There appears to be a sharper contrast in the frequency of middle and upper school meetings, with more 8-12 schools having a larger number of meetings than the 5-12s, and also a greater proportion having fewer meetings too.

Table 7.17 which gives details for the 9-13 schools reveals a marked increase on those schools transferring at 12+ in the percentage of subject specialists involved in liaison meetings and the figures now are much closer to those of foreign languages and science; also there is a substantially increased head of department role. Table 7.17 contrasts with the more primary orientation of the 5/8-12 schools where every teacher is expected to be able to cope with maths and english; in those schools transferring at 13+ this is no longer the case, as can be evidenced also from the drop in the combination of teachers involved in subject liaison. An interesting feature is the increased frequency over 8-12 schools of the humanities and remedial specialists and a corresponding decrease in the participation of senior staff in the latter.

For the upper schools, the head of department is the person the 9-13 middle school subject representative is most likely to see and the figures as a whole reveal a trend of much more clearly defined roles and responsibilities in this area. There is a sharp decrease compared with Table 7.15 in those schools which meet upper schools only occasionally and a significant increase in meetings taking place more than once per term. The figures for the 9-13 schools do seem to indicate a more systematic, coherent, and clearly defined pattern in the liaison with upper schools than is the case with middle schools transferring at 12. This would certainly be one benefit of a restricted pyramid structure typical of many 9-13 based tertiary schemes.

As one would expect, the 10-13 pattern (see Table 7.18) continues the trend of increase in the involvement of subject specialists, with the exception of the humanities specialist. A less consistent pattern emerges from the 10-13 schools compared with the 9-13, as there is a decrease in the number of schools where heads of department are involved and an increase in devolved responsibility; also there is a slight increase in the involvement of fourth year teachers especially for the humanities and in remedial subjects.

The upper school personnel remain similar to those for the 9-13 schools with the head of department principally involved, though a particularly large increase is shown for humanities and remedial subjects. A contrast with the 9-13 school is the increased involvement in liaison of the lower school subject head. The frequency of meetings is roughly comparable with that of the 9-13 schools with, if anything, a slight decrease.

Formal liaison meetings also take place between middle and upper schools to consider the details of administration. For nearly all the middle schools in the sample which engage in such meetings (see Table 7.19) these occur once per year usually about mid-way through the summer term. The numbers of schools involved in such an exercise again reveals the contrast between schools transferring at 13+ and those transferring at 12+ though perhaps the most significant inference one can make from Table 7.19 is the large number of schools which do not have meetings to discuss these matters. For those that do then the most likely teachers to be involved are the senior staff from both middle and upper schools, though with the exception of the 5-12 schools, the fourth year co-ordinator is also likely to play a part as well.

Liaison and transfer between schools should not only involve teachers but should include children as well and in this regard middle schools do have quite a good track record, for over 90% of the schools organise visits of their children to the upper schools prior to their actual transfer in September. Many head teachers feel that this reduces considerably the anxieties which children face on transfer to a large upper school and think that the exercise of moving large numbers of children to a number of different schools is well worth the time and trouble involved. Other than this the contact the children have between schools is naturally rather limited consisting for the most part of joint sporting and musical activities; there was mention occasionally of joint youth clubs and trips abroad but generally the contact middle school pupils have with upper school pupils is restricted to participation in orchestra and choirs, and the occasional sports day.

Summarising the evidence in liaison and transfer between schools one can say that the problems are not the same for all middle schools but vary according to the type of school and the numbers of institutions involved; it is very difficult to make generalisations applicable to all middle schools. However, one feature that is of considerable significance is the size of the school, for only if a school is large enough can it attract the resources, especially staff resources, to develop the flexibility to cover the many different aspects of liaison with other schools. It is for this reason that the combined and 8-12 schools suffer more than the 9-13 and 10-13 schools and find it difficult to maintain effective links with upper schools. It is not just a problem of appointing the appropriate staff to co-ordinate these links but also there are difficulties in providing sufficient flexibility to allow staff to be away from teaching duties to attend meetings and serve on committees.

A second feature affecting transfer is the number of schools involved and the survey has given valuable information concerning this aspect; the evidence presented here suggests that for many middle schools the large number of upper schools to whom they send pupils is a serious barrier to effective communication and curriculum harmonisation. It is not so much the case that middle schools are shy of other schools, for indeed they appear more extravert than most and many have set up specific structures to cope with this; it is rather that there are often too many schools for a hardpressed staff to cope with — in this case more does mean worse.

CHAPTER 8

The View from the Upper Schools

There is not a great deal of information available about the relationships which exist between upper schools and their feeder middle schools. Most of the research concerned with middle schools has concentrated on the curriculum and the internal organisation of the middle school itself and only a few writers, such as Burrows (1978), have viewed the middle school within the broader context of a three tier system of education. Some research in this field has been undertaken by Bryan (1980) and Piggott (1977, 1979) but this relates mainly to the pupil's perception of transfer from middle to upper school and does not examine the organisational features of transfer in general. It was to fill this particular gap in our knowledge of the three tier system that a Questionnaire was sent to upper schools in England and Wales which received pupils from middle schools and which were identifiable as part of a system with middle schools as feeders. The list of these schools was obtained from the 1978 edition of the Local Authorities Directory and the Questionnaires were sent to the head teacher of each school, together with a covering letter explaining the purpose of the research. The Questionnaire itself (see Appendix 2) was considerably briefer than that sent out to middle schools and although it was divided into five separate sections seeking information on the general background of the school, its staffing, organisation of the curriculum, links with feeder schools and a free response section at the end, the main thrust of the questions was focused on the transfer of pupils from the feeder middle schools. The basic aims, therefore, were to find out what the practice of transferring pupils at 12+ or 13+ actually entails and to assess the advantages and disadvantages which the upper schools perceive in accepting pupils at an age later than the traditional one of 11+.

Details of the sample of schools responding to the Questionnaire are given in Tables 8.1 and 8.2 where they are considered separately. In practice, of course, cation Volume 1 — Schools (HMSO, 1981) and comparison of these two sets of data enables an assessment to be made of the size and representativeness of the sample of upper schools. There are three main categories of upper school based upon age ranges of 12-16, 12-18 and 13-18 years and as with the middle school survey it was thought more appropriate and informative to organise the data into these major groupings so that any advantages and difficulties of transfer at either 12 or 13 years of age could be seen more clearly. In addition there were Questionnaires received from four schools whose age range was from 13 to 16

71

years and instead of creating a separate category for such a small number of schools their data was included with that from the 13-18 schools except in Tables 8.1 and 8.2 where they are considered separately. In practice, of course, the lack of a sixth form in the 13-16 schools makes them very different in character from their more conventional 13-18 counterparts but because of the shared age of transfer and the major focus of the Questionnaire it was thought that these schools would have more in common with 13-18 than with 12-16 schools.

Table 8.1 shows the number of schools in each age category responding to the Questionnaire and by comparing this with the total number of upper schools in England and Wales as reported in the Statistics of Education — Volume 1 (HMSO, 1981) the size of the sample can be calculated. Leaving aside the 13-16 schools, the highest response was from the 13-18 schools which showed a very commendable 63% return; the 12-16 schools' response rate was also satisfactory at 56.4% but the return from the 12-18 schools numbering less than 50% was disappointing.

Table 8.2 gives the total number and percentage of upper schools in England and Wales falling in each particular size band as published by the DES (HMSO, 1981) and places this information alongside that obtained from the sample responding to the Questionnaire; by comparing the characteristics of the survey sample with that of the total population some assessment of the sample's representativeness may be ascertained. Examination of the 12-18 schools reveals that the smaller establishments tend to be over represented in the sample while the larger schools in the 1201-1500 bracket are under represented; the two sets of percentages in each category are much closer together for the 12-16 schools but it can be seen also that the proportion of schools of size 401-600 pupils is larger in the sample than in the total population; for the 13-18 schools there is remarkable similarity in the proportions of the sample and total population in each size category with the single exception of the very smallest 13-18 upper schools where only one out of a possible nine returned the Questionnaire.

The overall relationship between the size and the number of schools in the sample and the total number of upper schools revealed in Table 8.2 is remarkably close with 28 out of 32 cells showing a deviance of less than 5%; of those four cells which do show a difference of more than 5%, one is for the small group of 13-16 schools and two others for the 12-18 schools show only a marginally greater difference than 5%; it is only in the 401-600 size of 12-16 school that there is a deviation as large as 10%.

Looking at the data from Tables 8.1 and 8.2 as a whole one can see that the size of the sample, comprising 56.9% of all the upper schools in England and Wales, is large enough to provide an adequate basis from which to make inferences about the population as a whole, though the information from the 12-16 schools, obtained from under 50% of the total number of such schools, should be treated with some caution. However, in assessing the representativeness of the sample in terms of the size of schools one can see that it follows the national pattern quite faithfully, even in the case of the 12-18 group, and so the data obtained from the survey may be treated with a reasonably high degree of confidence.

The wide variation in the size of upper schools renders the use of the average number of pupils in each type of school of limited value, and indeed the average sizes of schools do not appear in the DES Statistics of Education; however, it may be of some minor value in providing further evidence for the sample's representativeness as well as crystallising some differences between the various groups of upper schools. The survey data shows that the 12-16 schools, as expected, are the smallest of the three categories of upper schools, with an average number of 719 pupils on roll; the 12-16 are the largest schools with an average of 1008 pupils while the 13-18 schools are between the other two, containing on average 904 pupils. This pattern is clearly reflected in Table 8.2 where the modal band for 12-16 schools is 601-800, for 12-18 schools it is 1001-1200 and for 13-18 schools it is 801 to 1000. From this, therefore, one can see that upper schools are not particularly large institutions and the majority of them contain well below 1000 pupils.

A number of background details of the upper schools in the sample are given in Tables 8.3 to 8.5. Table 8.3 shows the years when upper schools were formally opened and, as with middle schools, this development reached its peak in the early 1970s followed by a tailing off towards the end of the decade. This table reveals no striking differences between the various types of upper school which is in marked contrast to the following table (Table 8.4) which does show quite different lines of historical development among the particular schools. Nearly three-quarters of the 12-16 schools in the sample were formerly secondary modern schools with only relatively small percentages of the remainder having more varied historical origins; this presents a different pattern of development to that of the 12 and 13 to 18 schools which have a much more diverse ancestry. Perhaps most significant is that about 40% of the 13-18 schools were former grammar schools with only 22.3% being formerly secondary modern schools. Only a relatively small percentage of 12-18 schools were formerly just grammar schools but a relatively large number were formed out of secondary modern and grammar schools amalgamating. An interesting comparison can also be found in Table 8.4 which shows the relatively high percentage of new purpose built 13-18 schools as contrasted with the number of new 12-18 and 12-16 schools. The physical arrangement of schools and their historical origins are important elements to bear in mind when looking at schools as frequently these factors play such an important part in the style and development of any new institution.

Table 8.5 shows the denomination of schools, the majority being non-denominational, and perhaps the interesting feature is the small number of denominational 13-18 and 12-16 schools and that these are equally divided between the Church of England and the Roman Catholics; by contrast the 12-18 schools have a much greater percentage of denominational institutions, especially Roman Catholic.

A particularly important feature of a three tier system of education is the number of middle schools which feed the upper schools and a comprehensive picture of the national pattern of transfer in this system is virtually non-existent. In a previous chapter this aspect was examined from the viewpoint of the middle schools, but seen from the upper schools' position the organisation of transfer has a quite different perspective. For example, if one looks at the number of different upper schools to which pupils transfer from a single middle school, one might find that they are dispersed among half a dozen or more upper schools; however, these same upper schools will receive pupils from other middle schools as well and in order to examine the complete picture of transfer information from both middle and upper schools is required. It is to complement the information obtained from middle schools that the series of Tables 8.6 to 8.10 has been compiled.

These tables show the number of middle schools which feed the upper schools and the number of pupils involved. Emerging quite clearly from this set of tables is a difference between the 13-18 schools and the rest in the organisation of transfer. Table 8.6 reveals that about 40% of 13+ transfer schools have no more than three separate feeder schools, whereas for those schools receiving 12 year old pupils the proportion is half of that; the 12-16 and 12-18 schools appear to have a much more varied pattern of intake than the 13-18 schools. Furthermore, size of upper school is not directly related to the number of feeder middle schools because the 12-16 schools, though smaller than the other upper schools, do not take in pupils from a smaller number of feeders. An exception to this is at the upper end of the scale where more than 16 feeder schools are involved, and where this occurs the 12-18 and 13-18 schools are more likely to be represented than the 12-16 schools.

As can be imagined the problems involved in liaising effectively with this number of schools are very great indeed, though the number of feeder schools alone does not give the total picture; this can only be seen when the numbers of pupils involved in the transfer between schools is given as well. An attempt to provide this information is given in Tables 8.7 to 8.10. Two cautionary points need to be heeded in the interpretation of these tables. Firstly, although each category of pupil numbers is exclusive, any one school may be represented in the series of tables more than once by being placed in more than one number band; for example, a 12-16 upper school which takes in 20 pupils, two each from ten middle schools and 195 pupils, 65 each from 3 middle schools, will be included in Table 8.7 and again in Table 8.10. The second point of caution is that the 12-18 schools contain a relatively high percentage of missing data; this may well be due to the fact that head teachers, in completing the Questionnaire, found it too time consuming to give all the details of pupil numbers especially as there was often such a large number of feeder schools involved.

Notwithstanding these two cautionary notes, however, these tables do underline the differences, already perceived, in the pattern of 13+ transfer from that at age 12+. For example, in Tables 8.7 to 8.9 the 'Not Applicable' category, signifying those upper schools which do not receive that particular number of pupils from the middle schools, is very much larger for the 13-18 schools than the other upper schools, while in the last table, Table 8.10, the percentage is smaller. This shows that a relatively greater proportion of 13-18 schools do not receive small numbers of pupils from a large number of feeders, a feature which is characteristic of many 12-16 and 12-18 schools.

The organisational patterns of pupil transfer from middle to upper schools are the result of the interaction of many different factors such as the designation and location of catchment areas, the siting of schools in a rural or urban environment, the degree of parental choice which is exercised and the relative sizes of lower and recipient schools. However, a useful classification of these organisational patterns can be drawn up based on the Questionnaire data and using the twin criteria of numbers of schools and numbers of pupils involved in the transfer.

The first type that can be identified is the restricted pyramid form of organisation which consists of a few, usually two to four, middle schools feeding one upper school; this is considered by many of the advocates of the three tier system to be the ideal type of structure because it facilitates the maximum degree of curricular compatibility between schools and minimises the number of transfer problems because of the small number of institutions involved. Although this appears a relatively neat arrangement from the bureaucratic viewpoint, to make it work effectively does entail some sacrifice of parental choice for administrative convenience. Many instances of this structural form occur in rural areas such as small market towns which are able to support only one upper school as is the case with Figure 1 from the Midlands:-

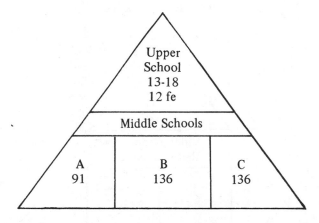

Figure 1. Restricted Pyramid

The upper school is a 12 form entry 13-18 school receiving 3 forms from Middle School A and 4½ from each of Middle Schools B and C. Notice that these 9-13 middle schools are relatively large and such a pyramid structure can only occur where the feeders are quite large schools, a characteristic which is not so common in the combined and 8-12 middle schools. Thus pyramid structures are much more common at 13+ than 12+ because relatively large middle schools feed moderately sized upper schools.

A second type of organisation – an extended pyramid – occurs where there are a few feeder schools supplying the upper school with the majority of its pupils, but in addition there are a small number of 'minor' middle schools each sending on a few pupils. Figure 2 provides an example of this model from north-east England which shows a 9 form entry 12-18 upper school receiving the majority of its pupils from 4 main middle schools and a handful also from 4 'minor' ones. This is a reasonably compact form of transfer as the majority of pupils come from the 4 main feeder schools and so liaison is not too difficult; coping with the remaining 10% of pupils scattered among four other middle schools may create some difficulties but in general these can be solved without too much trouble. The real problems of liaison and transfer begin to emerge when the 'minor' feeder schools begin to proliferate as the example from a typical 12-16 school in the Midlands illustrates. (Figure 3).

Two-thirds of the intake is supplied by three middle schools, but the remaining one-third of pupils are spread out over 20 different middle schools. The critical variables which lead to this pattern of transfer – the proliferated pyramid – are geographical location and the exercise of parental choice; if a large number of middle and upper schools are located close together in a compact urban environment so that pupils can travel easily to a number of them, and if parents are allowed to choose which upper school their child may go to, then this kind of transfer arrangement is likely to occur. Effective liaison in these

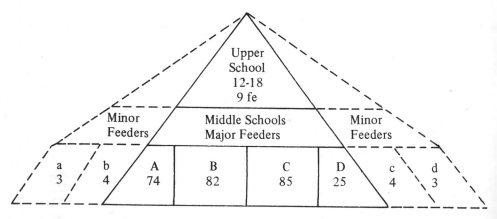

Figure 2. Extended Pyramid

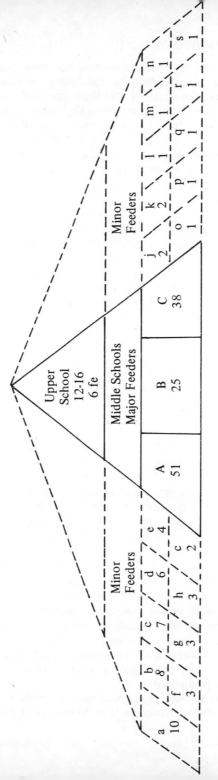

Figure 3. Proliferated Pyramid

circumstances becomes extremely difficult, not only because of the number of schools involved but also because the 'minor' middle schools are sending pupils to other upper schools as well and these may well have different curricular expectations and interests. The role of the LEA advisory staff in minimising the problems of transfer is crucial in this type of transfer pattern, especially by ensuring that there are not too many different maths, english, foreign language and science curricula in the various middle and upper schools. To enable this type of transfer system to work efficiently, therefore, entails some loss of traditional autonomy in the schools in planning and organising their curricula.

The fourth model of transfer, the dispersed pattern, is the most problematical one in terms of effective liaison between middle and upper school because this arrangement possesses no major feeder middle schools at all and the pupils come from a large number of 'minor' middle schools each sending fewer than a complete class of children to the upper school. The most extreme example of this which occurred in the survey came from the south of England and consisted of a 12-18 upper school which received pupils from no fewer than 52 different middle schools — a figure which would be quite hard to beat in the days of grammar school selection. The only feasible strategy open to the upper school in this predicament is to ignore all the individual variations in the middle school curricula and operate a 'clean break' philosophy as is the case with transfer at 11+. However, this particular arrangement does call into question some of the more exaggerated claims concerning the efficacy of the middle school system in creating an effective bridge between primary and secondary education; this may happen, but only if the organisation of transfer operates within certain quite well defined limits — it is certainly not an inherent quality of the system itself.

One final consideration in the organisation of transfer is the actual method of allocating pupils to any particular upper school and information concerning this is supplied in Table 8.11. Again some caution must be exercised in the interpretation of this data because a single method of distributing pupils to the upper schools is quite infrequent. However, Table 8.11 provides a useful guide to this process and indicates that there is little major variation between the different kinds of upper school, though one or two details are worth a mention. For example, the 12-18 schools have the smallest percentage of specific feeder schools and the largest percentage still maintaining a selective intake. Another noteworthy feature is the similarity in the proportions of schools operating a system of parental choice, especially when one considers this in relation to the data in Table 8.6 which reveals quite major dissimilarities in the percentage of feeder middle schools sending pupils to other upper schools. Again it would appear that the 9-13, 13-18 schools more frequently have a compact and tightly knit organisation, but where the 9-13 middle schools do send pupils to a variety of upper schools a major problem of subject continuity occurs because of the increased age of the pupils.

Summarising this section on transfer between middle and upper schools, as viewed from the latter's perspective, it is the very great diversity of organisation which is most readily apparent. Although the number alone of institutions involved in transfer does not determine the quality of liaison between schools nevertheless the number of feeder schools associated with many upper schools is very large and this does create administrative constraints which makes effective liaison very difficult indeed. Those problems seem to be most severe among the 12-18 schools which are, on average, larger than the other types of upper school, and yet receive pupils from the smaller middle school units — the combined and 8-12 schools; this naturally means that a large number of feeder schools are required to fill the places available in the upper school. Any degree of parental choice which is allowed by an LEA, whether at age 12+ or 13+, means that as a consequence, the upper schools are likely to be supplied from a large number of feeder middle schools — a situation which already exists in many urban areas and is likely to be exacerbated by the 1980 Act.

It was not intended that the Keele survey of middle schools would be concerned with an in-depth analysis of upper schools, but rather that it should include those aspects of upper school organisation which affected the relationship between them and their feeder schools. Thus the data which describes the staffing arrangements in upper schools is not detailed and comprehensive, and is included only because it sheds light on the overall pattern of organisation in a three tier system of education.

The Group number of a school is the principal factor which determines the staffing formula and the location of a school in a particular Group is largely a result of the number of pupils on roll and their ages, older pupils receiving a higher weighting than younger ones. Table 8.12 shows the distribution of the sample of upper schools in the Groups and, as one would anticipate, the 12-16 schools show a different arrangement compared to that of the other upper schools; being smaller and possessing no sixth form the 12-16 schools tend to fall in the lower categories and about three-quarters of them are Group 8-10 schools. The majority of 12-18 and 13-18 schools, however, are in Group 10-12, though there is a marked modal peak in the distribution of 13-18 schools with over 40% of these being in Group 11; the distribution of 12-18 schools is much more evenly divided between the three categories, although this type has the greatest proportion of very large Group 12 and 13 schools.

The average numbers of staff in each type of upper school are given in Table 8.13. As a result of their lower Group numbers the 12-16 schools have fewer staff than the 12- and 13-18 schools; the composition of those staffs, however, is also influenced by the origins of the upper schools and the relatively high proportion of non-graduates in the 12-16 schools is a reminder of the fact that most of these under the tripartite system were secondary modern schools. The highest proportion of graduate staff is in the 13-18 schools, many of which were former grammar schools, and this may also account for the slightly lower percentage of women teachers in these schools when compared to the numbers in the other upper schools. The distribution of scale posts within a school is largely decided by the head teacher though Table 8.14 shows a remarkable similarity in the percentage of teachers on each scale in the three types of school; the numbers may be smaller in the 12-16 schools than in the others but the pattern of scale post allocation shows a close resemblance to that of the 12- and 13-18 schools. However, some differences can be discerned in the distribution of these scale posts amongst the various subjects; for example, foreign languages has a departmental head in only half of the 12-16 schools compared with all of the 12-18 and 13-18 schools and these latter also tend to have separate heads for each of the three major sciences — physics, chemistry and biology — whereas the smaller 12-16s more frequently have a single head of science. In the 12-18 and 13-18 schools where a head of science is appointed this is often in addition to heads of the separate science disciplines — a situation quite different from that in the 12-16 schools.

While the pattern of distribution of departmental heads in science shows dissimilarities, in the arts subjects it is the general resemblance between the schools which stands out, although in nearly every case the 12-16 schools have just that fraction lower percentage than the other schools; the one notable exception to this is home economics.

Looking now at the ancilliary resources within the schools, Table 8.15 reveals the different levels of support in each of the three kinds of school, though many of these differences are due to the size of school rather than the type. The degree of support from ancilliary staff which a school can call upon may not be too critical when it is a case of determining whether there are two or three ancilliary personnel available, but it does become critical when size of school dictates whether there will be one person available, or no-one at all. The former appears to be the case in the deployment of secretarial staff, the latter with workshop and laboratory technicians, especially in the 12-16 schools, which frequently have only one such ancilliary member allocated to the school.

When pupils arrive at the upper schools from their middle schools they have to be organised into groups for learning and pastoral support. Sometimes the teaching groups and the pastoral groups are identical, as in those schools which have streaming, but where a more flexible grouping policy for teaching is adopted the welfare of pupils has to be organised separately. In addition to enquiring into this aspect of upper schools it was also thought useful to ascertain whether different patterns of grouping exist in different types of school and whether or not there are advantages for the choice of courses and examination subjects in transferring pupils at 12+ and 13+. Thus it is necessary to emphasise that consideration of the upper school curriculum is here limited to those aspects of organisation which may be affected by an age of transfer later than the traditional age of 11+.

Classifying the grouping procedures within any school is often very difficult because of the problem of defining in an unambiguous way the attributes of a particular system. For example, how narrow do 'broad bands' have to become before they are redefined as streams? How does one define a system which extracts a class of bright children to form an 'A' stream, with the remainder of the pupils being grouped in mixed ability classes? One school responding gave each of its pupils two groupings, one for arts subjects based on attainment in english and french and one for science subjects based on ability in mathematics; how would this system be categorised? It was because of this kind of problem that many of the upper school questions were open ended so that head teachers could describe briefly their systems many of which consisted of unique blends of setting, streaming and banding. In terms of research methodology, this does not solve the problem of classifying systems, but it does allow a more consistent categorisation by the researchers.

Table 8.16 shows the groups in which pupils are placed for registration when they newly arrive at the upper school; this is an important group for the pupils because in 90% of all schools this is where the pastoral support and welfare services are directed. The most common form of organisation is the mixed ability group, though this is found more frequently in the 13-18 schools than the others. Broad banding, where pupils are placed in one of two or three wide ability bands, is the second most popular system adopted by about one-quarter of schools. Streaming is found in a minority of upper schools particularly among the 12-16s. Many schools have a house system of some kind, but relatively few use this as the basis for morning and afternoon registration.

Whatever the form of grouping which is decided upon a policy has also to be devised for sorting out pupils coming in from the different feeder schools. Most schools report that their registration groups are designed to ensure the maximum integration of pupils from the feeders and, in addition to using middle school record cards, information on friendship groups is also used to make sure that pupils settle in quickly. Even when grouping by ability is adopted for registration groups many schools still attempt to accommodate friends and siblings and at the very least try to ensure that there are two pupils in the same class from the same middle school. Approximately 15% of 12-18 and 13-18 schools report 'disregarding' the feeder schools when grouping pupils for registration and group solely on a random basis — usually by alphabetical order. This is the most common method used where there is a large number of feeder schools each transferring small numbers of pupils and the upper school simply cannot take account of all the different middle schools in their grouping procedures; also this method is used when just a few large middle schools are the feeders, for a random grouping of pupils will automatically ensure that some pupils from the same middle school are in the same upper school class.

The manner in which teaching groups are arranged is even more important than the organisation of pastoral groups and Table 8.17 reveals quite significant differences in the patterns of organisation in the various types of school. For example, the proportion of schools streaming first year pupils is far greater among the 12-16s than among the others; and while schools which adopt streaming do so for both pastoral and academic purposes, those that have mixed ability groupings for pastoral support frequently have different teaching groups, especially amongst the 12-16 and 13-18 schools. The latter seem to favour broad banding more frequently than any other form of grouping, though a sizeable minority favour setting also; only a tiny proportion are streamed, or have complex combinations of systems difficult to classify in conventional categories.

The 12-18 schools seem to favour, in roughly equal proportions, broad banding and mixed ability groupings for their first year pupils and these systems account for the organisation in 70% of the schools, with only small numbers practising other forms of grouping. In the 12-16 schools the most popular form of grouping is broad banding, the same as that for the 13-18 schools, but those 12-16 schools which do not have this system are divided fairly evenly between the other four methods of grouping. Probably the most significant conclusion which can be drawn from Table 8.17 is that the age of transfer does not seem to be related to any particular form of internal grouping, for there is as much variation in grouping structures within those schools receiving pupils at 12+ as there is between them and those schools which accept pupils at 13+.

Methods of allocation to teaching groups vary too, though over 70% of all schools use the records passed on from the middle schools to help with the sorting procedure. Internal tests are employed by about 15% of schools, especially in mathematics and english. There seems to be a slightly more test orientated atmosphere in the 12-16 schools than in the other upper schools: more of these schools use standardised tests of some kind as their basis for grouping pupils and, rather significantly, 26.7% of 12-16 schools administer IQ tests to their children compared with only 15.9% of 12-18, and 8.3% of 13-18, schools. A small minority of schools use other criteria on which to base their grouping, such as the ability to begin another foreign language, assessment by personal interview and the specific recommendations of the middle school concerning likely future examination success.

Once assigned to a group in their upper schools the question can be asked as to how permanent is that grouping. Table 8.18 shows that, by the end of the first year, major regrouping occurs in approximately 40% of schools accepting 12+ pupils and in nearly 70% of those receiving pupils at 13+. The re-grouping in the 13-18 schools is different from that in the 12-16 and 12-18 schools, for it is in their first year that option choices have to be made in addition to decisions about the most appropriate examination course to follow. Further evidence of major changes in the 13-18 schools is given in Table 8.19 which shows the extent to which a common curriculum is pursued in the first and second years; in the 13-18 schools a common course virtually ceases after the first year when the pupils track off to their different courses. For the schools with a 12+ intake, however, re-grouping takes place on the basis of performance in the new school and frequently some form of setting is introduced during the first year and in the second year, among the 12-18 schools especially, some resorting occurs on the basis of ability to take up a second foreign language.

Few differences are found among the upper schools in their provision for, and identification of, remedial pupils. Over 80% of schools report having a remedial department and all of the upper schools indicate that middle school records play a vital part in the identification of pupils in need of extra help and support. About half of the schools use additional evidence to classify the remedial pupils, such as a standardised attainment test or some form of internal test of the school's own devising; a few schools use IQ tests and one or two call on the services of the LEA remedial department. On balance it would appear that remedial pupils are not unduly disadvantaged from a later age of transfer than 11+ and that the liaison which has been set up between middle and upper schools to cater for this minority of pupils works quite well.

By way of contrast a much more important consequence of transferring schools one or two years later than the traditional age of 11+ is that option courses have to be chosen when the pupils have spent less time in the upper school than is the case in the normal secondary school. To what extent is this perceived by the upper schools as advantageous or disadvantageous? An unequivocal answer to this question is given in Table 8.20; approximately two-thirds of all 12+ intake schools recorded some disadvantage while an even greater proportion — over 80% — of the 13-18 schools suggested some problem. The same picture emerges when the other side of the coin is examined — the positive advantages; the number of 12+ schools suggesting advantages was very small at around 5%, though among the 13-18 schools it was somewhat larger at 17.8%. Thus the balance of disadvantage outweighs quite considerably the perceived advantages and this does not show up the three tier system in a very favourable light. The small minority of schools which suggested advantages was not large enough to identify any major themes, though a number of schools claim that there is a greater enthusiasm among the pupils, especially the 13 year olds; some head teachers suggest that a later transfer age means a greater range of option choices available because of the larger number of pupils in any one age cohort, while others notice a greater maturity of approach to the problem of subject choice, especially amongst girls.

However, the overwhelming proportion of upper schools perceive difficulties rather than benefits in the later transfer age and the major categories of disadvantages are listed in Table 8.21. A major problem from the upper schools' point of view is that many of the pupils receive an inadequate foundation in many subject areas, particularly in the linear subjects such as foreign languages and mathematics, and in the practical subjects including science. This problem is more frequently experienced by the 12+ upper schools than the 13+ schools, and a possible reason for this might be the lack of specialist staff in the combined and 8-12 schools which is more common than in the 9-13 middle schools; however, even one-third of the 13+ schools feel that there is some inadequacy of preparation in one or more subject areas. Another principal area of concern for the 13-18 schools is the lack of sufficient time to carry out the whole decision-making process of choosing appropriate option courses and examination subjects; not only is it a case of the teachers having too little time to get to know the pupils and their strengths and weaknesses, but also the shortage of time allows too little opportunity for pupils to really comprehend what a subject entails — everything has to be carried out with undue haste. As anticipated these difficulties were not found as frequently in the 12+ intake upper schools.

Modern languages prove to be a testing subject area as in other comprehensive schemes and many 13-18 schools record that later transfer causes problems in introducing pupils to a second foreign language; other difficulties encountered by a minority of schools are the wide variation in standards among the feeder middle schools and the denial of extra time with specialist teachers which the upper schools heads believe so valuable; some schools feel that the middle schools prolong 'junior school' attitudes among their pupils and express disquiet at 12 and 13 year old children being unused to formal classrooms and regular patterns of homework.

The later age of transfer which a middle school system entails thus appears to create problems in the organisation of the upper school curriculum rather than ameliorate them and the undeniable drift of the comments from the head teachers of upper schools is that it would be far more beneficial, as well as convenient, to have pupils over the age of 11 in their own schools rather than in middle schools.

The previous section highlights some of the problems which upper schools face in organising the curriculum as a consequence of pupils transferring later than at 11 years, though these difficulties may be moderated by both upper and middle schools maintaining effective liaison with each other. One of the most important elements in this liaison is the information which the upper school receives from the middle schools about individual pupils and it is clear from the survey that many LEAs in recent years have done a great deal to organise on a more systematic basis the transmission of information about pupils from one school to another; a large number of LEAs have standardised record cards and an overwhelming majority of upper schools (72%) use these, though the proportions of 12-18 schools using standardised record cards is slightly lower than the others (66%). The comments of the head teachers indicate that a great deal of information is received from the middle schools including such items as the assessment of the child's general ability, frequently an IQ test score as well as data on reading ages; approximately 15% of upper schools receive results from a test in mathematics or english set by the middle school or by the upper school, and ability in languages is another key piece of information especially for the 13-18 schools; often these latter request specific recommendations from the feeder middle school concerning the take-up of a second foreign language, particularly where a school is forming a group of linguistically able children for advanced language study.

Only about 3% of upper schools suggest that there is inadequate information from the middle schools and so the general picture concerning the transfer of data from middle to upper school appears satisfactory; where problems emerge is in the way in which the cards are completed and some schools do feel that there could be a more standardised set of procedures, for example in the grades given to children, because sometimes these are not comparable between different schools.

It is this fact which leads some upper schools to administer standardised tests to pupils on entry and explains, to some degree, the use of IQ tests for pupil grouping. However, there is hardly any demand for pupils to sit an examination before moving on to the upper school, or for more testing by the upper school staff of middle school pupils in their final year.

The transfer of pupil records from middle to upper schools appears to work quite well and most upper school head teachers are satisfied with the quantity and quality of information received. In connection with this transfer of data it is encouraging to report that approximately one-third of upper schools have direct contact with the middle schools and often a deputy head, or head of lower school visits the feeder school to sort out the grouping of pupils for the new school and identify pupils in need of specialised help.

The other direct link which upper schools most commonly have with their feeder schools is the formal liaison meeting where, rather than discussing the needs of individual pupils, more general problems concerning the curriculum are examined such as subject continuity and the harmonisation of subject syllabi. Over 50% of upper schools have these meetings though there is some small variation according to type of school. The frequency of these meetings also varies and of those schools having formal liaison meetings it is more often the 12-16 and 13-18 schools which have them at least once per term with a greater proportion of the 12-18 schools meeting annually.

In addition to the formal liaison meeting there are other points of contact between upper and middle schools such as subject working parties, conferences organised by the LEA and meetings for heads of year although, with the exception of head teacher conferences, these involve a tiny minority of schools – at least on a regular basis. Meetings to discuss pastoral care show a marked variation in frequency of occurrence between different upper schools with the 13-18 schools having the largest percentage. As a rule these general meetings take place once per year and principally involve the upper school's senior staff and year tutors, though counsellors are also included where available; heads of subject departments are not usually present at these meetings.

The number of schools reporting informal contacts with their feeder schools was not large, consisting of 12.7% of the sample. It is difficult to identify any particular features of these exchanges but some schools, for example, send news letters to their feeder schools and others get together for theatre visits and sports meetings and informal visits by staff occasionally take place between the different schools.

About 15% of all upper schools have members of staff who teach in one or more of their feeders, and as one might expect, this occurs for the more critical subjects areas such as modern languages, which accounts for 39% of teachers engaged in such exchanges; other subjects involved include mathematics, music and science and two upper schools send their classics teacher to the middle school to teach latin. The number of upper schools reporting middle school teachers actively involved in their teaching programmes was very tiny, amounting to no more than seven schools, with the middle school teachers concentrating mainly on mathematics and science. Joint activities for pupils of both middle and upper schools occur in approximately 30% of the upper schools and consist mainly of musical and sporting activities.

Finally, in this section, a question was put to head teachers asking them to assess the scale of the problem of continuity between feeder and upper schools and a summary of their responses is given in Table 8.22; these figures, however, mask considerable contrasts between schools, for 70.1% of all 13-18 schools see this as a difficult problem with 12.1% of those perceiving this as the biggest problem in upper school organisation; the figures for the other upper schools — the 12+ intake schools — are considerably lower with 49.4% of 12-16s and 34.9% of 12-18s viewing this as a difficult, or the biggest, problem in upper school organisation; more of these schools see the problem of continuity as a minor one — irritating but not posing a serious difficulty to the organisation of the curriculum. The reason for these differences between 12+ and 13+ upper schools is not hard to find because in the case of the 13-18 schools one is coping with pupils who are two years into their 'secondary' school curriculum and who have to make important decisions very quickly on option courses and examinations; the 12-18 and 12-16 schools, on the other hand, often feel that continuity is not such a major problem because they have more time available to compensate for any work not covered in the 8-12 and combined schools — an opportunity not available for the 13-18 school.

One further problem of relevance to maintaining effective liaison between middle and upper schools is the number of feeder middle schools sending pupils to the upper school. Over two-thirds of all upper schools have some problems because of this and they appear especially frequently among the 12-18 schools which often receive pupils from a large number of middle schools. The biggest problems by far are those associated with modern languages, especially in those upper schools taking in pupils at 12+, where over 50% of the sample experience difficulty. The particular problems are many and varied. For example, there is a wide range in the quality of language teaching in middle schools and frequently different schools begin language teaching at different ages; sometimes some middle schools study german while other feeder schools teach french. In one particular career sequence pupils begin a modern language in the middle school, drop it after showing no aptitude for it only to resume it again on entry to the upper school. Although this case is an exceptional one it nevertheless emphasises the general point that pupils arrive at many upper schools with widely differing ranges of experience, from no language learning at all to four years of quite intensive study; this variation in the quality and quantity of teaching presents considerable difficulties in the organisation of languages in the upper school, especially in ensuring that pupils who have had little or no previous language experience are not disadvantaged. Although the Burstall findings (1974) showed that there was no particular advantage in starting french early this does not diminish the task of the upper schools in their attempt to equalise the pupils' linguistic opportunities.

A second major problem caused by the multiplicity of feeder schools is the variation in mathematics curricula; approximately 30% of 12+ upper schools experience problems associated with the teaching of different mathematics syllabi as well as with the quality of work done in the middle schools. With a larger number of middle schools supplying the 12+ upper schools, coupled with the fact that children from the same middle school may move on to different upper schools, the co-ordination of the mathematics curricula can be extremely difficult unless an LEA decides to organise this on regional lines. The 13-18 schools do not perceive this particular problem with mathematics as frequently as the 12+ schools and their second major area of concern is the more general problem of variations in the standards of the feeder schools. Head teachers appear to experience difficulty in describing their reservations in specific terms, but they frequently report differences not only in academic standards set by different middle schools, but in social attitudes as well.

Of course it is easy to criticise the quality of pupil or student intake which any institution may receive, and no doubt some of the comments made by head teachers could just as easily apply to primary schools; however, the problems may be exacerbated for the 12+ and 13+ upper schools because with a longer period out of the upper school the variation in attainments may show up more markedly.

These, then, are the major problems which upper schools associate with having several different feeder schools. There are minor difficulties too, for example in science and humanities where some schools have adopted an integrated course while others retain a more specialist approach; some schools find it difficult to organise craft because a part of their intake has had no experience of this subject. These are not widely experienced problems, however.

Summarising this section, therefore, one can say that the major concerns of upper schools in coping with pupils from different middle schools are modern languages and mathematics and integrating pupils with widely differing attainments; furthermore that the 13+ upper schools, more usually organised at the apex of a restricted pyramid system, experience these problems less frequently than do the other upper schools.

CHAPTER 9

The Head Teachers' Comments

In this chapter analysis will be made of the replies which the head teachers of the middle and upper schools gave to the last section of their Questionnaires which consisted of a set of open ended questions allowing them to express in their own words their views about the middle school system.

For the heads of middle schools the four questions covered the major aims of a middle school, the major problems associated with middle schools, their principal advantages and their future development; similar questions were put to the heads of upper schools though no question was asked about the future development of middle schools.

The replies were analysed by creating categories based upon the head teachers' responses and observations which approximated in meaning to an already existing category were assigned to that category. If a category had not been created which was close enough in meaning to the head teacher's reply, then a new category was formed. Thus, the very broad category of 'no premature specialisation' made up from the many responses to the question concerning the advantages of middle schools encompasses many individual replies such as 'encourages a wider curriculum', 'allows only a limited amount of specialisation' and 'allows a broad primary curriculum to be extended upwards'; so although the individual replies each have their own particular slant, it is nevertheless felt that they have sufficient in common for them to be included within the same broad category.

One other methodological point should be noted concerning the interpretation of these narrative replies and that is that schools may be included more than once in any particular table if they have provided more than one point to any of the questions; thus a head teacher who replies that the main aims of a middle school are 'to provide a bridge between the curricula of the lower and upper schools' and 'to make sure that the pupils have good manners and are well-behaved' will be included in two categories in the table listing aims.

The major aims of the middle school are listed in two tables, Table 9.1 giving the aims as perceived by middle school head teachers and Table 9.2 listing those produced by heads from the upper schools. Some caution must be exercised in the interpretation of these two tables as the categories are very broad indeed and are not mutually exclusive; for example, a middle school head teacher, writing that the major aim of a middle school is to provide a broadly based curricula, is more than likely to subsume in his reply the teaching of basic skills which occurs as another category; also in Table 9.2 the figures show that the percentage of upper school head teachers responding is quite low and many suggested that it would be far too presumptious of them to say what the aims of a middle school should be and thus they left this section blank. Given these reservations, therefore, perhaps the most profitable way of looking at Tables 9.1 and 9.2 is in the different emphasis which head teachers from different schools give in their replies.

Among the head teachers of middle schools there appears to be widespread agreement on two major aims one of which is academic and the other social. The need to provide a broadly based curriculum and to promote good behaviour and social skills are the two major aims perceived by the majority of schools, though differences in emphasis can be seen between those middle schools transferring pupils at 12+ and those at 13+, with a broadly based curriculum being considered more frequently the norm in the former than the latter where specialisation is considered to be of increasing importance. Many middle school heads responded to this question in terms of Plowden's famous phrase — combining the best features of primary and secondary education — a point of view shared by many upper school heads. Other middle school heads gave a rather different emphasis to their replies perceiving the middle school curriculum as a prophylactic, protecting their pupils from premature specialisation, believed to be a widespread feature in many secondary schools; naturally this is not a point of view shared by upper school heads who see the middle school curriculum as embracing many aspects of secondary education and not being confined to a mere upward extension of primary education.

Differences between middle schools in their philosophies can be detected in the second major aim listed — that is, socialising their pupils; all schools would have as an important aim the training and education of their pupils in appropriate social behaviour, yet the salience of this decreases as the pupils get older as can be seen quite clearly from the differences in the response given by 8-12 and combined schools and those schools keeping pupils until they are 13. The lack of any response in this specific category from the upper school head teachers perhaps shows how much this aspect of education is taken for granted by those who teach older pupils and reflects a lack of appreciation for the task which many of those involved with younger pupils see as a very important part of their work.

Training pupils in the basic skills of reading, writing and arithmetic is another aim which reveals differences in accentuation by the different middle schools and with the age-range of pupils being a considerable influence. The 10-13 and 9-13 schools have lower response rates in this category suggesting that the emphasis on basic skills is more important for the younger pupils; again it should be noted that the figures reflect differences in degree of emphasis rather than differences in kind, although the more secondary orientation of the 10-13 school is clearly revealed. It is worth noting that consolidation of the basic skills is regarded by many upper school head teachers as the basic goal of the middle school.

The transitional character of some middle schools is revealed in another aim given in Table 9.1, that of providing a bridge between the first school and the upper school. The 10-13 schools, keeping their pupils for only three, instead of the more usual four, years perceive quite clearly their intermediate status; as one head teacher put it they feel like the filling in the sandwich. The demands of the upper school do press down more heavily on those schools transferring pupils at 13+ than those transferring at 12+ because the children are two years into the secondary school curriculum and vital decisions soon have to be made covering subject choice; thus the pressures to prepare pupils according to the demands of the upper school are keenly felt by many 13+ middle schools.

The responses to the questions concerning the advantages and disadvantages of middle schools are given in Tables 9.3 to 9.8 and the first point to be noted is that from both middle and upper schools the percentage of head teachers regarding disadvantages outweighs those recording advantages. In the upper schools approximately 75% report some disadvantage while under 50% propose any advantages. These figures have considerable significance and indicate that within the three tier system itself many of the most senior personnel see it as problematical rather than beneficial so calling into question the way the middle school system is at present organised.

The middle school heads were asked to write down in their own words, the advantages of middle schools and the major categories derived from their responses are given in Table 9.5. The first thing which meets the eye is the low percentages recorded for any particular advantage, with only three response categories in the table being larger than 20%; this suggests quite clearly that there are no overwhelming categories of advantage in middle schools and that among the head teachers of these schools there is little unanimity as to their major benefits; this is in marked contrast to their perceptions of the problems of middle schools which do show a much greater uniformity. However, even though these percentages are low they do show up quite important differences in the kind of advantages as perceived by heads in different types of middle school. The lack of premature specialisation is seen as the greatest advantage by head teachers in 8-12 schools though far fewer 10-13 heads see this as an advantage since their schools have only half a foot in primary education and have a much more secondary orientated outlook. The advantages which a less specialised curriculum can bring is summed up by the head teacher who states,

'I am convinced that the extra year at primary level with its less rigid, formal and specialised approach is much more suitable for children of this age than transferring them to a secondary school at 11'.

Another head felt that this prevention of specialisation too early helps children who are late developers because it provides a less rigid framework in which pupils can develop their skills:—

'Late developers and those pupils with a weakness in one area of the basic skills are greatly improving their work in the middle school'.

For many head teachers, especially those in combined schools, the extra time spent in the middle school means that pupils are much better equipped to deal with the demands of the upper school, especially in terms of academic requirements.

This point is also echoed in the social and emotional advantages which the middle school can bring to its pupils and the head teachers, especially of 9-13 and 10-13 schools, believe that the extra years provide a happier school atmosphere for their children and affords a more appropriate environment for emerging adolescence. It was these social advantages which Blyth and Derricott (1977) claimed would be the distinctive features of middle school life and there is no doubt that this feeling was voiced by many middle school heads as this example from a 9-13 school illustrates:—

'the extra years seem to give a greater maturity to the child so that, on the whole, the school seems a more mature place to be in';

another head teacher, this time from an 8-12 school, felt that 'the extra year helps children's emotional well-being', while another suggested that 'we are more child-based'.

The lack of examination pressures is another major advantage seen by head teachers, chiefly in 9-13 and 10-13 schools; only a small number of 8-12 heads report this as a positive benefit and only a tiny proportion, just one or two heads, of combined schools suggest this as an advantage. It is interesting to examine this in the light of Edwards' strictures:

'The optimistic remark contained in one LEA memo on middle schools that "The middle schools will not suffer from the stranglehold of external exams" is partially true since many middle school pupils will not actually sit exams. But many of them will do so at the end of the third tier course and will have to begin the preparation for exams in the last two years of the middle school. To consider that, as another LEA memo stated, the new middle schools could "go a long way to breaking the grips of exams in education generally" is not only wishful, but irresponsible, thinking' (Edwards, 1972, p.91).

Whether the head teachers who think that the middle school releases pupils from exam pressures are likewise irresponsible or not is outside the scope of this analysis, but there is no doubt that many of them do believe that the middle school environment, by being less examination orientated, helps pupils to develop confidence and maintain their self esteem; whether this advantage for the middle schools is created at the expense of the upper school, that is the middle schools are merely postponing the acclimatisation of the pupils to examination orientated work and leaving the upper school with a difficult task to be accomplished later and in a short space of time, can be seen later in the chapter when the returns from the upper schools are analysed.

The advantages of size which a middle school system can bring to an area are seen rather differently by head teachers in the 5/8-12 and 9/10-13 schools with a considerable percentage of the latter giving this a high degree of importance.

It must be remembered, of course, that in the early days of middle school development it was the prevention of very large comprehensive secondary schools that was seen as one of the outstanding virtues of the system, though with the passage of time and the decrease in popularity of large secondary schools this may not appear to be so important today — certainly it does not seem to feature in the perceptions of head teachers in combined and 8-12 schools. However, there are still many heads of schools transferring pupils at 13+ who believe that smaller schools bring positive benefits to the pupils as this example illustrates:—

> 'One of the main advantages is the education of children of similar age and developmental problems as regards early adolescence in a much smaller school structure and supportive pastoral system than may be operated in large comprehensive schools'.

A particularly interesting advantage of middle schools, admittedly claimed by a relatively small number of head teachers, is that they provide an environment for their pupils which is particularly stimulating intellectually; this perceived benefit is somewhat surprising in view of the enormous staffing problems which many middle schools experience and the difficulties which schools face in meeting the needs of all their pupils. However, as Burrows suggests, the best of middle school education containing those better elements of primary education — the enquiry based learning and the lack of rigid boundaries between subjects — and the more systematic approach and discipline of the secondary school, may well stretch many middle school pupils. In these 'pacemaker schools' as he calls them,

> 'Both the curricula range and the actual quality of the pupils' attainment are hard to match, age for age, elsewhere. As for the pupils themselves, they emerge keen to acquire knowledge discriminating in their choice and use of it, versed in techniques of study, application and cooperation, maturing as persons with individual talents, not stamped in a standard mould' (Burrows, 1978, p.215).

It is encouraging that the survey reveals that there is still a degree of optimism in middle schools in spite of the many difficulties which they face.

As a counter to these views is the brutal pessimism expressed by a few head teachers, especially in the combined schools, who maintain that middle schools have no advantages at all over other systems:—

> 'There are no advantages. I think two schools is enough for every child's school life, especially for the insecure and the disadvantaged'.

Other heads feel that middle schools create extra difficulties for the upper school as in the case of this reply which hints at a decline in examination results consequent upon re-organisation to a middle school system:—

> 'At this moment in time I see very few advantages — re the C.S.E. grade 1 and the 'O'-level results in our area'.

Looking now at the response from upper schools, head teachers were asked a rather broader question than that asked of middle school heads, for instead of asking them to list the main advantages of middle schools it asked them for their opinions on the advantages of a three tier system and the bulk of the replies were mainly concerned with the benefits which the middle school system conferred upon the upper schools, rather than with the advantages of middle schools themselves. The percentage of responses, however, is not high in Table 9.6, but it does show that a major advantage seen by the 13-18 and 12-16 schools is the size of schools; a three tier system does allow an upper school to be smaller than a traditional secondary comprehensive school and it is interesting to note, in the light of the responses from the 9-13 and 10-13 middle schools, that over one-quarter of 13-18 schools perceive this to be an important advantage. However, size may bring disadvantages too, as can be seen later on in this chapter.

Apart from the advantages of smaller schools little agreement is shown by the upper schools on the other benefits which a three tier system may bring. For example, a number of head teachers in 12-16 schools feel that the only advantage of the system is a financial one: —

'In many cases the system was administratively convenient, being related to existing buildings — aims accrued to the system rather than preceding it'.

Another head teacher writes: —

'It is the only system which could be seen to work in this area. The school population could not support all-through comprehensive schools without closing two secondary schools and "bussing" children',

while another claimed the only advantage was

'the ability to abstain from expensive building programmes'.

While the efficient use of existing buildings is obviously a most important benefit which the three tier system may bring to both the taxpayer and rate-payer it is somewhat saddening to see this listed in many responses as the only advantage with no educational gains given at all: —

'There are no advantages except economies of scale in 6th form groupings and fuller use of primary school buildings at a time of falling rolls. (Not educational reasons!)'.

Head teachers of upper schools accepting pupils at 12+, especially the 12-18 schools, feel that the greater maturity of pupils is a distinct advantage as these replies indicate: —

'Pupils are more mature when they reach us',

and

'12+ transfer brings in pupils who are more mature',

and

'There is some advance in pupil maturity'.

Yet others appear to notice a new enthusiasm as well amongst their intake:—

'The pupils arrive at the secondary school more mature and confident and appear to be better motivated'.

'The youngsters are not ground down in the middle school because the removal of examination pressures allows them to be more flexible in their approach; the pupils appear more fresh and lively, eager, than their counterparts in the 11-18 system'.

This is a theme which is most frequently developed by head teachers of 13-18 schools, who report not only a new confidence and maturity among their pupils but also a reduction in the number of behaviour and discipline problems frequently found among 13 year olds in the traditional 11-18 school:—

'The 13+ year in the old system was bad behaviour-wise, but now it is the intake year, the problems are fewer'

and

'One major advantage is the positive attitude of the formerly disruptive third year pupils'.

Another respondent mentions this reduced behaviour problem especially with girls:—

'Some of the social and behaviour problems of 13 year old girls are overcome with a change of school and a chance to make a new start'.

It would appear to be the case in many 13-18 upper schools, therefore, that by transferring pupils at just this age, the rebellious tendencies of many adolescent 13 year olds are absorbed in beginning a new school career.

Many 13-18 head teachers list advantages of the three tier system which are more concerned with the effects which this has on the age structure of their school, for example because there are no younger pupils this seems to encourage a more unified and mature ethos in the school as these statements indicate:—

'. . . ours is very much a school for young adults',

'. . . the 13-18 school makes possible a more adult atmosphere and more adult attitudes',

'. . . there is more homogeneity — our pupils are all young adults',

'Without the 11 and 12 year olds the upper schools become institutions for the more mature and so can concentrate their teaching with an emphasis on preparation for leaving or further education'.

Also seen as an advantage is the fact that, size for size, the 13-18 school, by having a larger number of pupils in any one age cohort, provides a larger sixth form than an 11-18 school — a not inconsiderable benefit in the light of the Macfarlane Committee's Report (1980):—

'The sixth form is large, 'open' and offers a greater range of O-level, C.E.E. and A-level courses'.

'The 13-18 school can remain relatively small (round about 800) and still support a viable sixth form'.

Another size related gain is the wider range of subjects which can be offered to pupils at the end of the third year, again because there are a larger number of pupils in any one age group:—

'My school, at 16fe, offers a wide range of O-level and C.S.E. options to fit individual choice and ability level',

'The large numbers in each year means a more generous and flexible option choice'.

However, on a more cautionary note the advantages of being a smaller unit are not all one way, and the apparent benefits of flexibility which this may bring can evaporate as this head teacher of a 500 strong 13-18 upper school reports:—

'An extra problem is that an apparent advantage has a flaw in it. It at first seems that you can run, say, a sixth form entry school with a total roll of about 650 (540 = 3 x 180 + 90 sixth form). This keeps the school small, easy to run, and avoids having to build on a large scale.

However, the number of teachers in each department are still small so setting may be difficult and getting enough senior teachers to run, say, chemistry, physics and biology A-level may be difficult.

Even more difficult is the situation in french, german and music. French cannot be compulsory, even in the third year, so you may get three classes. The fourth and fifth year will get *at most* two sets. So the total french in the third, fourth and fifth is seven classes, which is less than one teacher's time. One teacher means that no setting is possible. The same situation, only worse for german; the same applies to music. Only one music teacher and no setting possible, and nobody to help with the out of school music. These subjects in an 11-16 or 11-18 school have a large compulsory base in the first and second forms taking 'teacher time' and building the size of the departments'.

Turning now to the problems of middle schools as perceived by their head teachers, the overwhelming difficulty for all types of school is the general shortage of teachers. Table 9.7 tells a sorry story, but also masks the strength of feeling which many heads have about this lack of staff:—

'Our biggest headache is insufficient staffing to ensure flexibility in organising specialist groups with sufficient staff to cover other areas. Lack of preparation time. Specialist teachers are still mainly class teachers as well, and at present they feel they can do neither job as well as they would like'.

The problem is made worse when good facilities exist in the school, but no staff to make full use of them:—

'We have a lovely school with excellent facilities, but much of our work is hampered and facilities are not used to the full simply because there are insufficient teachers to carry out the work we wish to do'.

For some middle schools, especially the smaller combined and 8-12 schools, the problem of adequately covering the specialist areas of the curriculum is keenly felt:—

'My existing school is too small to allow specialists to operate. I am convinced that if middle schools of 200 pupils are allowed to continue there will be limited progress in many aspects of the curriculum. We can cover english and mathematics but a second language and science — no'.

Although the problems of lack of specialist staff may be especially severe for the smaller middle school, the evidence from the survey indicates that for most schools transferring pupils at 12+, the lack of specialist teachers for languages, science and craft subjects is common:—

'Our main problem is staffing — the pupil-teacher ratio is not good enough for a proper range of specialist teachers',

'I cannot have the specialist staff with enough all-round experience to develop subject schemes',

'The smaller middle schools have difficulty offering the widest possible teaching from specialists, especially as they tend to be attracted to larger schools for obvious reasons'.

This means that sometimes schools are faced with difficult choices to make, as this head teacher reveals:—

'The main problem in this school is that we have no member of staff who feels competent to tackle the teaching of a foreign language. We are all agreed that to do the job properly one should be fluent in the language and therefore the children going to secondary school from here are at some disadvantage in having no french, but I feel that it is preferable to a bad start in the subject'.

An injustice felt very keenly by many middle school heads is the very high teacher-pupil ratios which they have to sustain, as compared to the secondary school; the consequence of this ungenerous staffing formula is that the full range of courses cannot be provided:—

'Compared with the secondary stage we have poor staff/pupil ratios which precipitates a lack of some specialist staff and resources to carry forward a satisfying programme in as many spheres as one would like. This also promotes parental doubts that the pupils in the final years at middle school are receiving the breadth of education the secondary phase would have offered had re-organisation been different'.

Instead of looking towards the secondary school as a guide for staff formulas, many LEAs have tended to base their staffing levels more on those of primary schools which means that acute problems arise:—

'Middle schools are just extended primary schools in this area. They are staffed as primary schools, they lack resources and they lack the availability of specialist staff. Many ideas of a middle school cannot be carried out'.

'We are middle schools in name only, evidently as a matter of economy. We have no extra resources such as specialist teaching staff; in fact until this term we had, as a primary school, one more member of staff than we did as a middle school, even though our numbers have increased. We are, in fact, a primary school with an extra year'.

Whereas for the 12+ middle schools it is the lack of specialist staff which is often most problematical, for the 13+ middle school, this is not so frequently the need, but rather there are difficulties in getting teachers who have the right blend of specialist and generalist skills — the sort of middle school teacher which Blyth and Derriott (1977) describe as performing several of the following roles:—

Generalist	Pastoral
Specialist	Community
Resourcing	Administrative
Consultant-adviser	Collaborative
Planning	

The evidence from the survey is that these skilled middle school teachers are extremely difficult to find with many teachers preferring the specialist role, as this head teacher indicates:—

'Teachers wishing to teach only one or two subjects are a great worry. Middle school teachers must be very FLEXIBLE, enthusiastic and have a wide spectrum of semi-specialist curricular strengths';

others echo this reply:—

'One of my biggest problems is finding quality experienced staff to fulfil the extremely demanding role expected in a middle school',

'The main problem is the shortage of trained middle school teachers. It is urgent that properly prepared mature men and women should volunteer for these schools'.

Perhaps the problem here is that one is dealing with ideal types and to expect teachers to fill these roles is simply asking too much of them. The problem is exacerbated by the low staffing ratios which simply do not allow all the various roles to be carried out; if one is spending all of one's time physically in front of a class, then it is almost impossible to fulfil all the other tasks expected of middle school teachers. Thus the feeling expressed by many heads in 8-12 and combined schools is that they are essentially primary schools given a middle school's job and the lack of flexibility in staffing means that the functions of a middle school teacher cannot be fulfilled.

The inadequacy of buildings is a second major problem for many 8-12 schools, no doubt reflecting the pressures experienced to provide their pupils with some form of specialist teaching but without the necessary physical resources — a need felt especially in the practical subjects such as science and home economics. Nearly one-quarter — 83 out of 355 — of 8-12 schools present this as a major problem as witnessed by this comment: —

'Our biggest problem is accommodation — we still have no other rooms apart from the requisite number of fully used classrooms'.

Lack of resources is another cri-de-coeur from these schools transferring pupils at 12+ and this lack of investment in middle schools leads to enormous frustration especially when parents have such high expectations and LEAs set ambitious goals to distinguish these schools from primaries; often the schools are multiply disadvantaged as this head teacher states: —

'There is simply insufficient staffing and lack of resources to do the work we would like to do in certain areas, i.e. modern languages, remedial, science, home economics and gifted children'.

Another writes: —

'Lack of facilities. No secondary school of this size would be left as we are with no proper gymnasium. Our music facilities are very makeshift. I think we may be luckier than many because we occupy ex secondary buildings but one gets the feeling that middle schools are expected to "rub along" on facilities which would not be tolerated in secondary schools'.

There is something of a contrast here with the 9-13 and 10-13 schools since only a relatively small percentage of their head teachers report that they have resource difficulties, so by comparison with other middle schools, these schools seem not too badly off. Their problems, of course, are more connected with the lack of staff so that they are not always able to maximise the utilisation of the resources which they possess.

The perception of career structure again shows up differences between schools with the 9-13 and 10-13 schools experiencing this as a pressing problem, no doubt because of the more specialist operation of the teachers coupled with the fact that many middle schools are quite small and cannot provide the higher scale posts to satisfy career aspirations. Here is a typical response from a head teacher of a 9-13 school: —

'Size is our main problem. Our school at 330 has certain problems. Chief of these is specialist staff. We have no art/craft specialist and no P.E. specialist. Indeed some activities our pupils do not get (gymnastics, pottery and metal work). Team games with other schools are not possible. Senior staff (all only on Scale 2) find promotion to other schools at Scale 4 or above difficult, even though in this school responsibility might have been the same'.

The number of head teachers from 8-12 and combined schools giving this as a problem is really extremely small and perhaps this is due to the fact that the expectations of the staff are really orientated towards those of the primary teacher. Many of the 9-13 schools, however, consist of teachers who were formerly in secondary schools and these may well think that the middle school does not provide sufficient opportunities for career advancement which a secondary school might have done. This contrast in perceptions between the 12+ and 13+ middle schools does emphasise an important point namely, that the frame of reference which one adopts to evaluate the organisation and staffing of these schools determines, to a considerable extent, the kind of judgment one makes; if one views the middle school from the primary end, it can be seen as an extension and enhancement of junior school education, whereas if one looks at it from the secondary perspective it appears to be a more constrained and confined institution, more limited in the range of activities which can be carried on there.

As far as the problem of liaison with upper schools is concerned large differences again exist between 12+ and 13+ middle schools with only a tiny minority of head teachers in combined and 8-12 schools seeing this as a difficulty at all. On the other hand, quite a number of 9-13 heads list this as a big problem though it is in the 10-13 schools where problems of liaison crop up most frequently mainly because of the particular necessity to maintain effective liaison at both ends of the age range and with pupils remaining in the school for only three years this can present major logistical difficulties. The relatively few 12+ schools reporting concern over liaison may be a reflection of the fact that the upper schools claim that they can just about 'lose' one year and compensate for it in their own schools, and thus liaison with schools may appear to be less pressing when viewed like this. If one is preparing pupils for a number of upper schools liaison with each becomes almost impossible because of the lack of available staff and time necessary to carry this out.

The disadvantage finally listed in Table 9.7 — the inability to cover the curriculum adequately — simply reinforces the points made earlier concerning the demands and expectations placed upon middle schools and their differential ability to meet these — yet again it is the combined and 8-12 schools who feel more frequently their inadequacy in this area.

Summarising the major problems in middle schools as seen by the head teachers, therefore, it would appear that these schools are simply not getting the staff necessary for them to carry out their function as perceived by the middle school enthusiasts and protagonists — a situation likely to have been exacerbated by the recent cuts in expenditure demanded by central and local governments. The subsequent major problems for combined and 8-12 schools centre on the unrealistic expectation that they should operationalise a middle school syllabus but without the necessary facilities. For the 9-13 and 10-13 schools, after staffing, their major pre-occupations are more with the shortcomings in the organisational aspects of the system, particularly the problem of maintaining effective liaison with upper schools and that of providing a suitable place for teachers to fulfil their career ambitions.

The main disadvantages of a three tier system as perceived by the head teachers of upper schools is given in Table 9.8. Many heads made similar comments about the problems of middle schools and this table should be regarded as reflecting particular emphases rather than exclusive categories; this will be seen in the individual comments made by the head teachers.

Many upper school heads feel that transfer to an upper school at an age greater than 11+ is really too late and this later age of transfer has a variety of consequences, each head teacher emphasising particular ones. A typical comment by a headmaster from a 12-16 school is:—

'We have found the age of transfer (12) a great disadvantage. It is the age when behaviour problems become manifest and we feel it would be a help to have pupils settled in with us for a year before this happens. In certain areas we feel that pupils are starting their courses a year late, and we have to fit into 4 years what was previously done in 5'.

A point constantly re-iterated is that the loss of the early years makes it difficult to socialise the pupils into the values and expectations of the school — foundation years which are so necessary for the success of pupils when they are older:—

'I believe middle schools continue the primary type of education for too long. I believe most boys and girls benefitted from transfer at 11+: I think transfer at 13+ is too late. High schools miss those marvellous 11+ and 12+ years when pupils are so receptive. I believe, therefore, that transfer at 13+ has no educational advantages and serious educational disadvantages'.

The head teacher of a 13-18 school writes that one disadvantage is,

'The loss of the younger pupils who are often the most enthusiastic and who are easier to inculcate with the school expectations in terms of work and behaviour at 11+ than 13+'.

Another comment, also from a 13-18 school, but consisting only of boys emphasises the difficulties of establishing the best teacher-pupil relationship:—

'We find 13 a rather high age for transfer on both pastoral and academic grounds. It is difficult to establish quickly the right personal relationships with boys at an age when they are beginning to value their privacy and are less naturally confiding'.

The disadvantage of late transfer to the pupils' social well being was another theme mentioned by many head teachers, as this reply illustates:—

'Socially: frequent break up of friendships at 13+ (a very sensitive age) so that pupils feel unhappy and uprooted, and take a long time to settle down. Some never do'.

For the 13-18 school the loss of two years' teaching of their younger pupils creates considerable academic difficulties especially in helping pupils to choose the best option courses and in gearing them up for the 'O'-level and C.S.E. examinations — '5 years' work to be done in three' is a common response:—

'There is a shorter time to get to know pupils well, to guide into option choices and to train and help those who are late developers or who have adolescent difficulties'.

101

A head teacher of a 13-18 school voices his disquiet over the brief time that the school has to prepare pupils for examinations:—

'Insufficient ground work covered in the 11+ and 12+ years followed by one year getting to know the pupils' abilities leaves 5 terms only to prepare for external examinations'.

This has the consequence, suggested by a number of heads, that upper schools tend to become something of an examination factory as the time available to prepare pupils for 'O'-level and C.S.E. is much reduced.

The 12-16 school, having pupils for only four years, seems to have specific problems because compared to the traditional 11-18 school it is truncated at both ends:—

'This secondary school only has the pupils for 4 years. There is very little time for general introductory courses before pupils have to choose options. Pupils are reluctant to leave school for the sixth form college especially when they have got to know the staff so well. It is also difficult to recruit sufficiently well qualified teachers in certain subjects'.

'The extra year in the middle school means that pupils are less mature when they transfer and they have missed the basic experience in the laboratories and workshops. There is also a certain loss of leadership that sixth formers can give'.

The lack of experience and basic skills which characterise many middle school pupils when they arrive at the upper school is frequently mentioned by head teachers from all types of upper school, and these problems are due to the lack of specialist teachers and adequate facilities in the feeder schools – the general feeling among a large number of upper school heads, therefore, is that middle schools are just junior schools writ large, as these comments illustrate:—

'In my experience of a good number of schools a change at 11+ is to be preferred to a change at 12+ since middle schools have not been given the proper facilities to do the job effectively'.

'Middle schools are at a disadvantage in ability to recruit specialist staff and their staffing ratios do not enable them to offer all the desirable specialist teaching'.

'Transfer at 12 is too late on the whole because pupils are denied the opportunity of undertaking certain types of work at an appropriate time in middle schools through lack of facilities and specialist staff'.

'In many curricular areas the training of pupils in basic skills is delayed one year, simply because feeders have neither facilities nor specialist staff in sufficient quantity'.

Many respondents mentioned the difficulties in specific subject areas:—

'A break at 13 does lead to some problems in languages and mathematics; also P.E. skills are often not well taught and 13 is too late to start serious gymnastics for instance'.

'There is a definite delay in certain subject areas, e.g. foreign languages, science and to some degree aspects of mathematics'.

'The shortage of specialist teachers and the lack of adequate facilities and equipment often means that some pupils are not educated to the required standard (e.g. in modern languages)'.

Another difficulty suggested is that not only do the pupils not possess the necessary basic skills, but poor teaching in some middle schools may put pupils off a particular subject:—

'The attempt of middle schools, generally with limited resources, to give their pupils some experience of practical subjects can deaden the appetite and there is no longer the thrill of starting new subjects in the high school. Science, too, can be affected in this way'.

Two other problems experienced particularly by 13-18 and 12-16 upper schools are those related to the continuity of the curriculum and liaison — not unconnected difficulties as this quotation indicates:—

'It may be considered a disadvantage that liaison between upper and middle schools is heavy on time and requires a degree of prescription if the upper school is to educate its pupils well';

and it takes time to weld together a new intake, especially when the pupils come from a number of feeder schools each with its own particular outlook:—

'Music loses out — our orchestra has gone — modern languages suffer. With twelve feeder schools each with its own ethos, aims and standards the first year is spent in ways other than learning'.

'A school like this, drawing on every middle school in the borough, has complicated problems of liaison especially with those middle schools whose allegiance is quite naturally to their neighbourhood upper school'.

More tersely one head teacher writes:—

'Too many feeder schools to liaise with — impossible!'

Finally in this section let us look at the future development of middle schools, as seen through the eyes of their head teachers and shown in Table 9.9. The percentage figures are generally quite low which may indicate a lack of clear cut directions for the future; in any case many teachers wished to see a period of consolidation to give the system time to prove itself. However, the response given by 25% of all middle school heads was the demand for more teachers. For middle schools the need for more teachers is especially important because for them the lack of teachers means that they cannot actually be middle schools, but rather become extended junior schools. Staff shortages, incurred as a consequence of severe financial cutbacks, present very serious difficulties for all kinds of schools in Britain today, but the unique problem for the middle school is that the very concept may well be threatened by teacher shortages, for if middle schools are not given appropriate staffing resources and thus cannot fulfil the expectations which the community has of them, then this type of school may well be abandoned — not through any inherent defect in the concept itself, but rather because of the way that it has been implemented in practice. Many heads in middle schools see a rather dark future:—

'If we have the same staff numbers as we have at present middle schools will not develop. As I see the future in such a pessimistic light I would prefer not to answer this question. I am disillusioned. A wonderful experience with eager enthusiastic teachers has become little more than an extended junior school with all the extra pressures because we will not willingly give up all that we did when we had three extra teachers';

Yet again the shortage of specialist teachers is mentioned:—

'Unless extra staffing is provided the specialist subjects, science, music, etc. will disappear from the timetable as french has already this year. We have specialist rooms with enthusiastic children but no specialist teachers'.

The need for more general resources for future development is again the plea from many combined and 8-12 schools. These demands simply underline the point made elsewhere in the chapter that unless these basic facilities are provided then the school will not be able to function as originally envisaged:—

'More resources to develop the specialist teaching. This one is frankly a junior school with a middle school job. No proper science room, domestic science room, art room, craft centre, and worst of all insufficient staff in excess of the number of classes to enable small group teaching'.

Greater liaison between schools is another area where improvements need to be made, especially according to 9-13 heads. The problems here are now well known though the possibilities of overcoming these are difficult, especially with severe financial constraints.

Some head teachers feel that if there are going to be middle schools, then a uniform pattern ought to be created instead of the wide diversity of schemes which exist at the present time. It is interesting to note that the only scheme which attracted the confidence of heads mentioning this, was the 9-13 pattern — an even greater percentage of 10-13 heads than 9-13 heads seeing this as the best scheme for future development.

Finally, a small number of head teachers, mainly in schools other than the 9-13 type, thought that middle schools should be abolished and the traditional pattern of the clean break established as this comment suggests:—

'Quite frankly I think that middle schools should be abolished. I think that all children should stay at one school for 5-11 years. At that age, after the most careful consideration of abilities and parental wishes they should go to small secondary schools'.

It is difficult not to end this collection of head teachers' comments on a pessimistic note, for although there are advantages given for the three tier system by the heads of upper and middle schools, the overwhelming trend of the comments emphasise the difficulties which middle schools have in carrying out what they perceive as their correct function, and the problems which this creates for the upper schools to which the pupils transfer. It is in these comments from experienced teachers who have to operate the three tier system that the gap between the rhetoric of the early pioneers and the reality of actual middle school development shows up most widely. A comment which epitomises this frustration and disappointment may be the fitting conclusion to this chapter:—

'Without doubt the middle school is a super system, but one gone off at half cock because of the reduction in staff and resources causing utter frustration in carrying out the original concept of middle schools'.

CHAPTER 10

The Future of Middle Schools

The birth of the English middle school did not take place as a result of widespread dissatisfaction or disenchantment with the educational provision for children in the 8 to 13 age range, but was the outcome of much more general pressures and developments which happened in the educational system as a whole. Specifically, middle schools were brought into being as a consequence of the move towards comprehensive education and the need to provide more school places created by the raising of the school leaving age to 16; the setting up of middle schools meant that in many areas these two demands could be satisfied more economically by making the most efficient use of existing school buildings. The major spur to middle school development thus lay at points in the system peripheral to the middle years of schooling and it is here suggested that the future course of the middle school is also likely to be determined by events which occur and decisions which are taken outside of the middle school system. Thus in considering the future of the middle school it is necessary to examine not only the internal features of their organisation, but also external influences as well.

However, to speak of 'the middle school' in the singular is somewhat misleading, for one fact which emerges clearly from the Keele survey is that the term middle school covers a wide diversity of institutions; the 8-12 middle school has little in common with the 9-13 school and even less with the 10-13 school, while the combined school, not even categorised as a middle school by the DES in their yearly statistical bulletins, is different again. Thus the middle school sector cannot be viewed as a homogeneous division within the education system and this fragmentation must influence its future development. Of course, it is a matter of judgment as to whether an institution is strengthened or weakened by such diversity, but in the case of middle schools the variety of different age ranges covered and the large number of different schemes implemented, many of which are the result of administrative convenience rather than sound educational objectives, must make it more difficult for them to develop into a coherent and united sector in the future.

This fragmentation of middle schools, bringing in its wake differing philosophies and curricula, is also a source of weakness because it occurs within a very small part of the education system; middle schools are now destined to hold a minority position within the total provision of primary and secondary education because it is extremely unlikely that there will be many more of such schools established in the future. The reason for this is not hard to find. Most local authorities have now completed their schemes for secondary comprehensive education and those which have based their provision on the traditional divide of 11+ are unlikely at this point in time to change the system yet again. Even if the middle school system had proved itself to be an outstanding success, with overwhelming advantages over the traditional system, it would still be extremely difficult for LEAs to justify the expense and upheaval involved in adopting the system. As middle schools have not turned out to be such an unqualified success not many more will be established and so the peak of their development is likely to occur in the early 1980s with a gradual diminution in their number after that date. Whether they survive into the twenty first century as a distinctive feature of the English educational landscape depends upon the solution of a number of basic problems.

One of these basic problems which is common to all forms of middle school is that of staffing and the consequent difficulties which this causes in providing a viable curriculum which combines specialist and generalist teaching. All schools in a period of financial retrenchment experience difficulties in covering adequately all parts of the curriculum, but the middle school, as it has developed in practice during the last decade, appears to have suffered from chronic understaffing because its staffing ratios have been determined within a system of primary and second provision which does not even admit the existence of middle schools. Middle schools, without doubt, are able to provide pupils with excellent class teaching but the real crux of the matter is whether they can provide adequate specialist teaching within the constraints of the middle school form of organisation; the answer to this problem is not wholly straightforward because of factors such as the size of school and the age range covered but there can be little doubt that many middle schools, especially those transferring pupils at 12+, cannot meet this objective. This is in no way a fault of the teachers or the heads of school, but is rather a disadvantage which has become inbuilt into the system, for although a middle school system may cost far less than a conventional 11+ based comprehensive system in terms of initial capital outlay, in terms of recurrent expenditure especially in staffing, it is more expensive — a point which has never been recognised by LEAs or the DES. To achieve a gradual transition from primary to secondary education, from non-specialist to specialist teaching, is a much more expensive process in terms of staffing resources than the clean break model yet no middle school receives a staffing formula which adequately recognises this. Staffing formulas in middle schools are not the equivalent of those in secondary schools and frequently fall at some point in between those established for primary and secondary education, usually nearer the former than the latter — it is just this very point which the NUT pamphlet (1979) emphasises.

While there is a justified criticism of the way in which staffing has been organised and financed in middle schools, it could also be claimed that the very idea of the combined specialist/generalist middle school teacher is intrinsically inefficient. If one has a teacher, a subject specialist, teaching that subject for only a proportion of the time, it is right to ask whether this represents an efficient utilisation of teaching skills. The idea of having specialist teachers, particularly in the scarcity subjects such as science, modern languages and mathematics, spending a good proportion of their time outside their range of specialist expertise, does, on the face of it, appear to be a waste of valuable skills and expertise. The survey indicates that the problem of staffing specialist areas of the curriculum is not so acute in the middle schools transferring pupils at 13+ as it is in those transferring pupils a year earlier, but it is often the case in 9-13 middle schools that poor staffing ratios combined frequently with inadequate resources creates an inflexible system which means that specialist teachers cannot be released from generalist teaching duties to teach their subject as much as they would like.

A continuing problem for middle schools, therefore, is the basic one of organising the gradual transition from generalist to specialist teaching; it is expensive in terms of staff resources and presents complex organistional headaches especially in smaller schools. These difficulties are exacerbated by the fact that a gradualist transition from primary to secondary education has not been adequately conceptualised and thus middle schools, with their differing philosophies, envisage this process happening in very different ways.

One further point can be made with respect to the generalist/specialist dichotomy in middle schools. Originally, these schools were perceived by their proponents as providing a much needed alternative to the somewhat rigid and overspecialised curriculum of the secondary school, and there can be little doubt that such inflexible programmes were typical of many secondary schools. However, within the last decade there have been changes and developments in the curriculum for the younger pupil in the secondary school as typified by the move towards a core curriculum, and thus the educational arguments for establising a separate middle school curriculum are not so forceful today as in the 1950s and 1960s.

Another fundamental problem facing the three tier system is that of ensuring a smooth transition in the curriculum from middle school to upper school; a similar problem may exist in the middle school's liaison with first schools but as this was not covered in any great detail by the Keele survey it is not possible to assess the extent of this problem. However, the dovetailing of the middle school curriculum with that of the upper school is fraught with difficulties which appear to be inherent in the system. The difficulties arise because of the number of middle schools which may feed any one upper school and the number of upper schools which are fed by any one middle school. As soon as one middle school is placed in the position of having to satisfy the expectations of more than one upper school, then problems can occur because of different emphasis in the curriculum; it is impossible for a middle school to satisfy the demands of two upper schools if both are teaching radically different mathematics syllabi — it is not practicable to teach two types of mathematics and the same goes for science and modern languages. Also, it is not until the end of their middle school career that most pupils will know which upper school they are going to attend, and so even if it were possible to teach different syllabi, it would not be possible to allocate children to the appropriate groups.

Of particular relevance to this problem of liaison is the amount of choice which parents are allowed in transferring their children to the upper schools for the encouragement of parental choice exacerbates the difficulties in effecting a smooth curricular transition. Where an LEA could limit parental choice, as was the case in the past, then there was the possibility for upper schools to have designated feeder middle schools which could encourage the formation of a compact and integrated system, as has been the case with restricted pyramid systems. However, the 1980 Education Act has changed this, for it requires every LEA,

> 'to make arrangements for enabling the parent of a child in the area of the authority to express a preference as to the school at which he wishes education to be provided for his child . . .'

and further, subject to certain exceptions,

> 'it shall be the duty of a LEA . . . to comply with any preference expressed'.

Thus, parents with children in a middle school have the right to express a preference for their child to go to any upper school and the LEA has an obligation to do its best in complying with that preference. The 1980 Education Act, therefore, is likely to make liaison with upper schools more difficult rather than easier, especially in urban areas where parents are likely to have several viable choices of upper schools to which to send their children. In rural areas the Act is likely to have little effect because often parental choice exists in name only with only one local upper school practically available; but in urban areas the Act will sustain and even extend the fragmentation of the transfer. A possible solution to this problem would be to harmonize the curricula of all the middle and upper schools in one area and this would ensure a smooth transition from middle to upper school. However, apart from the fact that this is unlikely to happen given the number of middle and upper schools involved, it is also very much against the English tradition of allowing schools to develop their own ethos and interests. Whether the middle school system has so many advantages as to be worth the price of uniformity over an entire LEA area is open to question. In any case it would be ironic that an education act is introduced to encourage parental choice, yet the most practical way of operating the act would be to make all the choices the same. It reminds one of Henry Ford's phrase that you could have a car of any colour so long as it was black!

The conclusion which appears to be inescapable is that any system of schooling in this country which deviates from the clean break which traditionally divides primary and secondary education and which claims as one of its principal advantages the smooth transition from a primary to a secondary curriculum is incompatible with free parental choice and curricular freedom.

The problems so far discussed — staffing, curriculum and liaison — are those which are internal to the middle school system and illustrate some basic weaknesses of it. However, the degree to which these weaknesses are manifested varies not only according to many local factors but according to the particular type of middle school as well. The combined school, for example, has the advantage that there are few transition problems for the 7 to 8 year old children as they are usually all under one roof, though in a number of cases pupils from other first schools do transfer to the middle part of the school to join those children who are already there; but there are many disadvantages as well because frequently these schools are small, have insufficient staff to provide any real move towards specialist teaching in the final year and thus experience many difficulties in maintaining an adequate curriculum for their 11 year olds.

These schools are very often under resourced and the staffing allowances which are given to them do not permit them to establish scale posts necessary to attract specialist expertise; their diminutive size often means that liaison with upper schools is difficult not only because so many other middle or combined schools are likely to be involved, but also because teaching staff do not have the time to meet with upper school colleagues. It is usually the head teacher only who can manage to attend such meetings. On balance, therefore, there are few advantages to be gained by continuing to keep the combined schools because they cannot fulfil the expectations which ought to be legitimately placed on schools educating children up to 12 years old.

The 8-12 middle school does seem to fare better than the combined school mainly because it is larger and so can go some way towards meeting the need for more specialist subject work. The difficulties experienced with liaison appear to vary according to local circumstance but the smaller 8-12 school, feeding into one or more 12-18 schools, is likely to have problems in ensuring a smooth transfer of pupils from primary to secondary education. Many 8-12 schools also have similar problems to those of the combined school — shortage of staff and material resources such as laboratories frequently means that there is little more offered than class teaching and in nearly all of the specialist areas these schools cannot compete with what is offered in the secondary school. It would appear that the ideal form of middle school teaching envisaged in the Plowden Report is the exception rather than the rule because there is simply not the availability of staff or the flexibility of organisation to allow the easy interchange of specialist and generalist teaching so favoured by Plowden.

The upper schools taking in pupils at 12+ seem to share this opinion of the 8-12 middle school and their most frequent claim is that the pupils in this system 'lose' a year when compared with those pupils transferring at 11+ and that their feeder schools are really nothing more than extended primary schools — a view difficult to refute when one sees how many of the 8-12 schools have developed in practice. An often claimed advantage for the 8-12 school is that pupils are more mature when they transfer to the upper school, but this would be expected of pupils who are one year older. On the other hand, there is little talk of the additional skills which middle schools have given to pupils — rather there is talk of having wasted a year which the upper schools have to compensate for.

The 10-13 school appears to have few advocates even within the middle school movement, for this school keeps the pupils for only three years at a critical period in their development, and it is difficult to find sound educational advantages for such an arrangement. Also the atmosphere of the 10-13 school is undoubtedly more like that of a secondary school and it is usually more convenient to organise the 10-13 school like a junior department of secondary school. In practice the effect of having a 10-13 system is that the age of transfer to secondary education is reduced from 11+ to 10+! Liaison with other schools is doubly difficult because 10-13 schools are large and therefore have a number of feeder first schools supplying them with pupils and therefore contacts have to be maintained with these schools in addition to the upper schools. The time and effort involved in maintaining effective liaison is disproportionately large in 10-13 schools. The educational benefits of such a system are hard to determine and, as one head recorded, these schools appear to be all width and no length and the large number of parallel classes found in these schools can produce a rather repetitive teaching situation for teachers.

This leaves the 9-13 school which, as it has developed, reveals the middle school system at its best. Not that these schools are without the staffing and resource problems experienced by other middle schools, but they have the span of age which enables them to make a serious and meaningful attempt to bridge the gap between primary and secondary education. They are large enough to support a body of generalist and specialist staff and because they have to educate children who are two years into the secondary age range, many have developed a sound base of more specialist subject work. The 9-13 schools are usually better equipped than other middle schools and in rural areas especially, where a restricted pyramid system is in operation, the problems of transfer and liaison with upper schools are much reduced. However, where the exercise of parental choice is a practical proposition this can make liaison at 13+ extremely difficult, and changes in teaching methods and curricula at this age can hinder pupil development. The major problem with the 9-13 school, however, is that it creates an especially difficult situation for the upper school because important decisions regarding subject choice and examinations have to be taken by the pupils after such a brief period in the new school. This is a profound and inherent disadvantage of the 9-13 middle school and coupled with the enhanced freedoms of the 1980 Act will make things more difficult for these schools, especially in urban areas.

Turning now to factors external to the middle school system which may affect their future development, there are two elements which need to be considered. The first concerns an event which has already taken place, namely the re-organisation of local authorities on April 1, 1974. Such a re-organisation could not have occurred at a worse time as far as middle schools were concerned because in many areas the implementation of the change to comprehensive education was only partially completed; also the tendency was for this re-organisation to create new local authorities which, instead of having homogeneous education schemes, now contain a variety of schemes with different ages of transfer. For example, a borough which had implemented an 8-12 middle school system in 1972, and which appeared to have a coherence and unity within its boundaries, but which in 1974 was re-organised and absorbed into the neighbouring county which had a scheme based on the traditional primary/secondary divide, now appears as a small island, different from the mainstream system operating in the county; thus the boundary changes and the change in status of many areas had the tendency to redefine middle schools as isolate and deviant from the normal system, a view enhanced by an often unsympathetic county hall administration. Furthermore, there are difficult problems created on the fringes of such systems where transfer to different schools at different ages is possible. An example of this fragmentation can be seen in Staffordshire where there co-exists 9-13, 8-12 and combined schools, together with conventional primary schools, in just one of its regional divisions. Such a hotch-potch of provision based on administrative quirks rather than sound educational criteria cannot but create difficulties for children and parents, especially mobile ones, and also put further pressure on middle schools as deviants from the mainstream system.

The second factor to influence middle schools is that of falling roles – a traumatic process affecting the whole of the education system and likely to be as instrumental in re-shaping it as was the expansion after 1945, though in a much more painful way. The direct effects on middle schools of a reduction in pupil numbers are unlikely to be very different from those occurring in primary and secondary schools, though there may be problems of maintaining particular specialist areas, which could upset the already precarious balance which exists between general and specialist teaching. The direct effects, however, are unlikely to be as profound as the indirect pressures, especially those concerned with maintaining the viability of upper schools. A scenario which may occur is that middle schools might lose their secondary age pupils to the upper schools in order for the latter to stave off, or at least reduce, the decline in pupil numbers and thus maintain their staffing ratios and keep their specialist teaching intact. Such a move might be more probable with systems based on a transfer age of 12+ where combined schools could revert back to conventional primary schools with relative ease and the 8-12 middle school would become a junior school with a 7 to 11 age range. There is little doubt that such a gradual re-absorption of the combined and 8-12 middle school back into a conventional 11+ system could be achieved with only minimal disruption to both pupils and teachers and there are signs that this is beginning to happen.

The future of those schools transferring pupils at 13+ is much more difficult to ascertain as they could not be easily transformed into conventional primary or secondary schools, the upheaval, cost and disruption would be too great. One possible influence will be the way in which LEAs plan their provision for the 16-19 age group in the face of falling roles. If the move towards collegiate provision for the 16-19 year olds becomes widespread in order to maintain viable sixth form courses, then this may pose a threat to the 13-18 school which could not really survive as a rump with a pupil age range of 13-16. Thus the arrangements made for the 16-19 age groups may ultimately affect the viability of the middle school system, especially those based on 9-13 or 10-13 schools. It is not possible at this point in time to see what the pattern of 16-19 provision will be especially as the Macfarlane Committee's Report (1980) was so ambiguous and did not give an unequivocal recommendation that there should be separate education for the 16-19 age group. In addition, an advantage of the 13-18 upper school rarely mentioned is that for a given size of institution it generates a larger and therefore more viable sixth form than an 11-18 school, and this fact may exert a more telling influence on planners than the pressure to separate students aged 16-19 in separate colleges; only time will tell.

Whatever the future may hold in store for the middle school the next five years are likely to be critical. If the 8-12 and combined schools are likely to disappear then this would also affect the other middle schools which would thereby be reduced to occupy an even smaller niche in the educational system, and thus in turn would find it more difficult to survive. If middle schools don't survive they are likely to be perceived as the education system's shock absorbers, thrown up to cushion the effects of rapid expansion and changes which occurred in the 1960s and 1970s. If they do survive into the 21st century and if they are to be viewed as something more than yet another eccentricity of a decentralised education system, then a much greater programme of investment of personnel, resources and research will be needed to make them viable.

Bibliography

ABRAMS, S. (1968), 'Profile of a middle school', *Where,* Supplement 14.

ALEXANDER, W.M. et al. (1969), *The Emergent Middle School* (2nd. ed.), Holt, Rinehart & Winston, New York.

ARDEN, E. (1972), 'Preparing to teach in a middle school: a report and a definition', *London Educational Review,* Vol. 1, No. 3.

ARMISTEAD, P. (1972), *English in the Middle Years,* Blackwell, Oxford.

ASSISTANT MASTERS' ASSOCIATION (1976), *The Middle School System,* AMA, London.

ASSOCIATION FOR SCIENCE EDUCATION (1975), *Science in Middle Schools. A Yorkshire Survey,* Study Series No. 5, ASE, Hatfield.

ASSOCIATION FOR SCIENCE EDUCATION (1976), *Science in the Middle Years,* Study Series No. 6, ASE, Hatfield.

BADCOCK, E.H., DANIELS, D.B., ISLIP, J., RAZZELL, A.G., ROSS, A.M. (1972), *Education in the Middle Years,* Schools Council Working Paper No. 42, Evans/Methuen Educational, London.

BARKER LUNN, J.C. (1970), *Streaming in the Primary School,* NFER, Slough.

BARNETT, J.V. (1972), 'Training teachers for the middle school', *Trends in Education,* January, 25.

BARRETT, R. (1977), '8-12 schools primary or middle' in Richards, C. ed., *New Contexts for Teaching, Learning and Curriculum Studies,* Association for the Study of the Curriculum.

BARRETT, R. (1977), 'Intent on languages – towards a policy', *Education 3-13,* Vol. 5, No. 2.

BARRETT, R., CUFF, C., MORAN, P. (1978), '8-12 middle schools – views of a local system', *Education 3-13,* Vol. 6, No. 1.

BENN, C. (1973), 'Middle school planning surveyed', *Forum,* No. 15.

BENN, C. & SIMON, B. (1972), *Half Way There,* (2nd. ed.), Penguin, Harmondsworth.

BENNETT, S.N. (1976), *Teaching Styles and Pupil Progress,* Open Books, Shepton Mallett.

BENNETT, S.N. & BATLEY, D. (1977), 'Open plan middle schools. Pupils' reactions to open plan', *Education 3-13,* Vol. 5.

BERNSTEIN, B. (1971), *On the Classification and Framing of Educational Knowledge,* Author's mss.

BLYTH, A. (1978), 'Middle years and middle schools now', *Education 3-13,* Vol. 6, No. 1.

BLYTH, A. (1977), 'Role-set, autonomy and middle school curricula', in Richards, C. ed., *New Contexts for Teaching, Learning and Curriculum Studies,* Association for the Study of the Curriculum.

BLYTH, A., COOPER, K.R., DERRICOTT, R., ELLIOTT, G., SUMNER, H., WAPLINGTON, A. (1976), *Place, Time and Society 8-13: Curriculum Planning in History, Geography and Social Science,* Collins – ESL, Bristol.

BLYTH, A. & DERRICOTT, R. (1977), *The Social Significance of Middle Schools,* Batsford, London.

BOOTH, N. (1971), 'Teaching in middle schools. 2. Middle school science', *Trends in Education,* October, 24.

BROOK, D. (1977), 'Language consultants – the role of the specialist in primary and middle schools', *Education 3-13,* Vol. 5, No. 2.

BRYAN, K.A. & HARDCASTLE, K. (1977), 'The growth of middle schools: educational rhetoric and economic reality', *British Journal of Educational Administration and History,* January.

BRYAN, K.A. & HARDCASTLE, K. (1978), 'Middle years and middle schools: an analysis of national policy', *Education 3-13*. Vol. 6, No. 1.

BRYAN, T.A. (1976), 'Syllabuses for a middle school', *The Head Teachers Review*, November.

BURROWS, J. (1969), 'The curriculum of the middle school', *The Head Teachers Review*, September.

BURROWS, J. (1978), *The Middle School. High Road or Dead End*, Woburn Press, London.

BURSTALL, C. et al. (1974), *Primary French in the Balance*, NFER, Slough.

BUTCHER, E.T. (1976), 'Kirklees surveys a new panorama of hopes and ideals' *Education*, August, 13.

CAMPBELL, R.J. (1973), 'The middle years of schooling: some priorities in curriculum planning', *Forum*, Vol. 15, Spring/Summer.

CHARLES, K. (1974), 'Aims, organisation and planning – an account of practice in one middle school', *Education 3-13*, Vol. 2, No. 1.

CENTRAL ADVISORY COUNCIL FOR EDUCATION (England), (1967), *Children and Their Primary Schools, The Plowden Report, 2 Vols.*, HMSO, London.

CENTRAL ADVISORY COUNCIL FOR EDUCATION (England), (1959), *15-18*, HMSO, London.

CENTRAL ADVISORY COUNCIL FOR EDUCATION (England), (1963), *Half our Future*, HMSO, London.

CLEGG, A. et al. (1967), *The Middle School – A Symposium*, Schoolmaster Publishing Company, Kettering.

CLEGG, A. (1963), 'The organisation of education in certain areas of the West Riding: Five to nine, nine to thirteen, thirteen to eighteen', pamphlet.

COLTHAM, J.B. (1978), 'Middle years without middle schools', *Education 3-13*, Vol. 6, No. 1.

CROSSLAND, R.W. & MOORE, S.F.D. (1974), *Environmental Studies Project 5-13*, Macmillan, London.

CULLING, G. (1972), *Projects for the Middle School*, Lutterworth, Guildford.

CULLING, G. (1973), *Teaching in the Middle School*, Pitman, London.

CURRICULUM DEVELOPMENTS ASSOCIATES INC. (1968), MACOS, Washington D.C. & Centre for Applied Research in Education, University of East Anglia.

DAVIES, E.R. (1973), 'Nine to thirteen middle schools', *Forum*, Vol. 15, No. 3.

DEPARTMENT OF EDUCATION AND SCIENCE (1977), 'Educating our children. Four subjects for debate; a background paper for the regional conferences', pamphlet, HMSO, London.

DEPARTMENT OF EDUCATION AND SCIENCE (1977), *Education in Schools: a consultative document*, HMSO, London.

DEPARTMENT OF EDUCATION AND SCIENCE (1977), *Gifted Children in Middle and Comprehensive Schools*, (HMI series), HMSO, London.

DEPARTMENT OF EDUCATION AND SCIENCE (1975), *A Language for Life*, (Bullock Report), HMSO, London.

DEPARTMENT OF EDUCATION AND SCIENCE (1970), *Launching Middle Schools. An Account of Preparations and Early Experiences in Division No. 15 of the West Riding of Yorkshire, Education Survey No. 8*, HMSO, London.

DEPARTMENT OF EDUCATION AND SCIENCE (1966), *New Problems in School Design, Middle Schools, Implications of Transfer at 12 or 13 Years, Building Bulletin No. 35*, HMSO, London.

DEPARTMENT OF EDUCATION AND SCIENCE (1965), *The Organisation of Secondary Education, Circular 10/65*, HMSO, London.

DEPARTMENT OF EDUCATION AND SCIENCE (1970), *The Organisation of Secondary Education, Circular 10/70*, HMSO, London.

DEPARTMENT OF EDUCATION AND SCIENCE (1974), *The Organisation of Secondary Education, Circular 4/74*, HMSO, London.

DEPARTMENT OF EDUCATION AND SCIENCE (1966), *School Building Programmes, Circular 13/66*, HMSO, London.

DEPARTMANT OF EDUCATION AND SCIENCE (1965), *The School Building Survey, 1962*, HMSO, London.

DEPARTMENT OF EDUCATION AND SCIENCE (1978), *Statistics in Education, Vol. 1, Schools*, HMSO, London.

DEPARTMENT OF EDUCATION AND SCIENCE (1970), *Towards the Middle School, Educational Pamphlet No. 57,* HMSO, London.
DEPARTMENT OF EDUCATION AND SCIENCE, HMI, (1977), *Curriculum 11-16,* HMSO, London.
DEPARTMENT OF EDUCATION AND SCIENCE, HMI, (1978), *Primary Education in England; a Survey,* HMSO, London.
DOE, B. & RAZZELL, A. (1976), 'How far have middle schools made a distinctive contribution to the education of children in their age group?' *Times Educational Supplement,* November 26.
DOUGLAS, J.W.B., ROSS, J.M., SIMPSON, H.R. (1968), *All Our Future,* Davies, Woking.
EDWARDS, R. (1972), *The Middle School Experiment,* Routledge and Kegan Paul, London.
EGGLESTON, S.J.E. (1965), 'How comprehensive is the Leicestershire Plan?', *New Society* 23.3.
FLOUD, J.E., HALSEY, A.H., MARTIN, F.M. (1956), *Social Class and Educational Opportunity,* Heinemann, London.
FOSTER, A., WHITFIELD, R., COXHEAD, P. (1977), 'Assessing curriculum balance in middle schools', Unpublished paper presented to British Educational Research Meeting, Nottingham.
FREELAND, G. (1973), 'Middle schools in Southampton', *Forum,* Vol. 15, No. 3.
FRYMIER, T.R. (1968), 'The middle school', *Theory into Practice,* Vol. VII, No. 3.
GANNON, T. & WHALLEY, A. (1975), *Middle Schools,* Heinemann Educational Books, London.
GORWOOD, B. (1973), 'The middle school – experiment?', *Forum,* Vol. 15, No. 3.
GORWOOD, B. (1978), '9-13 middle schools: a local view', *Education 3-13,* Vol. 6, No. 1.
GRAY, J. & SATTERLY, D. (1976), 'A chapter of errors: teaching styles and pupils' progress in retrospect', *Educational Research,* Vol. 19, No. 1.
GREAVES, J.G. (1976), 'Profile of a year', *Newcastle and Durham Institute of Education Journal,* No. 27.
GREIG, T.O. & BROWN, J.C. (1975), *Activity Methods in the Middle Years,* Oliver and Boyd, Edinburgh.
HARGREAVES, A. & TICKLE, L. (1980), *Middle Schools – Origins, Ideology and Practice,* Harper and Row, London.
HARGREAVES, A. & WARWICK, D. (1978), 'Attitudes to middle schools', *Education 3-13,* Vol. 6, No. 1.
HARLEN, W. (1975), *Science 5-13: A Formative Evaluation,* Schools Council Research Studies, Macmillan Education, London.
HAWKINS, J.W.B. (1973), 'Middle schools from within', *Head Teachers Review,* April.
HERTLING, J.E. & GETZ, H.G. (1971), *Education for the Middle School Years: Readings,* Scott Foresman, Glenview, Ill.
Howard, A.W. (1968), *Teaching in the Middle School,* International Textbook Company, New York.
JAMES, C. (1968), 'Childhood towards adolescence – the middle years', *Ideas,* March, 6.
KEFFORD, C. (1973), 'Taking the muddle out of the middle', *Education 3-13,* Vol. 1, No. 1.
LAWTON, D., CAMPBELL, J., BURKITT, V. (1971), *Social Studies 8-13,* Schools Council Working Paper No. 39, Evans/Methuen Educational, London.
LINES, C.J. & BOLWELL, L.H. (1971), *Teaching Environmental Studies in the Primary and Middle School,* Ginn, Aylesbury.
LONDON UNIVERSITY INSTITUTE OF EDUCATION, Centre for Teachers Research Club (1973), 'Report on the organisation of 9-13 middle schools with particular reference to the role of the year group leader and the subject head', pamphlet.
McGEE, T. & BLACKBURN, J. (1979), 'Administration of the middle school programme', *Theory into Practice,* February.
MACLURE, S. (1975), 'On trying to have our cake and eat it', T.E.S. July 4.
MARJORAM, D.T.E. (1971), 'Teaching in middle schools. Mathematics in the middle school', *Trends in Education,* October, 24.
MASON, S.C. (1964), *The Leicestershire Experiment and Plan,* 3rd ed. rev., Councils and Education Press, London.
NATIONAL UNION OF TEACHERS (1979), *Middle Schools – Deemed or Doomed?* NUT, London.
NEWBOLD, D. (1977), *Ability Grouping: The Banbury Enquiry,* NFER, Slough.
NICHOLSON, J.S. (1970), 'Delf Hill Middle School, Bradford', in E. Halsall, *Becoming Comprehensive: Case Histories,* Pergamon, Oxford.

117

NIE, N.H. et al. (1975), *Statistical Package for the Social Sciences*, McGraw Hill, New York.

O'CONNOR, M. (1968), 'Middle schools take shape', New Education, April.

OXFORDSHIRE COUNTY COUNCIL (1977), 'The child at thirteen, expectations in the field of humanities', Discussion paper.

OWEN, R. (1974), *Middle Years at School*, BBC, London.

PARTRIDGE, J. (1966), *Middle School*, Gollancz., London.

RAGGETT, M. & CLARKSON, M. eds., (1974), *The Middle Years Curriculum*, Vols. 1 & 2, Ward Locke Educational, London.

RAZZELL, A. (1978), 'Mixed ability teaching in the middle school – a personal view', *Forum*, Vol. 20, No. 2.

ROSS, A.M. (1968), 'The middle school'. *Comprehensive Education*, No. 9.

ROSS, A.M., RAZZELL, A.G., BADCOCK, E.H. (1975), *The Curriculum in the Middle Years*, Schools Council Working Paper No. 55, Evans/Methuen Educational, London.

SCHOOLS MATHEMATICS PROJECT (1972), *Mathematics in the Middle Years of School*, SMP, London.

SCHOOLS COUNCIL (1971), *Environmental Studies 5-13*, Rupert Hart Davies, London.

SCHOOLS COUNCIL (1972), *With Objectives in Mind: Guide to Science 5-13*, Macdonald Ed., London.

SHROPSHIRE COUNTY COUNCIL (1969), *Working Together in the Middle Years*, Ludlow.

SIMON, B. (1953), *Intelligence Testing and the Comprehensive School*, Lawrence and Wishart, London.

SIMPSON, A. (1973), 'The ten-plus first year base', *Forum*, Vol. 15.

STAFFORDSHIRE EDUCATION DEPARTMENT (1977), Curriculum Development, 5-16 Science, City of Stoke-on-Trent Schools, unpublished pamphlet.

SUMNER, R. & BRADLEY, K. (1977), *Assessment for Transition. A Study of New Procedures*, NFER, Slough.

WILLCOCK, J.B. (1969), *Education in the Middle Years of Schooling*, Schools Council Working Paper No. 22, HMSO, London.

WORCESTERSHIRE EDUCATION COMMITTEE (1968), 'Report of the Droitwich Working Party on middle schools', unpublished pamphlet.

Tables

School Type	Counties Numbers	Metropolitan Areas Numbers	Total Numbers
5-12	88	22	110
8-12	260	95	355
9-13	169	102	271
10-13	12	21	33
Other	12	1	13
TOTAL	541	241	782

TABLE 3.2   Total number of middle schools (1978) and sample size of the Questionnaire

School Type	Total Middle School Population 'n'	Keele Survey Sample 'n'	Keele Survey Sample %
Deemed Primary	702	359	51.14
Deemed Secondary	601	313	52.08
First & Middle	387	110	28.42

TABLE 3.2   Total number of middle schools (1978) and sample size of the Keele Survey

	51-100	101-200	201-300	301-400	401-600	601-800	801-1000	Not Known		
FREQUENCY	3	57	261	229	138	14	–	–	DES	DEEMED PRIMARY
%	0.4	8.1	37.2	32.6	19.7	2.0	–	–		
%	0.8	10.3	37.3	29.0	13.9	2.0	–	6.7	KEELE SURVEY	
FREQUENCY	3	37	134	104	50	7	–	24		
FREQUENCY	1	29	91	136	272	70	2	–	DES	DEEMED SECONDARY
%	0.2	4.8	15.1	22.6	45.3	11.7	0.3	–		
%	0.3	3.8	13.1	27.2	36.4	10.5	0.7	8.0	KEELE SURVEY	
FREQUENCY	1	12	41	85	114	33	2	25		

TABLE 3.3   Frequency and percentage of all middle schools and Keele survey sample of middle schools, by size of school

	26-50	51-100	101-200	201-300	301-400	401-600	601-800	Not Known	
FREQUENCY	2	10	46	21	6	2	–	23	KEELE
%	1.8	9.1	41.8	19.1	5.5	1.8	–	20.9	SURVEY

TABLE 3.4   Frequency and percentage of first and middle schools in Keele survey by size of school (middle school section only)

YEAR OF OPENING	TYPE OF SCHOOL							
	5-12		8-12		9-13		10-13	
	n	%	n	%	n	%	n	%
1968	–	–	2	0.6	4	1.5	2	6.1
1969	2	1.8	8	2.3	39	14.4	3	9.1
1970	10	9.1	32	9.0	13	4.8	10	30.3
1971	6	5.5	21	5.9	17	6.3	2	6.1
1972	7	6.4	52	14.6	60	22.1	4	12.1
1973	36	32.7	113	31.7	40	14.7	1	3.0
1974	16	14.5	42	11.8	45	16.6	–	0.0
1975	6	5.5	35	9.9	11	4.1	2	6.1
1976	15	13.6	28	7.9	25	9.2	7	21.2
1977	3	2.7	7	2.0	11	4.1	1	3.0
1978	1	0.9	8	2.3	4	1.5	–	0.0
Not Known	8	7.3	7	2.0	2	0.7	1	3.0

TABLE 4.1   Numbers and percentages of middle schools in the sample opening between 1968 and 1978

DENOMINATION OF SCHOOL	TYPE OF SCHOOL							
	5-12		8-12		9-13		10-13	
	n	%	n	%	n	%	n	%
Non Denominational	63	57.3	292	82.3	220	81.2	25	75.7
Church of England	31	28.2	53	14.9	38	14.0	5	15.2
Roman Catholic	16	14.5	10	2.8	13	4.8	3	9.1

TABLE 4.2   Denomination of middle schools in the sample – numbers and percentages

POPULATION AREA	TYPE OF SCHOOL			
	5-12	8-12	9-13	10-13
Large City	6.4	9.3	12.9	0.0
Town	15.5	30.2	25.8	45.5
Suburb	38.2	46.2	36.9	21.2
Village	36.4	10.7	14.8	21.2
Other	3.5	3.6	9.6	12.1
(E.g. combination of above)				

TABLE 4.3   Middle schools in the sample drawing the majority of pupils from different population areas (Percentage frequency of middle schools)

HOUSING TYPE	TYPE OF SCHOOL			
	5-12	8-12	9-13	10-13
Council Estate	12.7	20.9	20.3	12.1
Private Housing	34.5	21.4	10.4	15.2
Council Estate & Private Housing	43.7	40.3	52.0	57.5
Council Estate, Private and Sub-Standard Housing	7.3	14.6	15.5	15.2
Sub-Standard Housing	1.8	1.7	1.8	–
Other	–	1.1	–	–

TABLE 4.4   Various types of housing from which schools in the sample draw the majority of their pupils (Percentage frequency of middle schools)

BUILDING TYPE	TYPE OF SCHOOL			
	5-12	8-12	9-13	10-13
Purpose Built	24.5	21.1	25.5	24.3
Adapted Secondary	5.5	13.2	42.1	69.7
Adapted Primary	67.3	63.1	28.0	3.0
Other	2.7	2.6	4.4	3.0

TABLE 4.5   Type of building which applies to each middle school in the sample (Percentage frequency of middle schools)

TYPE OF SCHOOL			
5-12	8-12	9-13	10-13
33.6	33.2	43.9	45.5

TABLE 4.6   Middle schools in the sample with some part of their buildings open plan (Percentage frequency of schools)

	TYPE OF SCHOOL			
OPEN PLAN PROVISION	5-12	8-12	9-13	10-13
Predominantly Open Plan	48.6	36.1	32.5	33.3
Craft/Science Areas	21.6	28.1	30.8	26.7
Classroom Areas	13.5	26.6	14.2	40.0
Other	16.3	9.2	22.5	0.0

TABLE 4.7   Details of open plan provision. (Percentage frequency of middle schools with some part of their buildings open plan)

	TYPE OF SCHOOL			
SPECIALIST ROOM/AREAS	5-12	8-12	9-13	10-13
Craft	54.5	78.0	95.6	97.0
Music	29.1	43.1	67.9	78.8
Science	28.2	56.3	95.2	100.0
Home Economics	45.5	58.3	91.1	93.9
Language Laboratory	5.5	8.5	15.1	18.2
Gymnasium	21.8	37.2	64.2	84.8
Playing Fields	55.5	72.1	84.1	92.1
Outdoor Teaching Area	23.6	36.1	45.0	54.5

TABLE 4.8   Middle schools possessing specialist rooms/areas (Percentage frequency of schools)

ADDITIONAL BUILDING	TYPE OF SCHOOL			
	5-12	8-12	9-13	10-13
General Classroom Space	22.7	18.9	24.4	21.2
Music Room	19.1	14.9	11.1	6.1
Gym	10.9	12.1	22.9	27.3
Showers/Changing Rooms	11.8	20.3	12.5	12.1
Science laboratory/Area	19.1	14.6	14.4	9.1
Craft Area	18.2	14.1	9.2	12.1

TABLE 4.9　　Middle schools requesting additional building facilities
(Percentage frequency of schools)

	TYPE OF SCHOOL			
	5-12	8-12	9-13	10-13
Male	78.2	90.4	91.1	93.9
Female	20.9	9.6	8.5	6.1
Not Known	0.9	0.0	0.4	0.0

TABLE 5.1　　Sex of head teacher (Percentage frequency of schools)

	TYPE OF SCHOOL			
	5-12	8-12	9-13	10-13
Male	56.4	61.4	59.4	48.5
Female	40.0	34.6	21.0	27.3
Two Male	0.0	0.0	0.4	0.0
Two Female	0.0	0.3	0.4	0.0
One Male, One Female	1.8	3.7	17.7	24.2
Not Known	1.8	0.0	1.1	0.0

TABLE 5.2　　Sex of deputy heads (Percentage frequency of schools)

TYPE OF SCHOOL	AVERAGE NUMBER OF HOURS
5-12	8.0
8-12	7.5
9-13	6.5
10-13	6.1

TABLE 5.3   Average number of hours per week that head teachers spend in teaching

	MALE	FEMALE	TOTALS
Graduate	0.6	1.4	2.0
Non-Graduate	2.2	6.5	8.7
TOTAL	2.8	7.9	10.7

TABLE 5.4   Average numbers of full time teachers in 5-12 schools

	MALE	FEMALE	TOTALS
Graduate	1.0	1.6	2.6
Non-Graduate	3.0	6.4	9.4
TOTAL	4.0	8.0	12.0

TABLE 5.5   Average numbers of full time teachers in 8-12 schools

	MALE	FEMALE	TOTALS
Graduate	2.4	2.5	4.9
Non-Graduate	6.0	8.0	14.0
TOTAL	8.4	10.5	18.9

TABLE 5.6   Average numbers of full time teachers in 9-13 schools

	MALE	FEMALE	TOTALS
Graduate	2.4	2.6	5.0
Non-Graduate	6.5	9.1	15.6
TOTAL	8.9	11.7	20.6

TABLE 5.7   Average numbers of full time teachers in 10-13 schools

	TYPE OF SCHOOL			
	5-12	8-12	9-13	10-13
Primary Only	70.3	66.9	26.2	21.2
Secondary Only	3.9	3.5	36.1	32.3
Primary and Secondary	17.2	18.3	20.9	28.3
Middle School Trained	8.6	11.3	16.8	18.2

TABLE 5.8   Previous experience of staff. (Percentage frequency of teachers in schools)

	TYPE OF SCHOOL			
	5-12	8-12	9-13	10-13
Scale 1	38.2	33.3	32.8	38.8
Scale 2	39.7	38.9	35.2	30.6
Scale 3	22.0	19.4	20.7	19.8
Scale 4	0.1	8.4	11.3	10.8

TABLE 5.9   Teachers on scales 1, 2, 3 & 4 (Average percentage frequency of teachers in schools)

	TYPE OF SCHOOL			
	5-12	8-12	9-13	10-13
Subject Specialists	77.3	80.0	89.7	82.8
Year Co-Ordinators	42.3	51.6	76.0	46.4
Pastoral	14.8	24.0	27.3	21.9
Administration	1.8	1.4	3.3	0.0
Resources	19.1	18.0	26.2	6.1
Combinations (including Subject Specialists)	12.8	13.2	15.9	33.3
Other Combinations	1.8	2.5	0.8	0.0
Miscellaneous	13.7	9.9	12.9	13.1

TABLE 5.10   Reasons for allocation of scale 2 and above posts (Percentage frequency of schools)

NUMBERS OF SCALE 2 OR ABOVE POSTS	TYPE OF SCHOOL			
	5-12	8-12	9-13	10-13
1	9.1	6.2	2.2	6.1
2	12.7	11.8	4.1	6.1
3	13.6	10.7	4.4	3.0
4	13.6	13.0	9.6	12.1
5	6.4	12.7	10.0	9.1
6	4.5	8.2	12.9	6.1
7	8.2	8.2	7.7	9.1
8	3.6	4.8	7.4	12.1
9	0.9	2.8	8.1	3.0
10+	4.5	3.7	23.4	15.1

TABLE 5.11   Numbers of scale posts given for subject specialists (Percentage frequency of schools)

	TYPE OF SCHOOL			
	5-12	8-12	9-13	10-13
Maths	71.8	53.0	11.4	9.1
English	80.9	61.7	14.4	9.1
Science	70.0	39.2	7.9	9.7
Foreign Language	64.9	35.5	10.5	3.4
Art and Craft	53.3	39.7	7.4	3.6
Music	24.5	21.2	5.1	9.5

TABLE 5.13   Middle schools where specialists only teach their own class (Percentage frequency of schools)

	TYPE OF SCHOOL			
	5-12	8-12	9-13	10-13
Maths	29.4	29.6	58.2	67.5
English	30.4	44.4	60.6	70.2
Science	31.5	32.7	68.2	72.6
Foreign Language	23.3	31.8	69.7	80.6
Art and Craft	37.5	27.4	65.5	76.2
Music	27.0	38.9	62.8	75.1

TABLE 5.14   Average percentage of time specialists spend teaching their own subject

	5-12			8-12			9-13			10-13		
	2	3	4	2	3	4	2	3	4	2	3	4
Mathematics	25.5	12.7	0.9	29.6	12.7	0.6	42.1	34.7	0.7	30.3	54.5	3.0
English	30.9	6.4	0.9	32.7	14.6	0.8	39.5	35.8	0.4	27.3	33.3	3.0
Science	34.5	10.0	0.9	34.9	12.1	0.0	47.6	25.8	1.8	57.6	30.3	0.0
Foreign Language	29.1	3.6	0.9	35.2	7.0	0.0	54.2	14.8	1.1	60.6	24.2	0.0
Art/Craft	30.9	5.5	0.9	43.4	10.7	0.0	42.4	26.6	0.4	54.5	30.3	0.0
PE	32.7	5.5	0.0	54.9	11.6	0.0	50.2	14.8	0.7	57.6	12.1	0.0
Humanities	6.4	6.4	0.0	22.0	6.5	0.0	32.8	25.8	0.7	30.3	33.3	0.0
Music	35.5	7.3	0.0	45.9	11.3	0.3	51.3	14.0	0.4	45.5	12.1	0.0
Library	12.7	2.7	0.0	17.1	0.6	0.0	12.9	1.5	0.0	12.1	0.0	0.0
Home Economics	9.1	0.0	0.0	12.1	1.1	0.0	10.3	0.7	0.0	12.1	0.0	0.0
Drama	0.9	0.9	0.0	2.5	0.0	0.0	4.1	0.0	0.0	9.1	3.0	0.0
Joint	10.0	6.4	0.9	14.7	2.3	0.0	2.2	4.1.	0.0	0.0	0.0	0.0

TYPE OF SCHOOL

TABLE 5.12   Scale posts given for subject specialists (Percentage frequency of schools)

TYPE OF SCHOOL	ADVISING COLLEAGUES	LIAISING WITH UPPER SCHOOL
5-12	57.4	39.8
8-12	86.1	46.0
9-13	95.6	83.6
10-13	93.5	83.9

TABLE 5.15   Some duties of subject specialists not necessarily with a scale 2 or above post (Percentage frequency of schools)

	TYPE OF SCHOOL			
	5-12	8-12	9-13	10-13
Maths	9.0	8.2	8.4	0.0
English	10.9	8.5	7.7	6.1
Science	2.7	3.1	3.3	0.0
Foreign Language	16.3	14.1	10.7	6.1
Art/Craft	5.5	8.2	9.5	3.0
P.E.	5.5	4.8	7.4	3.0
Humanities	2.7	2.0	3.0	3.0
Music	10.0	11.0	5.2	6.1
Class Teacher	15.5	16.5	12.5	0.0

TABLE 5.16   Middle schools using part-time staff (Percentage frequency of schools)

	AGE OF PUPILS			
	9+	10+	11+	12+
9-13	1.5	4.4	10.3	13.3
10-13	-	6.1	12.1	15.2

TABLE 6.1   9-13 and 10-13 achools which stream their pupils for registration groups (Percentage frequency of schools)

TYPE OF SCHOOL			AGE OF PUPILS				
			8+	9+	10+	11+	12+
	5-12	Mathematics	20.0	23.6	37.3	44.5	
		English	12.7	14.5	22.7	28.2	
		Foreign Language	4.5	7.3	18.2	24.5	
		Science	0.0	0.0	4.5	6.4	
	8-12	Mathematics	23.9	31.3	50.7	64.5	
		English	11.3	14.4	22.0	30.4	
		Foreign Language	3.1	5.6	20.6	34.4	
		Science	2.0	2.0	6.8	10.7	
	9-13	Mathematics		32.5	45.4	73.1	75.6
		English		15.5	22.5	43.2	48.7
		Foreign Language		6.3	13.3	50.6	63.1
		Science		4.8	5.5	18.8	26.6
	10-13	Mathematics			45.5	54.5	66.7
		English			21.2	33.3	39.4
		Foreign Language			18.2	48.5	63.6
		Science			9.1	15.2	27.3

TABLE 6.2 Schools that set for subject teaching (Percentage frequency of schools)

	NUMBER OF CLASSES PER YEAR							
	1	2	3	4	5	6	7	8
5-12	57.3	32.6	9.2	0.9				
8-12	6.5	33.5	40.0	16.6	3.1	0.3		
9-13	1.8	11.4	24.4	37.6	18.5	5.5	0.4	0.4
10-13			15.2	9.1	27.3	33.2	6.1	9.1

TABLE 6.3 Number of classes per year (Percentage frequency of schools)

		AGE OF PUPILS				
		8+	9+	10+	11+	12+
Foreign Language	5-12	4.5	23.6	64.5	77.3	
	8-12	9.3	30.1	65.9	79.7	
	9-13		58.7	86.0	94.1	94.8
	10-13			84.8	87.9	96.9
Science	5-12	38.2	46.4	60.9	64.5	
	8-12	42.8	46.5	69.3	76.6	
	9-13		72.3	82.7	87.8	97.4
	10-13			75.8	87.9	97.0
Home Economics	5-12	14.5	19.1	26.4	40.0	
	8-12	14.9	18.6	36.9	52.7	
	9-13		26.2	38.7	59.0	60.1
	10-13			33.3	42.4	48.5
Drama	5-12	4.5	5.5	5.5	6.4	
	8-12	7.6	7.3	8.5	9.6	
	9-13		14.4	15.5	13.7	14.5
	10-13			18.2	18.2	21.2

TABLE 6.4   Schools teaching foreign languages, science, home economics and drama to pupils of various ages (Percentage frequency of schools)

	AGE OF PUPILS				
	8+	9+	10+	11+	12+
5-12	9.2	12.7	20.8	27.4	
8-12	9.4	12.8	21.6	29.9	
9-13		20.8	35.0	66.1	74.7
10-13			43.9	59.0	77.0

TABLE 6.5   Average percentage time which pupils of various ages spend with specialist teachers

		AGE OF PUPILS				
		8+	9+	10+	11+	12+
Mathematics	5-12	0.0	2.7	11.8	18.2	
	8-12	2.8	5.9	16.6	27.3	
	9-13		14.8	38.0	71.2	76.0
	10-13			33.3	75.8	84.8
English	5-12	0.9	3.6	4.5	6.4	
	8-12	1.4	2.8	7.3	11.8	
	9-13		11.1	26.9	53.1	65.7
	10-13			18.2	60.6	72.7

TABLE 6.6   Schools with pupils taught by mathematics and english specialists (Percentage frequency of schools)

		AGE OF PUPILS				
		8+	9+	10+	11+	12+
Foreign Languages	5-12	2.7	8.2	27.3	32.7	
	8-12	4.2	14.1	36.6	47.0	
	9-13		31.4	57.6	73.1	74.9
	10-13			63.6	78.8	81.8
Science	5-12	4.5	4.5	21.8	26.4	
	8-12	5.9	9.6	29.9	43.7	
	9-13		23.2	53.5	79.0	79.3
	10-13			57.6	81.8	84.8

TABLE 6.7   Schools with pupils taught foreign languages and science by specialists (Percentage frequency of schools)

	TYPE OF SCHOOL			
	5-12	8-12	9-13	10-13
School Mathematics Project	10.0	26.8	52.0	33.3
En Avant	42.7	61.1	76.8	36.4
Nuffield Combined Science	20.9	33.5	62.4	51.5
Science 5-13	22.7	23.4	14.4	18.2
Think Well	6.4	4.5	5.5	3.0

TABLE 6.8   Schools using selected national curriculum development projects (Percentage frequency of schools)

	AGE OF PUPILS				
	8+	9+	10+	11+	12+
5-12	24.6	28.3	43.7	59.0	
8-12	17.8	20.4	35.2	57.5	
9-13		39.9	51.7	81.5	89.6
10-13			75.7	93.9	97.0

TABLE 6.9   Schools that regularly set their pupils homework (Percentage frequency of schools)

	TYPE OF SCHOOL		
	8-12	9-13	10-13
Feeder school record	56.9	67.5	72.7
Standardised IQ test	11.3	11.4	12.1
Standardised attainment test	20.0	24.4	24.2
Internal test	16.9	21.0	21.2
Age of pupil	22.0	12.5	12.1

TABLE 6.10   Type of information used to group pupils in their first year (Percentage frequency of schools)

	AGE OF PUPILS				
	8+	9+	10+	11+	12+
5-12	31.9	33.6	44.6	65.5	
8-12	33.9	34.5	43.2	53.6	
9-13		32.5	29.5	27.3	33.6
10-13			39.4	33.3	33.3

TABLE 6.11   Schools giving IQ Tests to pupils of different ages (Percentage frequency of schools)

	YEAR											
	1			2			3			4		
	TERM			TERM			TERM			TERM		
	1	2	3	1	2	3	1	2	3	1	2	3
MATHS:												
Standardised attainment	6.4	13.6	13.6	3.6	11.8	16.4	7.3	14.5	18.2	6.4	14.5	20.0
Internal written	11.8	20.9	40.0	11.8	24.5	40.9	16.4	25.5	43.6	15.5	26.4	46.4
ENGLISH:												
Standardised attainment	5.5	11.8	14.5	1.8	10.0	16.4	5.5	14.5	15.5	6.4	13.6	19.1
Internal written	11.8	20.0	37.3	11.8	23.6	39.1	13.6	24.5	41.8	14.5	25.4	45.5
READING:												
Standardised attainment	32.7	27.3	41.8	26.4	23.6	44.5	30.0	26.4	43.6	29.1	28.2	44.5
Internal written	10.0	14.5	20.9	7.3	14.5	20.0	9.1	15.5	20.0	10.0	14.5	20.0

TABLE 6.12 Formal assessment of attainment in combined schools (Percentage frequency of schools)

	YEAR											
	1			2			3			4		
	TERM			TERM			TERM			TERM		
	1	2	3	1	2	3	1	2	3	1	2	3
MATHS:												
Standardised attainment	13.5	13.0	29.0	6.5	20.0	29.0	7.0	16.3	30.1	9.3	24.0	29.6
Internal written	12.7	20.0	46.5	12.7	19.7	47.0	14.7	20.6	48.2	15.2	22.3	49.9
ENGLISH:												
Standardised attainment	9.6	13.0	26.8	4.8	18.0	26.2	5.4	15.5	27.0	8.7	21.1	28.2
Internal written	11.0	17.7	45.1	11.0	18.0	44.5	13.5	19.7	47.3	14.9	22.0	46.8
READING:												
Standardised attainment	45.6	25.4	56.1	30.4	26.2	55.2	29.3	23.9	54.1	27.9	27.6	52.4
Internal written	9.6	12.7	21.7	8.5	9.9	22.0	9.0	10.1	22.5	9.0	10.7	22.5

TABLE 6.13 Formal assessment of attainment in 8-12 middle schools (Percentage frequency of schools)

	YEAR											
	1			2			3			4		
	TERM			TERM			TERM			TERM		
	1	2	3	1	2	3	1	2	3	1	2	3
MATHS:												
Standardised attainment	21.8	10.7	16.6	11.8	15.1	15.9	9.2	12.2	15.1	10.7	19.2	18.8
Internal written	19.2	21.8	50.9	18.1	25.5	58.7	19.2	29.2	59.8	18.8	26.6	58.3
ENGLISH:												
Standardised attainment	19.6	12.5	13.7	11.1	17.3	13.7	8.5	14.4	12.8	8.9	19.9	16.6
Internal written	14.8	21.0	48.0	14.4	25.5	55.4	16.2	26.9	57.2	15.1	25.1	57.9
READING:												
Standardised attainment	54.2	18.8	35.1	31.4	20.7	35.1	22.9	13.7	26.9	21.0	19.2	25.5
Internal written	9.2	11.1	24.4	7.7	10.0	27.3	8.1	8.9	23.6	7.7	9.6	25.8

TABLE 6.14 Formal assessment of attainment in 9-13 middle schools (Percentage frequency of schools)

	YEAR								
	1			2			3		
	TERM			TERM			TERM		
	1	2	3	1	2	3	1	2	3
MATHS:									
Standardised attainment	11.8	15.1	15.9	15.2	18.2	9.1	12.1	18.2	18.2
Inrernal written	18.1	25.2	58.7	30.3	21.2	66.7	18.2	24.2	51.5
ENGLISH:									
Standardised attainment	11.1	17.3	13.7	21.2	15.2	6.1	12.1	21.2	18.2
Internal written	14.4	25.5	55.4	21.2	15.2	51.5	15.2	18.2	45.5
READING:									
Standardised attainment	31.4	20.7	35.1	21.2	6.1	12.1	12.1	12.1	27.3
Internal written	7.7	10.0	27.3	6.1	0.0	15.2	3.0	0.0	18.2

TABLE 6.... Formal assessment of attainment in 10-12 middle schools (Percentage frequency of schools)

NUMBER OF FEEDER FIRST SCHOOLS	TYPE OF MIDDLE SCHOOL			
	5-12	8-12	9-13	10-13
1	[1]89.5	58.5	6.3	—
2	5.8	23.4	13.3	—
3	0.9	10.7	17.3	18.2
4-5	2.9	4.8	28.1	24.2
6-7	0.9	2.0	16.9	36.4
8-9	—	0.3	5.6	3.0
10+	—	0.3	12.5	18.2

TABLE 7.1   Middle schools receiving pupils from various numbers of feeder
first schools (Percentage frequency of schools)

[1] This refers to own children in combined schools

	TYPE OF MIDDLE SCHOOL		
	8-12	9-13	10-13
Specific Feeder First Schools	29.0	17.0	3.0
Pupil's Residence	39.2	22.9	45.5
Parental Choice	5.6	25.8	12.1
Some Combination of the above	26.2	34.3	39.4

TABLE 7.2   Middle schools showing methods of allocation from feeder first
schools (Percentage frequency of schools)

NUMBER OF UPPER SCHOOLS	TYPE OF MIDDLE SCHOOL			
	5-12	8-12	9-13	10-13
1	19.1	26.2	44.7	54.4
2	22.7	18.0	18.1	9.1
3	10.9	14.4	9.6	9.1
4-5	30.0	23.5	15.5	24.3
6-7	15.5	14.1	6.2	3.1
8-9	0.9	1.9	2.2	—
10+	0.9	1.9	3.7	—

TABLE 7.3   Middle schools transferring pupils to various number of upper
schools (Percentage frequency of schools)

135

	⟨10 PUPILS		11-30 PUPILS		31-50 PUPILS		⟩50 PUPILS	
	5-12	8-12	5-12	8-12	5-12	8-12	5-12	8-12
Not applicable	28.3	34.9	40.0	56.6	66.4	65.1	75.5	36.9
1	11.8	15.2	38.2	23.1	21.8	25.1	12.7	55.5
2	12.7	13.2	9.1	9.0		2.2		
3	13.6	11.5		3.4				
4-5	16.4	12.7	0.9	0.3				
6-7	3.6	2.6						
8-9	0.9	1.4						
10+	0.9	0.9						
Not Known	11.8	7.6	11.8	7.6	11.8	7.6	11.8	7.6

TABLE 7.4[1] Middle schools (5-12 and 8-12) sending various numbers of pupils to upper schools (Percentage frequency of schools)

NUMBER OF UPPER SCHOOLS	⟨10 PUPILS		11-30 PUPILS		31-50 PUPILS		⟩50 PUPILS	
	9-13	10-13	9-13	10-13	9-13	10-13	9-13	10-13
Not applicable	55.0	66.6	64.2	69.6	76.8	69.6	18.1	9.1
1	12.9	6.1	14.8	6.1	11.4	6.1	69.0	72.7
2	7.8	9.1	9.2	6.1	3.7	9.1	4.8	3.0
3	5.5		2.6	3.0				
4-5	4.9	3.0	1.1					
6-7	2.9							
8-9	2.5							
10+	0.4							
Not Known	8.1	15.2	8.1	15.2	8.1	15.2	8.1	15.2

TABLE 7.5[1] Middle schools (9-13 and 10-13) sending various numbers of pupils to upper schools (Percentage frequency of schools)

NOTE 1. When comparing these tables with Table 7.3 remember that transfer may be made of different numbers of pupils to different schools: i.e. a 5-12 school sending pupils to 7 different upper schools may send 1 block of 50 pupils to one school, with 1 group of 11-13 going to another and 5 groups of 2 or 3 pupils going to 5 different schools.

	TYPE OF MIDDLE SCHOOL			
	5-12	8-12	9-13	10-13
Pupil Residence	10.0	11.5	9.6	3.0
Selective System	32.2	18.1	0.7	0.0
Parental Choice	33.3	32.1	40.5	17.2
Parental Choice & Residence	5.4	12.1	4.5	25.4
Not applicable	19.1	26.2	44.7	54.4

TABLE 7.6   Reasons for allocation to more than one upper schools
(Percentage frequency of schools)

	TYPE OF MIDDLE SCHOOL		
	8-12	9-13	10-13
Head Teacher	22.8	5.3	3.1
1st Year Co-Ordinator	38.4	60.3	54.5
Deputy Head	3.4	4.2	9.1
Other Teacher(s)	35.4	30.2	33.3

TABLE 7.7   Members of staff responsible for liaison with first schools
(Percentage frequency of those schools having a specific member
of staff)

	TYPE OF MIDDLE SCHOOL		
	8-12	9-13	10-13
More than once per term	13.8	15.5	9.1
Once per term	24.2	31.0	36.4
Once per year	30.1	35.8	51.5
Rarely	19.7	16.2	3.0
Not At All	12.2	1.5	—

TABLE 7.8   Frequency of formal meetings with colleagues in feeder first
schools (Percentage frequency of schools)

TYPE OF MIDDLE SCHOOL			
5-12	8-12	9-13	10-13
72.7	86.2	93.4	93.9

TABLE 7.9   Schools with a member of staff specifically responsible for liaison
with upper schools (Percentage frequency of schools)

	TYPE OF MIDDLE SCHOOL			
	5-12	8-12	9-13	10-13
Head Teacher	29.0	26.3	6.8	6.5
Deputy Head Teacher	8.9	7.9	7.5	9.7
Final Year Co-Ordinator	16.5	21.7	44.9	35.4
Team of Teachers	45.6	42.1	37.7	45.2
Teachers with a Scale Post for Liaison	0.0	2.0	1.2	0.0
Others	0.0	0.0	1.9	3.2

TABLE 7.10 The member of staff responsible for liaison with upper schools (Percentage frequency of schools having a specific member of staff)

TYPE OF MIDDLE SCHOOL			
5-12	8-12	9-13	10-13
0.9	3.4	4.4	0.0

TABLE 7.11 Middle schools whose staff teach in upper schools (Percentage frequency of schools)

TYPE OF MIDDLE SCHOOL			
5-12	8-12	9-13	10-13
7.3	10.1	14.0	6.1

TABLE 7.12 Middle schools who have upper school staff teaching in them (Percentage frequency of schools)

TYPE OF MIDDLE SCHOOL			
5-12	8-12	9-13	10-13
52.7	62.5	84.9	81.8

TABLE 7.13 Middle schools holding formal liaison meetings with upper schools to discuss specific subject areas (Percentage frequency of schools)

	TYPE OF MIDDLE SCHOOL			
	5-12	8-12	9-13	10-13
Mathematics	86.2	86.9	87.8	100.0
English	69.0	65.8	75.2	77.8
Foreign Language	60.3	72.8	87.8	96.3
Science	60.3	64.4	82.6	85.2
Humanities	19.0	27.9	57.4	48.2
Remedial	15.5	37.8	48.7	44.4

TABLE 7.14   Middle schools reporting formal liaison meetings to discuss specific subject areas with upper schools (Percentage frequency of schools having formal liaison meetings)

		MATHEMATICS	ENGLISH	FOREIGN LANGUAGES	SCIENCE	HUMANITIES	REMEDIAL
MIDDLE SCHOOL STAFF	Subject Specialist	23.2	23.3	54.1	38.9	25.0	18.2
	Head Department	1.9	2.3	2.7	2.8	–	9.1
	Subject Coordinator	–	2.3	–	2.8	–	–
	Senior Staff	3.8	11.6	2.7	5.6	8.3	27.2
	All Staff	1.9	–	–	–	–	–
	4th Year Teachers	11.5	11.6	2.7	2.8	8.3	9.1
	Combination of Above	53.9	44.2	32.4	41.5	50.0	18.2
	Not Known	3.8	4.7	5.4	5.6	8.3	18.2
UPPER SCHOOL STAFF	Head Department	44.3	41.9	54.1	58.2	25.0	36.3
	Subject Head (Lower School)	3.8	4.7	5.4	5.6	16.8	9.1
	Subject Teacher	3.8	2.3	–	2.8	8.3	9.1
	Whole Dept.	3.8	4.7	–	–	–	–
	Senior Staff	1.9	–	–	–	8.3	9.1
	Combination of Above	36.5	39.5	35.1	27.8	33.3	18.2
	Not Known	5.9	6.9	5.4	5.6	8.3	18.2
FREQUENCY OF MEETINGS	More than One Meeting per term	7.6	4.7	13.5	11.2	–	9.1
	One Meeting per Term	23.2	18.6	18.9	19.4	–	9.1
	One Meeting per Year	55.8	60.5	62.2	61.1	91.7	72.7
	Less than One Meeting per year	13.4	16.2	5.4	8.3	8.3	9.1

TABLE 7.15   5-12 Middle schools having formal subject liaison meetings – staff in middle and upper schools and frequency of meetings
(Percentage frequency of those 5-12 schools having such meetings)

		MATHEMATICS	ENGLISH	FOREIGN LANGUAGES	SCIENCE	HUMANITIES	REMEDIAL
MIDDLE SCHOOL STAFF	Subject Specialist	25.6	21.1	56.0	51.6	22.9	28.9
	Head Department	0.5	1.3	1.2	0.6	1.4	2.1
	Subject Coordinator	8.2	7.7	2.9	3.2	5.7	4.1
	Senior Staff	5.8	6.4	2.3	2.6	7.1	12.4
	All Staff	1.0	1.9	–	–	–	–
	4th Year Teachers	10.6	12.2	3.5	4.5	12.9	8.2
	Combination of Above	34.3	43.0	30.1	31.0	38.6	34.0
	Not Known	14.0	6.4	4.0	6.5	11.4	10.3
UPPER SCHOOL STAFF	Head Department	55.6	50.0	66.5	66.5	50.0	47.5
	Subject Head (Lower School)	2.4	4.5	3.5	2.6	4.3	5.1
	Subject Teacher	3.4	5.8	3.5	2.6	4.3	5.1
	Whole Dept.	2.9	1.9	1.2	1.9	–	–
	Senior Staff	–	–	–	–	–	–
	Combination of Above	29.0	31.4	21.3	20.6	31.5	28.9
	Not Known	6.7	6.4	4.0	5.8	9.9	13.4
FREQUENCY OF MEETINGS	More than One Meeting per term	10.6 / 28.5	8.3 / 25.0	5.8 / 32.9	5.8 / 31.6	7.1 / 15.7	3.1 / 20.6
	One Meeting per Term One Meeting per Year	44.0	50.6	46.2	43.9	57.2	63.9
	Less than One Meeting per year	16.9	16.1	15.1	18.7	20.0	12.4

TABLE 7.16   8-12 Middle Schools having formal subject liaison meetings – staff in middle and upper schools and frequency of meetings (Percentage frequency of those schools having such meetings)

		MATHEMATICS	ENGLISH	FOREIGN LANGUAGES	SCIENCE	HUMANITIES	REMEDIAL
MIDDLE SCHOOL STAFF	Subject Specialist	49.8	44.7	59.5	56.5	51.0	46.9
	Head Department	12.3	12.1	13.5	13.5	10.0	10.0
	Subject Coordinator	1.8	4.7	2.3	1.9	4.0	3.1
	Senior Staff	0.9	1.6	–	–	1.3	3.8
	All Staff	–	–	–	–	–	–
	4th Year Teachers	2.8	3.2	1.3	1.0	3.4	1.6
	Combination of Above	24.6	24.8	15.3	18.8	20.2	21.5
	Not Known	7.8	8.9	8.1	8.3	10.1	13.1
UPPER SCHOOL STAFF	Head Department	51.2	57.9	64.0	59.4	53.0	53.8
	Subject Head (Lower School)	1.4	2.6	0.9	1.0	3.4	1.6
	Subject Teacher	3.2	4.7	4.5	3.4	5.4	4.6
	Whole Dept.	2.8	4.2	3.6	5.3	6.0	4.6
	Senior Staff	0.9	0.5	0.4	0.5	0.7	2.3
	Combination of Above	20.4	19.5	16.2	19.8	17.4	17.7
	Not Known	10.1	10.6	10.4	10.6	14.1	15.4
FREQUENCY OF MEETINGS	More than One Meeting per term	14.6	9.5	16.2	12.1	6.0	10.7
	One Meeting per Term	42.0	37.9	39.7	40.6	29.5	24.6
	One Meeting per Year	39.3	46.8	40.1	41.1	55.0	59.3
	Less than One Meeting per year	4.1	5.8	4.0	6.2	9.5	5.4

TABLE 7.17   9-13 Middle schools having formal subject liaison meetings –
staff in middle and upper schools and frequency of meetings
(Percentage frequency of those schools holding such meetings)

		MATHEMATICS	ENGLISH	FOREIGN LANGUAGES	SCIENCE	HUMANITIES	REMEDIAL
MIDDLE SCHOOL STAFF	Subject Specialist	55.6	57.1	57.8	61.0	46.1	50.0
	Head Department	3.7	9.5	11.5	4.3	7.7	25.0
	Subject Coordinator	–	–	–	4.3	7.7	–
	Senior Staff	3.7	–	3.8	–	–	–
	All Staff	–	–	–	–	7.7	–
	4th Year Teachers	3.7	4.8	3.8	4.3	7.7	8.3
	Combination of Above	33.3	28.6	23.1	26.1	23.1	16.7
	Not Known	–	–	–	–	–	–
UPPER SCHOOL STAFF	Head Department	59.3	57.1	57.8	56.6	69.2	75.0
	Subject Head (Lower School)	7.4	4.8	7.7	4.3	–	–
	Subject Teacher	7.4	4.8	7.7	8.7	7.7	16.7
	Whole Dept.	–	4.8	3.8	4.3	–	–
	Senior Staff	–	–	–	–	–	–
	Combination of Above	25.9	28.5	23.0	26.1	23.1	8.3
	Not Known	–	–	–	–	–	–
FREQUENCY OF MEETINGS	More than One Meeting per term	14.8	14.3	11.5	17.3	7.7	–
	One Meeting per Term	37.0	33.3	34.6	26.1	15.4	8.3
	One Meeting per Year	37.0	38.1	46.2	34.8	53.8	75.0
	Less than One Meeting per year	11.2	14.3	7.7	21.8	23.1	16.7

TABLE 7.18   10-13 Middle schools having formal subject liaison meetings –
staff in middle and upper schools and frequency of meetings
(Percentage frequency of those schools holding such meetings)

	TYPE OF MIDDLE SCHOOL			
	5-12	8-12	9-13	10-13
Pastoral	33.6	44.5	61.6	60.6
Administrative	17.3	23.9	41.0	30.3

TABLE 7.19 Middle schools holding formal liaison meetings with upper schools to discuss pastoral care and administrative matters (Percentage frequency of schools)

AGE RANGE	TOTAL NUMBER OF UPPER SCHOOLS[1] (1978) IN ENGLAND AND WALES	NUMBER OF UPPER SCHOOLS RESPONDING TO QUESTIONNAIRE	PERCENTAGE RESPONSE
12-16	133[2]	75	56.4
12-18	137	63	46.0
13-16	5	4	80.0
13-18	243	153	63.0
TOTAL	518	295	56.9

TABLE 8.1 Size of sample of upper schools responding to Questionnaire

Note 1 Source: DES Statistics
Note 2 DES Statistics give this as 12-15/16 rather than just 12-16 and so the total number of 12-16 schools only is likely to be less than this figure.

	TYPE OF SCHOOL		
	12-16	12-18	13-18
1968 or before	6	3	19
1969-73	32	29	88
1974-1978	37	31	50
TOTAL	75	63	157

TABLE 8.3 Year of opening (Numbers of upper schools)

	TYPE OF SCHOOL		
	12-16	12-18	13-18
Secondary Modern	73.3	36.5	22.3
Grammar	10.7	14.3	39.5
Technical	1.3	–	2.5
Adapted Comprehensive	4.0	9.5	6.4
Purpose Built Comprehensive	–	6.3	6.4
New School	–	1.6	11.5
Secondary Modern and Grammar	8.0	28.6	10.8
Not Known	2.7	3.2	0.6

TABLE 8.4   School type prior to reorganisation (Percentage frequency of upper schools)

		UP TO 400		401-600		601-800		801-1000		1001-1200		1201-1500		1501-2000		OVER 2000	
		n	%	n	%	n	%	n	%	n	%	n	%	n	%	n	%
12-15/16 Schools	Population	7	5.3	27	20.3*	46	34.6	29	21.8	17	12.7	7	5.3	–	–	–	
	Sample	4	5.3	23	30.7	24	32.0	13	17.3	8	10.7	3	4.0	–	–	–	
12-18 Schools	Population	–	–	6	4.4	21	15.3*	31	22.6	35	25.6	31	22.6*	12	8.8	1	0.7
	Sample	–	–	5	7.9	13	20.7	14	22.2	14	22.2	11	17.5	6	9.5	–	–
13-16 Schools	Population	1	20.0	3	60.0*	–	–	1	20.0	–	–	–	–	–	–	–	–
	Sample	1	25.0	2	50.0	–	–	1	25.0	–	–	–	–	–	–	–	–
13-18 Schools	Population	9	3.7	26	10.7	56	23.1	64	26.3	47	19.3	38	15.7	3	1.2	–	–
	Sample	1	0.7	17	11.1	40	26.1	42	27.5	30	19.6	21	13.7	2	1.3	–	–

*Indicates a difference of more than 5% between population and sample

TABLE 8.2 A comparison of the distribution by size of school between the total population of Upper schools and the sample responding to the Questionnaire

	TYPE OF SCHOOL		
	12-16	12-18	13-18
Church of England	6.7	1.6	5.1
Roman Catholic	6.7	14.3	6.4
Non-Denominational	86.6	84.1	88.5

TABLE 8.5 Denomination of schools in the sample (Percentage frequency of upper schools)

NUMBER OF FEEDER	UPPER SCHOOLS		
MIDDLE SCHOOLS	12-16	12-18	13-18
3 or less	20.0	15.9	39.3
4-6	29.3	27.0	24.1
7-9	18.7	15.9	9.0
10-15	21.3	15.9	12.4
16 or more	10.7	22.2	14.5
Not Known	0.0	3.1	0.7

TABLE 8.6   Upper schools receiving pupils from feeder middle schools
(Percentage frequency of upper schools)

NUMBER OF FEEDER	TYPE OF SCHOOL		
MIDDLE SCHOOLS	12-16	12-18	13-18
1, 2	18.7	17.5	15.3
3-6	21.3	9.5	10.8
7-10	21.3	4.8	7.6
11-14	5.4	11.2	4.5
15+	1.3	6.2	7.0
Not Applicable	24.0	27.0	43.3
Not Known	8.0	23.8	11.5

TABLE 8.7   Upper schools receiving 10 or fewer pupils from various middle
schools (Percentage frequency of upper schools)

NUMBER OF FEEDER	TYPE OF SCHOOL		
MIDDLE SCHOOLS	12-16	12-18	13-18
1, 2	45.3	31.8	24.2
3-6	13.3	11.1	13.4
7-9	2.7	1.6	1.3
Not Applicable	30.7	31.7	49.6
Not Known	8.0	23.8	11.5

TABLE 8.8   Upper schools receiving 11-30 pupils from various middle schools
(Percentage frequency of upper schools)

147

NUMBER OF FEEDER MIDDLE SCHOOLS	TYPE OF SCHOOL		
	12-16	12-18	13-18
1, 2	48.0	27.0	27.4
3-6	6.6	7.9	4.5
Not Applicable	37.4	41.3	56.6
Not Known	8.0	23.8	11.5

TABLE 8.9   Upper schools receiving 31-50 pupils from various middle schools (Percentage frequency of upper schools)

NUMBER OF FEEDER MIDDLE SCHOOLS	TYPE OF SCHOOL		
	12-16	12-18	13-18
1, 2	61.4	25.4	47.8
3-6	10.6	25.4	30.6
Not Applicable	20.0	25.4	10.1
Not Known	8.0	23.8	11.5

TABLE 8.10   Upper schools receiving 51 or more pupils from various middle schools (Percentage frequency of upper schools)

	TYPE OF SCHOOL		
	12-16	12-18	13-18
Specific Feeder	16.0	7.9	12.4
Pupil Residence	24.0	15.9	15.9
Parental Choice	28.0	27.0	35.1
Combination of Above	28.0	39.7	34.5
Selection	1.3	7.9	0.7
Not Known	2.7	1.6	1.4

TABLE 8.11   Methods of allocating pupils to upper schools (Percentage frequency of upper schools)

GROUP NUMBER	TYPE OF SCHOOL		
	12-16	12-18	13-18
6	2.7	–	–
7	4.0	3.2	–
8	16.0	1.6	0.7
9	22.7	4.8	4.1
10	36.0	25.4	25.5
11	14.7	23.8	41.4
12	2.7	27.0	19.3
13	1.2	9.5	6.2
Not Known	–	4.7	2.8

TABLE 8.12   Group number of upper schools (Percentage frequency of upper schools)

		TYPE OF SCHOOL					
		12-16		12-18		13-18	
		AVERAGE NUMBERS	%	AVERAGE NUMBERS	%	AVERAGE NUMBERS	%
Graduates	Male	9.8	39.5	19.2	55.8	23.5	62.9
	Female	6.5		12.3		12.3	
Non Graduates	Male	13.1	60.5	12.8	44.2	11.5	37.1
	Female	11.9		12.2		9.6	
All Teachers		41.3	100.0	56.5	100.0	56.9	100.0

TABLE 8.13   Average numbers of full-time teachers in upper schools

	TYPE OF SCHOOL					
	12-16		12-18		13-18	
	AVERAGE NUMBERS	%	AVERAGE NUMBERS	%	AVERAGE NUMBERS	%
Scale 1	11.5	27.8	16.0	28.3	16.6	29.2
Scale 2	11.1	26.9	15.8	28.0	14.6	25.7
Scale 3	9.6	23.2	12.9	22.8	12.8	22.5
Scale 4	6.1	14.8	7.5	13.3	8.7	15.3
Deputy Head/ Senior Teacher	3.0	7.3	4.3	7.6	4.2	7.3

TABLE 8.14   Average numbers and percentages of scale posts in upper schools

	TYPE OF SCHOOL		
	12-16	12-18	13-18
One Secretary	32.0	28.6	19.1
Two Secretaries	37.3	23.8	25.5
Three Secretaries	30.7	47.6	55.4
One Laboratory Technician	57.3	26.5	21.0
Two Laboratory Technicians	40.0	71.3	78.4
Workshop Technician	46.7	55.6	63.1
Librarian	70.7	74.6	80.9

TABLE 8.15   Ancillary assistance in upper schools (Percentage frequency of schools)

	TYPE OF SCHOOL		
	12-16	12-18	13-18
Mixed Ability	50.7	52.4	63.1
Streamed	17.3	9.5	5.1
Broad Banded	28.0	25.4	26.1
Other (e.g. Houses, Vertically grouped)	4.0	12.7	5.7

TABLE 8.16   Registration groups in upper schools (Percentage frequency of schools)

	TYPE OF SCHOOL		
	12-16	12-18	13-18
Mixed Ability	14.6	35.0	19.8
Streamed	17.3	9.5	5.1
Broad Banded	42.7	34.9	44.6
Setting	13.4	7.9	21.7
Mixture of Various	12.0	12.7	8.8

TABLE 8.17   Teaching groups in the first year of upper schools (Percentage frequency of schools)

TYPE OF SCHOOL		
12-16	12-18	13-18
40.0	41.3	69.4

TABLE 8.18   Schools making significant changes in initial grouping of pupils during the first year (Percentage frequency of schools)

	TYPE OF SCHOOL		
	12-16	12-18	13-18
Common Curriculum in 1st Year	81.3	87.3	82.2
Common Curriculum in 2nd Year	70.7	63.5	14.0

TABLE 8.19 Upper schools having a common curriculum in their first year and continuing it into their second year (Percentage frequency of schools)

	TYPE OF SCHOOL		
	12-16	12-18	13-18
No disadvantage	36.0	30.2	17.8
One or more disadvantage	64.0	69.8	82.2
No advantage	96.0	93.7	82.2
One or more advantage	4.0	6.3	17.8

TABLE 8.20 Upper schools recording advantages and disadvantages in organisation and choice of option courses as a result of pupils transferring at an age greater than 11+ (Percentage frequency of schools)

	TYPE OF SCHOOL		
	12-16	12-18	13-18
1. Inadequate foundation in various subjects	48.0	44.5	36.8
2. Too little time to allow most effective option choices	12.0	12.7	31.8
3. Difficult to introduce 2nd foreign language	1.3	6.3	10.2
4. Variation in standard of feeder middle schools	0.0	3.2	6.4
5. Specialist teachers lose valuable time with pupils	5.3	4.8	2.5

TABLE 8.21 The major disadvantages in option choice caused by transfer later than 11+ (Percentage frequency of upper schools)

TYPE OF SCHOOL		
12-16	12-18	13-18
65.3	77.8	72.0

TABLE 8.22 Upper schools reporting problems arising out of receiving pupils from several feeder schools (Percentage frequency of schools)

151

	TYPE OF SCHOOL		
	12-16	12-18	13-18
General difficulties with modern languages	52.0	57.1	35.0
Different curricula in Maths	29.3	30.2	19.7
General variation in standards of different Middle Schools	14.7	11.1	29.3

TABLE 8.23   Major problems as perceived by upper schools in receiving pupils from several feeder middle schools (Percentage frequency of schools).

	TYPE OF SCHOOL			
	5-12	8-12	9-13	10-13
To provide a broadly based curriculum	75.7	70.4	63.8	51.5
To promote social skills and good behaviour	54.5	52.1	48.3	33.3
To train pupils in the basic skills	20.0	22.0	17.0	12.1
To provide a bridge between lower and upper schools	8.2	10.4	16.2	27.3

TABLE 9.1   Main aims of middle schools according to middle school head teachers (Percentage frequency of schools)

	TYPE OF SCHOOL		
	12-16	12-18	13-18
To consolidate basic skills	33.3	28.6	33.8
To combine the best of primary with the rigour of secondary education	22.7	25.4	38.9
To develop the individual pupil's potential	12.0	7.9	8.3
To provide a broader curriculum for the middle years of schooling	1.3	9.5	4.5

TABLE 9.2   Main aims of middle schools according to upper school headteachers (Percentage frequency of schools)

	TYPE OF SCHOOL			
	5-12	8-12	9-13	10-13
One or more disadvantage	78.2	83.4	80.1	81.8
One or more advantage	42.5	56.3	77.5	75.8

TABLE 9.3   Middle school headteachers recording advantages and disadvantages of middle schools (Percentage frequency of schools)

	TYPE OF SCHOOL		
	12-16	12-18	13-18
One or more disadvantage	64.0	69.8	82.2
One or more advantage	40.0	36.5	59.9

TABLE 9.4   Upper school headteachers recording advantages and disadvantages of middle schools (Percentage frequency of schools)

	TYPE OF SCHOOL			
	5-12	8-12	9-13	10-13
No premature specialisation	13.6	20.3	16.2	9.5
Better equipped for upper school	16.4	14.9	16.6	12.1
Secure environment for early adolescence	9.1	9.9	18.8	21.2
No exam pressure	0.9	7.6	21.0	15.2
Size	1.8	3.4	14.0	18.2
Greater intellectual stimulation	2.7	2.0	9.5	9.1

TABLE 9.5   The major advantages of middle schools according to the middle school headteachers (Percentage frequency of schools)

	TYPE OF SCHOOL		
	12-16	12-18	13-18
Allows a smaller school	10.7	4.8	26.8
Saved money	8.0	−	−
Pupils are more mature	5.3	12.7	−
Easier liaison with fewer Middle Schools	−	6.3	−
Absence of younger pupils − more unified ethos	−	−	15.9
Provides 6th form of larger size	−	−	9.6
Absence of a difficult third year	−	−	7.6
Greater range of option choices	−	−	6.4

TABLE 9.6   The main advantages of a 3-tier system according to upper school headteachers (only responses of more than five per cent are shown). (Percentage frequency of schools)

	TYPE OF SCHOOL			
	5-12	8-12	9-13	10-13
1. General shortage of teachers	30.9	38.3	28.4	18.2
2. Shortage of specialist teachers	20.9	22.3	16.6	12.1
3. Inadequate buildings	15.5	23.4	15.9	15.2.
4. Lack of resources	22.7	21.1	7.0	3.0
5. Shortage of skilled Middle School teachers	6.4	7.9	12.5	9.1
6. Lack of career structure	6.4	5.4	14.0	18.2
7. Liaison	1.8	3.1	14.8	18.2
8. Inadequate coverage of curriculum	7.3	8.2	3.7	0.0

TABLE 9.7   Major problems of middle schools according to middle school headteachers (Percentage frequency of middle schools)

	TYPE OF SCHOOL		
	12-16	12-18	13-18
Lack of specialist staff in Middle Schools	12.0	7.9	12.7
Lack of sixth form — problems attracting staff	18.7	—	—
Continuity of curricula	8.0	—	10.8
Transfer too late (lose first year)	20.0	15.9	14.0
Difficulties of liaison	5.3	—	5.1
Large task of orientating quickly because of external exams	—	9.5	26.8
Increased problem of option choices	—	6.3	14.0
Low level of attainment in key subject areas	—	—	5.7
Lack of appropriate work habits in children	—	—	5.7

TABLE 9.8   Main disadvantages in 3-tier system as seen from upper schools (only responses of more than five per cent are shown) (Percentage frequency of schools)

	TYPE OF SCHOOL			
	5-12	8-12	9-13	10-13
More teachers	27.3	25.9	25.1	21.2
More general resources	11.8	11.5	8.9	6.1
Greater liaison	3.6	5.1	11.8	6.1
9-13 pattern	4.5	2.5	10.0	12.1
Abolition	4.5	2.5	0.7	3.0

TABLE 9.9   The future development of middle schools according to middle school headteachers (Percentage frequency of middle schools)

Appendix 1

1. *Please indicate your answers by a tick unless otherwise requested.*
2. *If insufficient space has been left for any responses please continue these on a separate piece of paper.*
3. *Unless otherwise stated questions refer to your school in September 1978.*
4. *All information supplied on this questionnaire will be treated in the strictest confidence and will not be revealed to anyone.*

1. BACKGROUND INFORMATION

1.1 Name of school: 1 _____

1.2 L.E.A.:   2 _____

1.3 When did your school become, or open as a middle school?   3 _____
Month _____ Year _____   4 _____

1.4 Official designation: Primary ☐   Secondary ☐   5 _____

1.5 Age range of pupils in September 1978:

     8-12 ☐   10-14 ☐

     9-13 ☐   11-13 ☐

                Other *(please specify)*   6 _____   7 _____

1.6 Number of pupils on roll in:

     September 1977   Boys _____ Girls _____   9 _____

     September 1978   Boys _____ Girls _____   10 _____

1.7 Number of pupils in each year: 11 _____

     1st Year _____ 3rd Year _____   12 _____

     2nd Year_____ 4th Year_____   13 _____

1.8 Is your school: 14 _____

     Non-denominational ☐   Roman Catholic ☐

     Church of England ☐   Other *(please specify)* ☐   15 _____

1.9 From which kind of population area does your school draw the majority of its pupils?

     From the middle of a large city
(population 200,000 or more) ☐

     From a town *(population 5000-200,000)* ☐

     From a suburban area *(on outskirts of town or city)* ☐   16 _____

     From a village or surrounding countryside
(population under 5000) ☐

1.10   From which kind of housing does your school draw the
       majority of its pupils?

       Mostly from council estate(s)
       Mostly from private housing   17 _____
       From a mixture of council and private housing
       From a mixture of council, private and sub-standard
          housing
       Mostly from an area of sub-standard housing
       From other *(describe below)*

1.11   Number of first schools FROM which pupils have transferred
       TO your school:
          1976_____1977_____1978_____   18 _____

1.12   In which ways are pupils allocated to your school?   19 _____

       From specific feeder schools   20 _____

       From a catchment area defined by pupil's residence

       By a system of parental choice   21 _____

       Other *(please specify)*

1.3   Names of upper schools to which your pupils normally
       transfer;

Name of upper school	Approximate numbers transferred in July 1978
		22 _____
		23 _____

1.14   If pupils transfer to more than one upper school please state:
       a) Reasons for allocation   24 _____
       b) By whom the decisions are made   25 _____

1.15   Type of building that applies to your school:

       Purpose-built middle school

       Adapted from a previous secondary school   26 _____

       Adapted from a previous primary school

       Other *(please specify)*

1.16   Is any part of your school open plan?   Yes ☐   No ☐   27 _____

       If yes, please give brief details   28 _____

1.17   Does your school have specialist rooms/areas as well as
       classrooms?   29 _____

                                 Yes ☐   No ☐

       If yes, please indicate which ones: 30 _____

       Craft Room   ☐   Gym   ☐   31 _____
       Music Room   ☐   Playing Fields   ☐   32 _____
       Science Laboratory ☐   Outdoor teaching areas   ☐   33 _____
       Home Economics   (e.g. greenhouse, pond et.)
       Room   ☐   Others *(please specify)* ☐   34 _____
       Language Laboratory ☐   35 _____

156

1.8 If you had additional funds to spend on buildings, what would you spend the money on?

36 _____
37 _____
3 8 _____

40 _____
41 _____

2. STAFFING

2.1 Head Teacher   Deputy Head Teacher   42 _____

     Male ☐   Male ☐

     Female ☐   Female ☐   43 _____

2.2 If the Head Teacher is involved in teaching, approximately how many hours per week does this entail?_____ 44 _____

2.3 Number of teachers *(excluding Head Teacher)*

	Full-time		Part-time		
	Men	Women	Men	Women	
Graduates					45 / 46 / 47 / 48
Non-graduates					49 / 50

Full time equivalent of all the part-time staff:_____   51

2.4 How many teachers in your school have had experience in: 52

    primary schools only   _____

    secondary schools only   _____   53

    both primary and secondary schools _____   54

How many teachers in your school have been trained specifically for middle schools?   _____   55

2.5 Group number of your school *(for salary purposes):*_____   56

Number of teachers on: 57

Scale 1_____ Scale 2 _____Scale 3____Scale 4_____   58

2.6 How many teachers have scale posts: 59

    As subject specialists?   _____   60

    As year group leaders/co-ordinators? _____   61

    For other pastoral duties?   _____   62

    For other reasons? *(please specify)*   _____   63

2.7 Please insert in the table below the numbers of staff who have scale posts in the following subject areas:

Scale Posts

	2	3	4
Mathematics			
English			
Science			
Foreign Languages			
Art/Craft			
P.E.			
Humanities			
Music			
Others *(please list)*			

2.8 Approximately what percentages of their time do your subject specialists devote to teaching:
Maths_____ English _____ Science_____Art/Craft_____
Foreign Languages_____ P.E. _____ Humanities _____
Music_____Others? *(please list)*

2.9 Please list the subjects taught in your school by peripatetic and part-time teachers and the groups of pupils whom they teach *(If class teaching, write CT)*
Peripatetic:
Part-time:

2.10 Please indicate which of the following your school employs or has attached to it *(If member of staff, write 'S', if part-time, write 'PT')*
Secretary_____ Librarian_____ Laboratory assistant_____
Workshop technician_____ Guidance/Counsellor _____
Any others *(please specify)*

2.11 Do any of your staff have a scale post as a remedial teacher?
Yes ☐   No ☐
If yes, which children are taught by this member of staff?
Year 1:
Year 2:
Year 3:
Year 4:

2.12 If your remedial children are taught separately for any of the following subjects please state by which type of teacher *(e.g. class teacher, subject specialist, remedial teacher etc.)*

	Year 1	Year 2	Year 3	Year 4
Maths				
English				
Science				
French				
Others *(please specify)*				

64
65
66
67
68

69
70
71
72
73
74
75
76

77
78
79

81
82
83
84
85
86
87
88
89
90
91
92
93
94
95
96

97
98

2.13　If you could have more staff resources how would you use these additional teachers?　　　<u>99</u>

3.　GROUPING OF PUPILS

3.1　in what kinds of groups are the children placed for registration?

	Years			
	1	2	3	4
Mixed ability				
Streamed				
Vertical				
Other *(please specify)*				

3.2　In what kinds of groups are the pupils placed for teaching purposes?

Mixed ability				
Streamed				
Set for: Maths				
English				
French				
Science				
Other *(please specify)*				

3.2　What are the sizes of your teaching groups in the following subject areas in Years 3 and 4 *(or pupils in the last two years in your school)?*

	Year 3		Year 4	
	Average	Maximum	Average	Maximum
Maths				
English				
French				
Science				
Others *(please specify)*				

3.4   Are your remedial pupils taught:

	Year			
	1	2	3	4
Together with other pupils?				
Separately in all subjects?				
Separately in: Maths?				
English?				
French?				
Science?				
Others?				

(please specify)

3.5   If your remedial pupils are taught separately from other pupils please indicate the size of the group:

Maths				
English				
French				
Science				
Others *(please specify)*				

100 ___
101 ___
102 ___
103 ___
104 ___
105 ___
106 ___
107 ___
108 ___

3.6   Are there any other groups within your school?

Year groups   ☐ Tutor Groups   ☐

House Groups   ☐ Others *(please specify)* ☐

Upper/Lower School ☐

109 ___
110 ___
111 ___

Please give brief outline of the functions of such groups *(e.g. sport, gifted children, clubs, pastoral care, academic, etc.)*

4.   ORGANISATION OF THE CURRICULUM

4.1   Approximately what proportion (%) of the pupils' time is spent with

112 ___
113 ___
114 ___
115 ___
116 ___
117 ___

	Years			
	1	2	3	4
Class teaching				
Specialist subject teaching				

118 ___
119 ___

4.2   If relevant, please add any further information on the organisation of generalist and specialist teaching in your school:

160

4.3   YEAR 1 PUPILS

Number of classes or teaching groups: _____   120 ___

Are children in Year 1 taught by subject
specialists?   Yes ☐   No ☐   121 ___

If yes, who teaches the following
subjects?

*(The numbered boxes 1-6 refer to classes and are provided for
those schools with more than one class in each year. Please tick
appropriately for each class).*

	Subject specialist with scale post						Other subject specialist						Peripetatic						Other *(please specify)*					
	1	2	3	4	5	6	1	2	3	4	5	6	1	2	3	4	5	6	1	2	3	4	5	6
Maths																								
English																								
French																								
Science																								
Music																								
P.E.																								
Others *(please specify)*																								

Any special reasons for this arrangement?

4.2   YEAR 2 PUPILS

Number of classes or teaching groups: _____   122 ___

Are any children in Year 2 taught by subject
specialists?   Yes ☐   No ☐   123 ___

If yes, who teaches the following subjects? *(The numbered
boxes 1-6 refer to classes and are provided for those schools
with more than one class in each year. Please tick
appropriately for each class).*

	Subject specialist with scale post						Other subject specialist						Peripetatic						Other *(please specify)*					
	1	2	3	4	5	6	1	2	3	4	5	6	1	2	3	4	5	6	1	2	3	4	5	6
Maths																								
English																								
French																								
Science																								
Music																								
P.E.																								
Others *(please specify)*																								

Any special reason for this arrangement?

4.5   YEAR 3 PUPILS

Number of classes or teaching groups _____   124

Are any children in Year 3 taught by subject
specialists?   Yes ☐   No ☐   125

If yes, who teaches the following subjects? *(The numbered
boxes 1-6 refer to classes and are provided for those schools
appropriately for each class).*

	Subject specialist with scale post						Other subject specialist						Peripetatic						Other *(please specify)*					
	1	2	3	4	5	6	1	2	3	4	5	6	1	2	3	4	5	6	1	2	3	4	5	6
Maths																								
English																								
French																								
Science																								
Music																								
P.E.																								
Others *(please specify)*																								

Any special reasons for this arrangement?

4.6   YEAR 4 PUPILS

Numbers of classes or teaching groups: _____   126

Are any children in Year 4 taught by subject
specialists?   Yes ☐   No ☐   127

If yes, who teaches the following subjects? *(The numbered
boxes 1-6 refer to classes and are provided for those schools with
more than one class in each year. Please tick appropriately for
each class.)*

	Subject specialist with scale post						Other subject specialist						Peripetatic						Other *(please specify)*					
	1	2	3	4	5	6	1	2	3	4	5	6	1	2	3	4	5	6	1	2	3	4	5	6
Maths																								
English																								
French																								
Science																								
Music																								
P.E.																								
Others *(please specify)*																								

Any special reasons for this arrangement?

4.7 What subjects are taught to your children in the following years?
Year 1:
Year 2:
Year 3:
Year 4:

4.8 If you have subject specialists, do they have responsibility for:
Planning individual subject teaching for

1st ☐ 2nd ☐ 3rd ☐ 4th ☐ years?
Advising non-specialist teachers? ☐

Meeting upper school staff ☐

Other activities *(please specify)* ☐

128
129

130
131
132
133
134

4.9 Please specify if you use a published scheme of work *(e.g. Fletcher Maths)* or curriculum material from national projects *(e.g. Nuffield Combined Science)* for
Maths:
English;
French:
Science:
Humanities:
Others:

135

4.10 Please specify if you use any scheme of work or unpublished curriculum material from:
Local teacher groups
Advisory staff
Others

4.11 If your school is mixed sex are there any subjects *(excluding sports)* open only to:
Boys?
Girls?

4.12 Please indicate if any of your pupils regularly do homework:

Yes ☐   No ☐

If yes, please indicate approximately how much time (in hours) are they expected to spend on it each week?
Year 1_____ Year 3 _____
Year 2_____ Year 4 _____

136
137
137
138
139
140
141

4.13 Do you have a homework timetable?   Yes ☐   No ☐

If yes, please state which subjects are included

5. ASSESSMENT PROCEDURES
5.1 If you group pupils in the first year on what basis is this made? *(Tick more than one box as appropriate)*

Feeder school record ☐   Internal test ☐

Standardised IQ test ☐   Age of pupil ☐

Standardised attainment test ☐   Others ☐
(please specify)

142
143
144
145
146
147

5.2 Please indicate if standardised I.Q. tests are given to any pupils
in:

Year 1_____ Year 3 _____

Year 2_____ Year 4 _____

148
149
150
151
152

5.3 Please give brief details about the informal assessment
procedures carried out in your school.

5.4 **Year 1 Pupils**
Please indicate when formal assessment of attainment *(if any)*
takes place.

	Standardised attainment test			Internal written test			Other *(please specify)*			Other *(please (specify)*		
	Term			Term			Term			Term		
	1	2	3	1	2	3	1	2	3	1	2	3
Maths												
English												
Reading												
Others *(please specify)*												

Please give brief details of any other relevant assessment procedures.

5.5 **Year 2 Pupils**
Please indicate when formal assessment of attainment *(if any)* takes
place

	Standardised attainment test			Internal written test			Other *(please specify)*			Other *(please (specify)*		
	Term			Term			Term			Term		
	1	2	3	1	2	3	1	2	3	1	2	3
Maths												
English												
Reading												
Others *(please specify)*												

Please give brief details of any other relevant assessment procedures.

5.6 **Year 3 Pupils**
Please indicate when formal assessment of attainment *(if any)* takes place.

	Standardised attainment test			Internal written test			Other *(please specify)*			Other *(please specify)*		
	Term			Term			Term			Term		
	1	2	3	1	2	3	1	2	3	1	2	3
Maths												
English												
Reading												
Other *(please specify)*												

Please give brief details of any other relevant assessment procedures.

5.7 **Year 4 Pupils**
Please indicate when formal assessment of attainment *(if any)* takes place.

	Standardised attainment test			Internal written test			Other *(please specify)*			Other *(please specify)*		
	Term			Term			Term			Term		
	1	2	3	1	2	3	1	2	3	1	2	3
Maths												
English												
Reading												
Other *(please specify)*												

Please give brief details of any other relevant assessment procedures.

16. **LINKS WITH OTHER SCHOOLS**
Feeder First Schools

6.1 Do you have a member of staff specifically responsible for continuity between your school and feeder first school(s)?

Yes ☐   No ☐   153

If yes, indicate position: 154

Head Teacher ☐   Deputy Head Teacher ☐

Year Year Co-Ordinator ☐   Other *(please specify)* ☐   155

6.2 How frequently are *formal* meetings arranged with colleagues from feeder first school(s)?

Once per term ☐   Once per year ☐

More than once per term ☐   Rarely ☐

165

Upper Schools

6.3 Do you have a member of staff specifically responsible for continuity between your school and upper school(s)?

Yes ☐   No ☐   156 ___

If yes, indicate position:

Head Teacher ☐   Deputy Head Teacher ☐   157 ___

Fourth Year Co-ordinator ☐   Other *(please specify)* ☐

6.4 Are any of your staff involved in teaching in the upper school(s)?

Yes ☐   No ☐

If yes, please give brief details   158 ___

6.5 Do any upper school(s) staff teach in your school?

Yes ☐   No ☐   159 ___

If yes, please give brief details

6.6 If there are any *informal* contacts with staff in the upper school(s) please give brief details.

6.7 Are formal liaison meetings held between your school and   160 ___
the upper school(s) to discuss specific subject areas?

Yes ☐   No ☐

If yes, please complete the table indicating the nature and frequency of those meetings.
(Space is provided for the case of liaison with more than one upper school. An example is given at the top of the table illustrating meetings with two upper schools).

	Subject	Middle school staff	Upper school staff	Frequency of meetings:			
				once term	more than once term	once year	less than once year
Ex.	Science	1. SUBJECT SPECIALIST 2. 4ᵗʰ YEAR Co-ORDINATOR	1. HEAD OF SCIENCE 2. HEAD OF SCIENCE	✓		✓	
	Maths						
	English						
	French						
	Science						
	Humanities						
	Remedial						
	Others						

6.8 Please indicate if there are any *formal* liaison meetings held   161 ___
between your school and the upper school(s) to discuss: 162 ___

Pastoral care ☐   Other matters *(please specify)* ☐

Administration ☐   163 ___

Would you give brief details of these meetings, their frequency   164 ___
and the staff involved?   165 ___

6.9 Do your children visit their upper school(s) prior to going there?   166 ___

Yes ☐   No ☐

6.10 Do your pupils meet pupils from the upper school(s) for joint activities *(e.g. clubs, societies, sports, etc.)* ˙ Yes ☐ No ☐   167

If yes, please give brief details

6.11 Please give full details of the information which is passed on to the upper school(s) receiving your pupils.

7. ETHNIC MINORITY GROUPS
(Please complete this section only if you have any children from ethnic minority groups).   168

7.1 Approximately how many children of ethnic minority groups do you have in your school?

Indian _____   Cypriot _____

Pakistani _____   Others *(please specify)*

West Indian _____   _____

7.2 What do you consider to be the main problems in providing for the needs of any of these children?

7.3 Do you make specific provision for any of these children?

Yes ☐   No ☐   169

If yes, please give details

7.4 What do you consider to be the main advantages *(if any)* of a middle school form of organisation for pupils of ethnic minority groups?

7.5 What do you consider to be the main disadvantages *(if any)* of a middle school form of organisation for pupils of ethnic minority groups?

8. GENERAL ORGANISATION

8.1 If your school has *either* a parent teachers' association *or* a parents' association: 170

   171

State the percentage of parents belonging to it _____   172

Indicate its main functions: 173

To provide financial aid for the school ☐

To provide information for parents on curriculum and other developments ☐

   174

To provide information on individual pupils' progress ☐   175

To consult parents on matters of school policy ☐   176

Others *(please specify)* ☐

If your school has *neither* a parent teachers' association *nor* a parents' association, please give details of parental contact other than to give information on individual pupils' progress

8.2 Please give brief details of any specific provision for pastoral care in your school

State briefly if any additional pastoral support is given to children of eleven years and over.

8.3 Do you have a health education programme in your school?

Yes ☐   No ☐   177

If yes, please give brief details for each year

8.4 Are any of the following carried out in your school:

Team teaching? ☐ Individualised learning? ☐ 178

Integrated curricula? ☐ 179

If you have ticked any of the above, please could you describe it briefly, mentioning which staff are involved. 180

8.5 How many of your staff attended an in-service course during the last school year? _____ 181

86. Please indicate which of the following facilities you have in addition to your normal classroom provision: 182

School library ☐ Departmental resource ☐ 184

Central audio visual ☐ collections 185

resources Others *(please specify)* ☐ 186

If you had additional funds to spend on resources, what would you spend the money on?

8.7 Please list the out of school activities provided by the school for your pupils:
'Subject' clubs *(e.g. History Club, Science Club, etc.)*
Sports
Hobbies *(e.g. stamps, pets, etc.)*
Cultural *(e.g. music, drama, etc.)*
Others *(please specify)*

8.8 What do you see as the main behaviour problems presented by your most difficult pupils?

8.9 To what extend do you seek assistance and guidance from local support agencies? *(e.g. school psychological service, social services, welfare officers, etc,)*

8.10 What do you consider to be the main aims of a middle/junior high school?

8.11 What, in your experience, are the main problems associated with middle schools?

8.12 What do you think are the main advantages of a middle school in a three tier system of comprehensive organisation?

8.13 In your opinion, how should middle schools develop in the future?

Thank you very much for your help in completing a long and difficult questionnaire. We greatly appreciate the co-operation that you have kindly given. If you could send us copies of record cards, timetables, prospectuses or any other information about your school we would find them extremely useful. If you have any further comments on middle schools we would be grateful if you could make them below.

Appendix 2

NATIONAL SURVEY OF MIDDLE SCHOOLS – UPPER SCHOOLS

1. *Please indicate your answers with a tick unless otherwise requested.*
2. *If insufficient space has been left for any responses please continue these on a separate piece of paper.*
3. *Unless otherwise stated questions refer to your school in September 1978*
4. *All information supplied on this questionnaire will be treated in the strictest confidence and will not be revealed to anyone.*

1 BACKGROUND INFORMATION

1.1 Name of school:

1.2 Name of Local Education Authority:

1.3 When did your school re-organise to become part of a three tier form of organisation?   Month_____Year_____

1.4 What form of school were you before this re-organisation:

Secondary modern? ☐   Comprehensive *(purpose built)*; ☐

Grammar?   Other *(please specify)*

Technical?

Comprehensive *(adapted)*? ☐

1.5 Age range of pupils in September 1978:

12-16 ☐   12-18 ☐

13-16 ☐   13-18 ☐

14-16 ☐   14-18 ☐

1.6 Number of pupils on roll: Boys_____ Girls_____

1.7 Number of pupils in each year:
12+_____ 13+_____ 14+_____ 15+_____

16+_____

1.8 Is your school:

Church of England? ☐   Non-denominational? ☐

Roman Catholic? ☐   Other *(please specify)*? ☐

1.9 Number of middle/junior high schools from which pupils transfer to your school:

Names of middle/junior high schools from which pupils have transferred:

Names of middle/junior high schools *Approximate numbers transferring in September 1978*

1.10 In which ways are pupils allocated to your school?

From specific feeder schools ☐ By a system of parental choice ☐

From a catchment area defined ☐ Other *(please specify)* ☐
by pupil's residence

Are pupils from your feeder schools also allocated to other upper
schools?

Yes ☐ No ☐

If yes, please indicate any problems which occur.

1.11 How many of the following specialist rooms/areas does your school
have?

Craft Room_____ Science Laboratory_____ Playing fields _____
Music Room_____ Home Economics Room___Outdoor teaching areas_____
(e.g. greenhouse, pond etc.)
Gym _____ Language Laboratory_____Others *(please specify)*_____

1.12 If you had additional funds to spend on buildings, what would you spend
the money on?

2 STAFFING

2.1 Number of teachers *(excluding Head Teacher:)*

	Full-Time		Part-Time	
	Men	Women	Men	Women
Graduates				
Non-graduates				

Full-time equivalent of part-time staff_____

2.2 Group numbers *(for salary purposes)*
Unit total:
Number of teachers on:
Scale 1_____ Scale 2 _____ Scale 3_____ Scale 4 _____
Deputy Head Teacher Scale_____ Senior Teacher Scale_____

2.3 How many departmental heads has your school? _____

Could you tick those subjects listed below which have a departmental
head?

English ☐	Welsh ☐	Newsom ☐	
French ☐	Religious Education ☐	Mathematics ☐	
Commerce ☐	Other Language ☐	Home Economics ☐	
German ☐	Technical ☐	Foreign Languages ☐	
Physics ☐	Remedial ☐	Classics ☐	
Chemistry ☐	Geography ☐	Music ☐	
Biology ☐	Art ☐	Science ☐	
History ☐	Engineering ☐	Physical Education ☐	
		Others *(please specify)*	

Any other not listed above *(e.g. faculty heads)*.

2.4   Could you tick which of the following your school employs or has attached to it *(If more than one give number; if member of staff write 'S')?*

Secretary	☐	Laboratory Technician	☐
Workshop technician	☐	Guidance Counsellor	☐
Careers teacher	☐	Adult education officer	☐
Welfare officer	☐	Librarian	☐

Any others not listed *(please specify)*

3.   CURRICULUM AND ORGANISATION
Registration Groups
3.1   How is your intake allocated to registration groups?

mixed ability ☐   broad-banded ☐   vertical grouping ☐

streamed ☐   houses ☐   other (please specify) ☐

3.2   Give brief details of your school's policy with regard to the grouping of pupils from different feeder schools.

3.3   Are your registration groups the principal pastoral unit?

                                                    Yes ☐   No ☐

If *not,* please give details of your pastoral organisation.

Teaching Groups
3.4   How is your intake initially grouped for teaching purposes?
(Please give details for the basis of any grouping, e.g. middle school record, standardised attainment test, I.Q. test, internal test, etc.)

3.5   Are there any significant changes made to the initial groups during their first year?   Yes ☐   No ☐

If yes, please give details.

3.6   *(Please answer this question only if your age of intake is 12.)*
Give brief details if there are any changes in the grouping of pupils in their second year at your school.

3.7   Option Courses *(for GCE, CSE and non-examination groups).*
Please list any advantages and disadvantages in the organisation and choice of option courses which you have found in your school as a result of pupils transferring at an age later than 11.
Advantages:
Disadvantages:

Remedial
3.8   Does your school have a remedial department?   Yes ☐   No ☐
What procedures do you employ for identifying your first year pupils in need of remedial provision?

Curriculum
3.9   Does the first year in your school have a common course or curriculum?
(i.e. all pupils pursuing the same basic subjects even if at a different pace or depth).   Yes ☐   No ☐

Is this continued into the following year?   Yes ☐   No ☐

3.10   Please give brief details of the subjects taken and organisation of the curriculum during the first year.

4. LINKS WITH FEEDER SCHOOLS

4.1 Please give brief details of the information received by your school from the feeder schools about new pupils.
In what ways is this information used by your school?
If you feel that this information is not adequate what further details would you require?

4.2 If *formal* liaison meetings are held between your school and the feeder schools to discuss specific subject areas, please give details of the nature and frequency of those meetings.
If *formal* liaison meetings are held between your school and the feeder schools to discuss *pastoral care, administration and/or other matters,* please give details of the nature and frequency of those meetings *and* the staff involved.

4.3 If there are any *informal* contacts with staff in the feeder schools, please give details.

4.4 Are any of your staff involved in teaching in the feeder schools?

Yes ☐   No ☐

If yes, please give brief details

Do staff from any of the feeder schools teach in your school?
If yes, please give brief details   Yes ☐   No ☐

4.5 Do your pupils meet pupils from the feeder schools for any joint activities *(e.g. clubs, societies, sports etc.)?*   Yes ☐   No ☐

If yes, please give brief details

4.6 What scale of problem does continuity pose between the feeder schools and yourselves:

a) the biggest problem in upper school organisation?

b) a difficult problem?

c) a minor problem?

Any further comments on this aspect of transfer would be welcome.

5. MISCELLANEOUS

5.1 Are there any problems arising out of having pupils from several feeder schools *(e.g. in mathematics, modern languages and integrated studies etc.)?*

Yes ☐   No ☐

If yes, please give details.

5.2 With regard to your system of three-tier organisation outline its main advantages and disadvantages
Advantages:
Disadvantages:

5.3 What do you consider to be the main aims of the middle/junior high school in a three tier system?

Thank you very much for your help in completing this questionnaire. We greatly appreciate the co-operation that you have kindly given. If you can send us time-tables for your twelve and thirteen year old pupils, record cards, prospectuses or any other relevant information we would be most grateful. If you have any further comments on the three tier system of comprehensive organisation, please would you make them below.

Appendix 3

ETHNIC MINORITY GROUPS IN MIDDLE SCHOOLS

A number of authors (e.g. Blyth and Derricott, 1977) have suggested that middle schools provide a particularly supportive environment for pupils' social and emotional development during early adolescence and so a small section of the Questionnaire included some open ended questions on ethnic minority groups whose problems might be reduced in such institutions. Only those schools having ethnic minority pupils were requested to respond and a total of 383 schools — approximately 49% of the sample — completed this section. There were no significant differences emerging from the various types of middle school suggesting that the age-range of the schools was not an important variable in this context and so analysis was undertaken of all the middle schools in the sample as a whole. The largest ethnic groups, as one would expect, are from West Indian, Indian and Pakistani backgrounds, though there are sizeable minorities also of Cypriot and other European groups.

As anticipated the most frequently reported problem was with language and 39.5% of schools with ethnic minority groups made some kind of special provision for these pupils either within school, for example language remediation programmes (27.9%), or outside school, such as visits to language centres (8.1%). A handful of schools mentioned other activities to help with minority groups such as arranging specific cultural festivals and getting parents in to assist with reading and other language skills. Problems other than language were mentioned by relatively few schools, though a lack of specialist teachers appeared to be a problem in 5.5% of middle schools having ethnic minority pupils; other difficulties listed included individual communication with the parents of such pupils, and the rather different attitudes to education which some pupils displayed. Only 2% of schools mentioned colour prejudice as a problem.

As regards the advantages and disadvantages of a middle school form of organisation in dealing with problems of ethnic minority groups, the percentage of head teachers responding was low indicating that this form of schooling had little effect, one way or another, on such children. However, among those head teachers responding, 10.0% felt that middle schools did give a greater flexibility in dealing with the needs of ethnic minority children, for example in being able to withdraw fairly easily groups for special attention; 5.0% of head teachers thought that middle schools provided extra time to master the english language before moving on to the less sensitive atmosphere of the upper school. Another perceived advantage was the provision of a large range of practical subjects and these allowed pupils with language difficulties to achieve success quite quickly which helped the children's self esteem and made them more motivated; 3.1% of head teachers replied in this vane.

There were few reports which suggested that middle schools were specifically disadvantageous to ethnic minority pupils, though 4.2% of the heads wrote that it was sometimes difficult for the class teacher to make contact with pupils

173

because of the relatively large amount of time spent with specialist teachers — obviously the organisation of the school was an important consideration here. Only 1.3% of head teachers with minority pupils claimed that transfer between schools created additional difficulties for ethnic minority children.

On the whole, the Keele survey revealed only a limited amount of useful information on ethnic minority groups and a more detailed investigative procedure would be necessary to look at the particular problems of these children in the English middle school. Also the regional variations in the number of such children in middle schools is considerable, and any analysis of this phenomenon would need to take account of the geographical distributions.

Appendix 4

MISCELLANEOUS DATA ON MIDDLE SCHOOLS

PARENT-TEACHERS' ASSOCIATIONS
PASTORAL CARE
HEALTH EDUCATION
TEACHING ORGANISATION
RESOURCE FACILITIES
OUT OF SCHOOL ACTIVITIES
BEHAVIOURAL DIFFICULTIES
TABLES APPENDIX 4

Parent-Teachers' Associations

The percentage of schools having a parents' association or a parent-teachers' association are given in Table A4.1 and while individual variation is indicated between the types of school this does not relate to age of transfer. The 8-12 schools have the fewest PTAs at only 60.8% while the 10-13 have the greatest number at 87.9%.

The functions of PTAs do not vary greatly among the middle schools, and for the majority they provide a means whereby the parents can give financial help to the school and also provide the schools with a forum to disseminate information to parents. Few schools use the PTA to give information about the progress of individual pupils. Fewer 5-12 schools than the other middle schools use the PTA to consult parents on matters of school policy. About one-quarter of those schools having a PTA emphasise its value in encouraging informal contacts between teachers and parents.

Of those schools without a parent-teachers' association a significant number of combined schools maintain parental contact via the church or community activities — a reflection, possibly, of the more rural situation of many 5-12 schools. In spite of there being no formal parents' organisation communication with parents is maintained through a number of activities such as parents' evenings, concerts and regular newsletters. In many schools, especially the 5-12s, parents are invited to give general help with school functions. All these activities would no doubt feature among those schools with a formal parent-teachers' association, but no data is available on this.

Pastoral Care

An open ended question was asked concerning specific provision for pastoral care and the returns indicate only one or two differences between different types of middle school. Approximately 15% of schools (10.9% of combined schools) have a member of staff whose responsibility is for boys' or girls' welfare and a few schools, especially 5-12s, mention the involvement of clergy in their pastoral support system. Other schools receive visits by social workers, but by and large pastoral care is seen as the responsibility of senior staff.

For the 11+ children a significant difference emerged based on transfer age for of the 9-13 and 10-13 schools; 35.1% report that pastoral support for these pupils is the responsibility of the year co-ordinator, while in the 5-12 and 8-12 schools only 5% regard this as the year co-ordinator's function. Few schools report any other specific provision for children over 11 years old.

Health Education

A majority of middle schools run a health education programme of some kind, though of the 5-12 schools only 45.5% run such courses (see Table A4:4). The most popular arrangement is to include health education as part of other curriculum areas such as science and home economics rather than to treat it as a separate topic. Many schools devise their own particular scheme, especially the 9-13s, although the Schools' Council Project Material 'Think Well' is also popular. Other schemes used include 'Your Body', 'Growing Up' and 'Education for Family Life'; many schools also mentioned a broadcast series called 'Merry Go Round'.

Apart from these the health education provision was extremely varied — some schools arranging visits by external speakers such as a nurse, or arranging one whole day specifically set aside for health care; one or two schools arrange talks with children and parents together while others organised visits for their pupils to visit such places as hospitals.

Teaching Organisation

Team teaching was reported to be undertaken by about 50% of those schools transferring at 13+, with slightly less for the 12+ transfer schools. The impression given that middle schools are innovatory, largely inferred on the basis of a few case studies, is not borne out by the data given in Table A4.5, and the idea given by some early reports such as that from the Droitwich Working Party (Worcester Education Committee, 1968) that team teaching had particular potential in middle schools, has not materialised in practice, especially among those schools transferring at 12+. The explanation for this is probably the shortage of staff and resources which limit the flexibility of the school and thus the opportunities for teachers to get together into teaching teams.

Individualised learning is reported by approximately one-third of all schools with no great difference between the different types of middle school.

A rather interesting finding revealed in Table A4.5 is that in spite of their more secondary orientation the schools transferring at 13+ more frequently report the adoption of integrated curricula, whereas one would expect this to be a feature of the more primary orientated middle schools transferring pupils at 12.

The percentage of teachers attending an in-service course of some kind was similar among the combined, 8-12 and 9-13 schools, with the latter showing the largest number attending at just under 50% of the staff. The lowest average to attend in-service courses was in the 10-13 schools where an average of 35.9% of staff were involved (see Table A4.6). These figures show a relatively high rate of participation in in-service education by middle school staffs, a situation which may have changed due to financial cut backs.

Resource Facilities

The Keele survey indicated that the majority of middle schools possess a library of some kind, though the size and scope of these is not known; however it is somewhat disconcerting to find that a significant minority of middle schools of all types, have no library (see Table A4.7). Central audio visual resources are available in over three-quarters of middle schools, with the combined schools as the exception for only 60% of these claim such facilities.

Departmental resource collections do vary in frequency according to the type of school, with the 12+ transfer schools having fewer than the other schools. This difference in the distribution is probably as much a reflection of the way in which a school organises the curriculum as of shortage of finance, though many schools do seem short of audio-visual facilities (see Table A4.8). After audio-visual equipment, the most frequently demanded resources are books — especially in the combined and 8-12 schools; in the latter type over 40% of schools need more books. Other resource facilities are needed, but only by a relatively few schools, and these include science and office equipment and more storage facilities. Thus the need in middle schools seems to be for more basic general resources rather than specialised equipment. In terms of resource facilities generally, the 10-13 schools seem to be better off than the others.

Out-of-School Activities

No attempt has been made to provide a detailed analysis of the out-of-school activities provided by middle schools, but rather the data is presented to give some overall impression of the scope of activities on offer.

There are fewer subject clubs in middle schools than of other types, though the 9-13 schools appear to have more of these than other middle schools (Table A4.9). The most frequently mentioned clubs in this category are art and science.

Sports activities naturally feature as the largest group of out-of-school activities, and again it is the 9-13 middle school which has the largest average number of sporting activities available to pupils. Almost every sport one could think of is done in some middle school somewhere. Surprisingly the 10-13 schools offer the smallest range of sports to pupils.

Hobbies clubs, consisting of such activities as electronics, pets, gardening and chess feature widely among all kinds of middle schools as do cultural activities, especially music; the range of musical activity is immensely encouraging with orchestra groups, bands, choirs, guitar, recorder and other instrumental groups frequently listed. These along with other activities too numerous to mention give the impression that a tremendous amount of activity is taking place in middle schools and that in this regard the quality of education is as good as in any other sector of the system. The 10-13 schools, however, do seem to offer slightly fewer extra curricular activities than the other schools – even fewer than the combined schools, many of which must find it very difficult to sustain such a varied extra curricular programme.

Behavioural Difficulties

The data given in Table A4.10 is in response to the question 'What do you see as the main behaviour problems presented by your most difficult pupils?' As this is an open-ended question the statistical information needs to be treated with caution; nevertheless the data does give some idea of the most difficult behaviour problems with which middle school teachers have to cope.

Perhaps the first point which can be made is that a large majority of head teachers were very keen to point out the relatively low incidence of behaviour problems in their schools. Typical comments repeating this are 'At the moment we do not suffer from behaviour problems' and,

'We have relatively few behaviour problems. In the main these come from children who should be at special schools but are not either because of parental refusal, shortage of psychologists over the past three years or lack of special school places';

another head teacher writing in the same spirit says,

'No major behaviour problems exist in the school, Some minor ones are encountered from time to time but these are quickly and easily dealt with'.

It is important to bear this overall lack of major behavioural problems in mind when examining Table A4.10, for the data refers only to the nature of the behaviour problems, if and whey they occur, and is not a table indicating frequency

Of the behaviour problems listed it is possible to select three major areas of difficulty, namely social relationships with peers, relationships with adults and personal problems.

The most often perceived difficulties are in the relations between teachers and pupils – general discipline problems – which feature particularly highly in the returns from the 8-12 schools. A typical comment in this category is 'Dis-

177

obedience: Usually done, I believe, due to lack of sufficient care and discipline at home'. Another head teacher echoes this, especially in the cause of the problem:

'A desire to flout authority. A good number of our children seem to do as they wish at home and expect to be able to do so, or at least try to do so, at school'.

Another head writes,

'Reaction against authority within the school and a lack of respect for property'.

A second area of behaviour problems relates to the relationship between pupils; the most often reported difficulty here is concerned with bullying and generally aggressive behaviour of some pupils towards others. The frequency of head teachers' reports of this does not vary greatly between types of schools, though it is mentioned more frequently by heads in 8-12 schools. Another related problem is that of social adjustment involving a general lack of care and consideration for other pupils — often this form of behaviour comes from children from good homes who teachers perceive as being 'spoilt' or who show 'lack of respect for others'.

The personal difficulties of pupils manifests itself in two major areas. Firstly, there are emotional problems which in the opinion of many head teachers are the result of broken homes. The importance of the home background of pupils is nearly always mentioned in this context, as these examples show: —

'I am worried about the increasing number of children who "have a chip on their shoulder" or under perform because there are problems at home — divorce, separation etc.'

and

'Emotional problems, usually because of a disturbed home background'

and

'Problems resulting from insecurity caused by broken homes'.

In fact a very large number of head teachers refer to home background in their answers to this question, even though they were not asked specifically to give reasons for behaviour problems. In view of this, every time a head teacher mentioned home background in connection with behaviour problems this was recorded and as a result 32.3% of all middle school heads give this as a reason for pupils' difficulties.

Many teachers also see poor parental attitudes as the key to the other most frequently reported individual difficulty — lack of motivation. The general drift of responses here is that some pupils tend to be apathetic, and have a general lack of interest in the life of the school.

'Lack of motivation to be interested in school or what school stands for'

is a typical reply, as is 'Lack of desire to work'. For some reason the 10-13 schools report this twice as often as the other schools.

Most of the other behaviour problems, though more serious, are reported by only a few schools, and reflect a general low level of incidence. Even truancy was mentioned by less than 3% of all head teachers.

Most head teachers use the local support agencies if and when the situation demands it, especially the school psychological service though opinion is divided on the speed with which the psychological service responds to their call, no doubt reflecting local factors and organisation. Welfare Officers are also widely used.

TYPE OF MIDDLE SCHOOL			
5-12	8-12	9-13	10-13
73.6	60.8	63.1	87.9

TABLE A4.1   Middle Schools with a Parent-Teachers Association (Percentage frequency of schools)

	TYPE OF MIDDLE SCHOOL			
	5-12	8-12	9-13	10-13
Providing financial aid	97.5	95.3	93.5	89.6
Providing information for parents on curriculum and other developments	65.4	69.4	73.1	62.0
Providing information on pupils' progress	17.3	21.3	22.2	31.0
Consulting parents on school policy matters	24.7	35.2	39.7	34.5
Promoting informal teacher/parent contacts	28.4	25.9	22.2	27.6

TABLE A4.2   Functions of Parent-Teachers' Association (Percentage frequency of those schools having a Parent-Teachers' Association)

	TYPE OF MIDDLE SCHOOL			
	5-12	8-12	9-13	10-13
Church and/or community activities	13.8	2.2	3.0	25.0
Parents' evenings	27.6	36.7'	22.0	25.0
Concerts	17.2	33.8	21.0	0.0
Regular newsletter	13.8	9.3	17.0	25.0

TABLE A4.3   Ways of maintaining contact with parents in schools without a Parent-Teachers' Association (Percentage frequency of schools without a PTA)

TYPE OF SCHOOL			
5-12	8-12	9-13	10-13
45.5	61.1	67.2	57.6

TABLE A4.4   Middle schools having a health education programme (Percentage frequency of schools)

	TYPE OF SCHOOL			
	5-12	8-12	9-13	10-13
Team teaching	31.8	42.0	50.6	51.5
Individualised learning	33.6	36.1	36.2	33.3
Integrated curricula	40.0	38.0	50.9	63.6

TABLE A4.5   Middle schools carrying out team teaching, individualised learning and integrated curricula (Percentage frequency of schools)

TYPE OF SCHOOL			
5-12	8-12	9-13	10-13
44.8	48.3	49.2	35.9

TABLE A4.6   Teachers attending an in-service course during the previous school year (Percentage frequency of schools)

	TYPE OF SCHOOL			
	5-12	8-12	9-13	10-13
School library	86.4	89.3	86.0	90.9
Central audio visual resources	60.0	77.5	75.6	78.8
Departmental resource collections	26.4	38.3	51.3	66.7

TABLE A4.7   Middle schools possessing various resource facilities (Percentage frequency of schools)

	TYPE OF SCHOOL			
	5-12	8-12	9-13	10-13
More audio visual resources	38.2	43.4	38.7	42.4
Books	37.3	40.3	36.2	24.2
Science equipment	2.7	4.2	1.8	3.0
Office equipment	3.6	3.1	6.6	0.0
Storage facilities	5.5	7.1	6.6	3.0

TABLE A4.8   Middle schools requesting additional resources (Percentage frequency of schools)

	TYPE OF SCHOOL			
	5-12	8-12	9-13	10-13
Subject clubs	1.0	1.1	3.2	1.1
Sports clubs	6.5	7.6	9.4	5.8
Hobbies clubs	2.5	2.4	4.7	1.7
Cultural clubs	3.3	3.7	5.3	2.7

TABLE A4.9   Average numbers of clubs in middle schools

	TYPE OF SCHOOL			
	5-12	8-12	9-12	10-13
Lack of social adjustment	10.9	10.1	7.7	9.1
Vandalism	1.8	1.7	3.3	3.0
Stealing	–	3.1	4.4	3.0
Swearing	–	1.1	1.1	–
General discipline problems	13.6	19.7	14.4	9.1
Dishonesty	–	0.6	0.4	–
Problems with school uniform	–	–	1.1	–
Aggression towards other pupils	14.5	17.5	14.0˙	12.1
Attention seeking	1.8	5.4	3.7	–
Emotional problems	11.8	8.2	5.2	6.1
Truancy	–	2.3	5.2	1.2
Apathy/distinterest	7.3	5.6	5.9	12.1

TABLE A4.10 Responses to the question — What do you see as the main problems presented by your most difficult pupils? (Percentage frequency of schools)

Appendix 5

LOCAL EDUCATION AUTHORITIES FROM WHICH THE
MIDDLE SCHOOL SAMPLE WAS DRAWN

METROPLITAN DISTRICTS

London Boroughs of:
  Ealing
  Harrow
  Merton

Greater Manchester:
  Rochdale
  Wigan

Merseyside:
  Wirral

South Yorkshire:
  Barnsley
  Doncaster
  Sheffield

Tyne and Wear:
  Gateshead
  Newcastle-upon-tyne
  North Tyneside

West Midlands
  Birmingham
  Dudley
  Walsall

West Yorkshire:
  Bradford
  Kirklees
  Leeds
  Wakefield

NON-METROPOLITAN COUNTIES

Bedfordshire
Berkshire
Buckinghamshire
Cambridgeshire
Cheshire
Derbyshire
Devon
Dorset
East Sussex
Hampshire
Hereford and Worcester
Hertfordshire
Humberside
Isle of Wight
Kent
Lincolnshire
Norfolk
Northamptonshire
Northumberland
Nottinghamshire
Oxfordshire
Shropshire
Somerset
Staffordshire
Suffolk
Surrey
Warwickshire
West Sussex
Wiltshire

Jex

Reference to tables in italics

Also from Trentham Books:

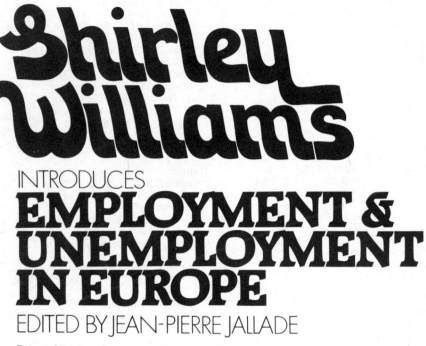

Shirley Williams

INTRODUCES

EMPLOYMENT & UNEMPLOYMENT IN EUROPE

EDITED BY JEAN-PIERRE JALLADE

Price: £7.95 or $16.   ISBN: 0 9507735 0 6

EMPLOYMENT AND UNEMPLOYMENT IN EUROPE presents the most thorough-going analysis to date of one of the major issues affecting Western European society. It includes contributions by most of the major European experts including the new Finance Minister of the Mitterand Government, Mr. Jacques Delors. The volume-is introduced by Mrs. Shirley Williams, who has worked closely with the contributors both in her ministerial career and in her recent studies with the Policy Studies Institute. The introduction alone will ensure it receives widespread attention.

Trentham Books
30 Wenger Crescent
Trentham
Stoke-on-Trent, ST4 8LF